# CHANGING GOVERNMENT
## POLICIES FOR THE
## MENTALLY DISABLED

# CHANGING GOVERNMENT POLICIES FOR THE MENTALLY DISABLED

LFogarty Memorial Conference (1st ; 1980;
Newport, R.I.

*Edited by*
JOSEPH J. BEVILACQUA

Proceedings of the First Annual
Fogarty Memorial Conference,
Newport, Rhode Island
August 1980

SCHOOL OF
CALIFORNIA PROFESSIONAL
PSYCHOLOGY
LOS ANGELES

BALLINGER PUBLISHING COMPANY
Cambridge, Massachusetts
A Subsidiary of Harper & Row, Publishers, Inc.

International Standard Book Number: 0-88410-384-6

Library of Congress Catalog Card Number: 81-10968

Printed in the United States of America


**Library of Congress Cataloging in Publication Data**

Fogarty Memorial Conference (1st : 1980 : Newport, R.I.)
  Changing government policies for the mentally disabled.

  Bibliography: p.
  Includes index.
  1. Mentally handicapped—Government policy—United States—
Congresses. I. Title.
HV3006.A3F63  1980          362.3'56'0973          81-10968
ISBN 0-88410-384-6                                  AACR2

# CONTENTS

# LIST OF FIGURES

# LIST OF TABLES

# FOREWORD

The John E. Fogarty Foundation for the mentally retarded was delighted to join with the governor of Rhode Island in sponsoring what was hoped would become an annual convocation of distinguished citizens, professionals, and scholars to discuss and to analyze the problems of the mentally disabled. The foundation and the conference are named for John E. Fogarty, a giant of a man who is sadly missed by everyone who knew him personally or by reputation. Certainly he is missed by a legion of dedicated professionals in medicine and research. He is missed especially by those whom he loved dearly and served nobly—the sick and the old, the blind and the deaf, the disabled and the poor, and of course the mentally retarded. It was to these disabled and often disenfranchised citizens that he directed his special attention and consuming efforts. John Fogarty frequently observed that illness is a national problem that knows no barriers of race or religion and has its most crippling effects on those who can least afford to cure it or even to resist it.

One of the most eloquent tributes to his memory appeared in the *New York Times* on January 15, 1967, just five days after his death. In the eulogy Dr. Howard A. Rusk, America's foremost medical writer, commented:

> If hospitals, research laboratories and institutes for the aged, infirm and retarded had flagpoles, every flag would have flown at half-staff this past week to mourn the loss of John E. Fogarty. . . . Flags at half-staff . . . would also have been in evidence in thousands of homes throughout Rhode Island and

the nation. . . . No one in the history of this country has done more to promote more and better health services, more and better health facilities and more and better health research than Representative Fogarty.

John Fogarty came to the U.S. Congress from Rhode Island at the age of 26 after working ten years as a bricklayer. Although he did not receive much formal education, no one was more avid in the pursuit of knowledge nor more earnest in its application. He never tried to impress, but he never failed to impress. He was never loud or flamboyant, but his message was clear and convincing. For over twenty years he presided as chairman of the House Appropriations Subcommittee on Health, Education, and Welfare.

His years of service on that committee beckoned the dawn of a new era in medical research. It is impossible to overstate the impact the quiet and determined John Fogarty had on health care in America. During his tenure in Congress, the national government's annual investment in medical research rose from about $3 million to $1.5 billion. The budget of the U.S. Public Health Service alone during that same period rose to $2.5 billion, which was forty times greater than it was when John Fogarty entered Congress. In 1955 Representative Fogarty succeeded in getting Congress to appropriate for the first time funds to help retarded children. When he died twelve years later, over $3 million was being spent annually on research into the cause of retardation. It was primarily John Fogarty who summoned Congress to appropriate these monies, and it was John Fogarty who aroused the concern of Congress on health care and focused its attention on medical research and the immense benefits to mankind that can be derived therefrom.

Perhaps the best way to illustrate John Fogarty's eloquence and deep compassion for suffering people and his continuing, restless search for new attacks on disease is to quote from one of the hundreds of speeches he delivered on the floor of the House of Representatives in support of new and larger appropriations for medical research. The *Congressional Record* for Spring 1956 carries the transcript of a somewhat heated debate on the value of increasing the appropriation for the National Institute of Health. The debate lasted five full days. John Fogarty singlehandedly opposed those who contended that not enough progress was being made to justify the increase he was advocating in health care appropriation. He said,

I do not know how much we have expended on cancer research. I do not care. I do not know whether it is $1 million or $3 billion, but if any part of that was a help in finding a new technique in diagnosing cancer of the cervix in women, every dime that we have spent has been well expended by the Congress of the United States.

Dr. Sidney Farber, the outstanding expert in the field of leukemia in children has pioneered the use of an antifolic compound in the treatment of leukemia. He used these compounds to treat a boy 10 years ago. He discovered the use in Boston and with the help of funds from this appropriation, if you please. As a result of that discovery for the first time in medical history a young boy afflicted with acute leukemia is still living after 10 years. How much is his life worth? I do not know, but to me, it is worth every dime we have put into these programs over the past 10 years.

We also have the testimony of people in the mental health field like Dr. Menninger. He told us of new advances that have been made in the drugs that have come out within the past two years, with the help of some of our appropriations. He told us that the discharges from mental institutions have increased 25% this past year because of the use of these new drugs. Ladies and gentlemen, I do not know what the cost has been for the developing of those new drugs, but if it is doing what Dr. Menninger suggests, we are not spending enough, in my opinion, in that field.

How many people would have believed me if I had said to them two years ago that we had information from leading experts in the field of polio that there might be developed a vaccine that would prevent polio? But that has happened, because of a program supported by the National Institute of Health for which the appropriations we are now discussing are made. That vaccine is now being given to children and has proven 80% effective. The goal was to make it 100% effective. As a result of that discovery, the heartaches of mothers and fathers and the suffering of little children, not only in this country but all over the world, will be relieved. I do not know how much money it cost to develop that vaccine, and I do not care. It is worth every dime we have spent.

Concluding his magnificent extemporaneous address, the Honorable Mr. Fogarty voiced his profound disagreement with those who would move slowly against the major killers and cripplers of our time:

We are sometimes told that we must move at a measured pace — that a program of research to find the prevention and cure of disease must go along slowly. I need not say to you that death and disability make their own pace and speed. They do not accommodate themselves to the tempo we set for research. They strike swiftly and relentlessly. Our vote today is to declare if we are willing to meet them on their own terms and show the way to better health for the people of this nation of ours. Our vote today will indicate whether or not we really intend to help those who so desperately need assistance — the sick and the poor.

The *Congressional Record* shows that following intense debate the House of Representatives voted—in the face of great odds (at the very same time, the Congress was sharply reducing expenditures in almost every other segment of the budget)—to approve Representative Fogarty's recommended increases in the medical appropriations.

Of all the causes for which John Fogarty fought so hard, none was more important to him than helping the mentally retarded. His heart went out to the people who through no choosing of their own were viewed as hopelessly sick and whose future was circumscribed by public misconception. He tried to help them any way he could. He dedicated himself to leading thousands of retarded children beyond the darkness of their affliction to a life of light and promise, to careers of productiveness and self-fulfillment.

In 1959, when he became the first person outside the medical profession to receive the prestigious Albert Lasker award for championing the advancement of medical research in public health, he immediately donated the funds to the Rhode Island Parents Council for Mentally Retarded Children. A few years later, as a winner of the leadership award from the Joseph P. Kennedy Foundation, John Fogarty used the money to establish his own foundation for the mentally retarded. It was the one memorial by which he wanted to be remembered.

To the award he added numerous personal contributions, donated honoraria from speaking engagements, sponsored fund-raising activities, and solicited others to contribute to the foundation. Through his efforts he hoped that one day the foundation would be capable of bringing meaningful help to the mentally retarded.

Unfortunately John Fogarty died before he could see that hope fulfilled. Since then, however, many persons have undertaken to strengthen his memorial. The dream of a foundation for the retarded is becoming a reality, not just through efforts to increase the foundation, but even more through the spirit that emanated from John E. Fogarty himself. The foundation provides money for rehabilitation of the mentally retarded and hopes someday to have enough money to distribute fellowships for research in all areas of mental health. During the 1970s the foundation awarded over $100,000 in grants. But, as John Fogarty would have said, that is not nearly enough. We have to do more.

This country needs more people like John Fogarty—leaders who demonstrate great compassion and understanding, leaders who have the vision and the will to encourage government to realize the truth of an observation made long ago by Disraeli: "The health of the people is really the foundation upon which all their happiness and all their powers as a state depend."

There is no better way to honor John Fogarty than to participate in a conference such as the one the chapters in this volume record. John Fogarty was not interested in hollow praise or pious intonations. He was interested in sincere dedication to the fight against illness, disease, and disability. Those committed to better health policy in this country are to be congratulated and it is hoped that they will be inspired by the life of John Fogarty and remember the lesson he so eloquently taught: The fight for better health for all Americans must be as relentless and unending as the disease and disability it seeks to conquer. It must be waged with courage and conviction. Not every battle can be won, but for the soldiers of John Fogarty, there will be no rest until disease and disability are subdued, and the ravages of illness are tamed.

**James J. Skeffington**

# ACKNOWLEDGMENTS

The original suggestion to have a conference honoring John E. Fogarty came from Gunnar Dybwad, the internationally recognized scholar on mental retardation and developmental disabilities. Rhode Island Governor J. Joseph Garrahy committed his office and staff to the idea of a conference designed to examine national policies for the mentally disabled. Those who encouraged the idea included Frank Rocco, a Washington, D.C. based expert on organization science; William Datell, a prominent research psychologist; Mary Anne Allard, an authority on service for the handicapped; Harry Schnibbe, executive director of the National Association of State Mental Health Program Directors, as well as Jack Noble and Valerie Bradley whose papers appear in this volume. Joseph Byron, Past President of the Fogarty Foundation and James L. Maher who has been closely associated with the Foundation, were wonderfully supportive, providing the necessary funds to help pay for the conference.

My own staff at the Department of Mental Health, Retardation and Hospitals worked very hard with the myriad of details involved. Sister Mary Patrick, my administrative assistant, and Robert Holmes, coordinator of drug abuse training and education programs, co-chaired the conference effort with amazing thoroughness and grace.

I would also like to extend a special thanks to Sister Lucille Mc-Killop, RSM, PhD, president of Salve Regina College, which hosted the Conference, and Dan Caley, the Department's public information officer, who assisted me in organizing the papers for this volume.

Joseph Bevilacqua

# CHANGING GOVERNMENT POLICIES FOR THE MENTALLY DISABLED

# INTRODUCTION

*Joseph J. Bevilacqua*

As the 1980s began, a review of recent national legislation affecting the mentally disabled pointed to important policy developments. The Mental Health Systems Act (PL 96-398), passed in 1980, enlarged the role of the states in managing the mental health system. It emphasized meeting the needs of the elderly, children, and minorities, all of whose access to mental health services has traditionally been limited. Community-based provision of services was fostered by the act in its requirement for better planning and program development for the mentally disabled discharged from hospitals, particularly those clients who had been institutionalized for long periods of time. The formal structuring of an advocacy system was also addressed.

A number of significant pieces of legislation were passed in the 1970s (Office of Handicapped Individuals, 1980).

1. Intermediate care facility (ICF) amendments (PL 92-223) to the Social Security Act in 1971 made institutions for the mentally retarded eligible for reimbursement under Medicaid. This provided significant impetus for communities' efforts to develop residential services.

2. Under the Social Security Act amendments of 1972 (PL 92-603) and modifications passed in 1973 (PL 93-233) Congress created

1

Title XVI of the act, which authorized a broad set of new cash payment mechanisms or Supplemental Security Income (SSI) for needy aged, blind, and disabled adults.

3. Through the Rehabilitation Act of 1973 (PL 93–112) the federal government mandated that state vocational rehabilitation focus on services to severely handicapped clients.

4. The Social Services Act amendments of 1974 (PL 93–647) consolidated social service grants under a new Title XX of the Social Security Act, which also established social service goals, revised eligibility criteria specified planning requirements, and clarified operating procedures for programs designed to prevent inappropriate institutional care and promote client independence.

5. The Public Health Services Act of 1974 (PL 93–641), in addition to establishing a "certificate of need" for regulating health services, placed the authority for approval of state health plans, grants, and contracts under the umbrella of state health coordinating councils or state health systems agencies.

6. The Developmental Disabilities Services and Facilities Amendments of 1970 (PL 91–517), the Developmental Disabilities Assistance and Bill of Rights Act of 1975 (PL 94–103) and later developmental disabilities legislation had a wide-ranging impact on community based services. The bills affected the definition of clients eligible for services and protection of client rights as well as program planning, evaluation and supervision.

7. Title III of the Special Health Revenue Sharing Act of 1975 (PL 94–63) significantly revised and expanded the Community Mental Health Centers Act of 1963 (PL 88–164) by providing funds for planning and eight-year operational grants in addition to mandating a broad range of community mental health services.

8. The 1975 Education for all Handicapped Children Act (PL 94–142) significantly expanded earlier programs to provide a multi-billion dollar federal commitment to assist in the education of handicapped children.

Broad consequences of this legislation focused nationwide attention on the chronically ill or incapacitated high-risk populations, institutions, community supports, and legal rights. The applications of financial, program, and regulatory requirements of the various major federal agencies at the end of the 1970s provided significant and important management and resource allocation for the mentally disabled populations. But allocation was not evenhanded by any means and did not represent a single coherent policy position. Rather, it was a potpourri of activities and forces that included not only formal legislation but various issues affecting the mentally disabled that were under litigation in many states. Moreover, Medicare, Medicaid, and housing, education, vocational training were all being reviewed as critical parts of the whole program for the mentally disabled (U.S. General Accounting Officer, 1977). Different parts were being applied more and more in response to political pressure. The unevenness of focus can be seen, for example, in Title XIX funds being extended from institutional support to community residential services for the mentally retarded whereas the federal funding policy for the mentally ill excluded those patients between the ages of 21 and 64 who reside in psychiatric hospitals.

Growing alarm among professionals concerning these apparently disparate and disjointed policies suggested the desirability of convening a national meeting to assess policy patterns. It was hoped that certain courses of action could be identified that would build a broader foundation for providing services for the mentally disabled.

Governor J. Joseph Garrahy of the State of Rhode Island, in his role as chairman of the human services subcommittee of the National Governors Association, believed it would be useful to convene a conference in which the general direction of these governmental policies would be examined. Reviewing current policies and recommending change was the general agenda given to invited presenters and participants by Governor Garrahy.

Honoring the late Congressman John Fogarty by this endeavor was seen as a testimony to his work in first charting much of the national health policy in the early 1960s, pointing the way to the future.

The climate of the country for the mentally disabled at the end of the 1970s was not calm. Mandates for services to the mentally disabled had been broadened to include housing, community support services, and there was heightened awareness of the need for greater social integration. Client and patient services were shifting from public to private settings, but the phenomenon of deinstitutionalization was beginning to show signs of a backlash. Just as federal health and welfare financing mechanisms were becoming overloaded, constituencies and lobbying efforts for the mentally disabled were beginning to coalesce. There were also increasingly sophisticated strategies for packaging money and services and dealing with the political systems of federal and state government. The directions of these complex and multifaceted trends were often contradictory. For example, in the maze of financing during deinstitutionalization allocation of monies and regulations often reinforced the upgrading of large institutions while creating fund shortages for community programs.

In rapid fashion the policy climate changed when President Reagan assumed office in January 1981. In one sense it meant acceleration of what had been identified in President Carter's Mental Health Systems Act, a move toward more state management and control. The emphasis of the new administration has been total rather than partial or incremental. The Reagan administration in 1981 proposed block grants with nearly total operation being the responsibility of the states. Funding responsibility is also diverted more to state government with initial federal reductions of 25 percent and higher, depending on inflation.

Such changes will have a profound impact on how the social and health services will be developed and implemented during the 1980s in the United States. They also indicate a very different role for the government, both state and federal, in the human service sector.

The conference on national policy and potential changes was called because of a general sense of need for change. Ironically, it was immediately followed by a dramatic shift in the very infrastructure of governmental policymaking and implementation which presents an interesting opportunity to view the administrative transition with more clarity and understanding than is usually possible. It is a compliment to the insight and sagacity of the authors of the conference papers presented in this book that they remain highly pertinent and germane in spite of these major structural changes. (Two of the papers, Chapter 1, by John H. Noble, and Chapter 4 by William C. Copeland and Iver A. Iverson, were revised but maintain essentially the original analysis.) Presented in August 1980, the papers have not lost their relevance. Indeed, besides clarifying the political and administrative future transition, they highlight the policy ramifications for the future.

The authors who were invited to contribute papers to the First Annual Fogarty Memorial Conference represent an interesting spectrum of professional interests and talents. The broad policy review by John Noble (Chapter 1) comes from his extensive experience in the federal government. He has worked in the technical management of federal contracts with a number of research and evaluation projects in public agencies and private universities as well as consulting firms. His work with the World Health Organization has provided a very helpful international view of social and physical rehabilitation. Noble's discussion of cooperatives and of health maintenance organizations, for example, show the advantages not only of integrating the mentally disabled into society but of earlier intervention and self-help.

Elizabeth Boggs, educated as a physicist, has been in the forefront of national policy development for the mentally retarded and developmentally disabled. She has worked through national associations such as the National Association for Retarded Citizens and has served on many national task forces and commissions for the handicapped. She currently serves on the President's Committee for the Handicapped. In Chapter 2 she analyzes the politics of fiscal behavior for the mentally disabled, moving across this diverse landscape with acute insight and understanding. Her analysis describes brilliantly what is happening in the field, and her recommendations are pivotal for viewing the transition to state control and management and the change in entitlement programs in human services.

Clark Ross's careful compilation of the complex national infrastructure of the mental disabilities constituencies (Chapter 3) represents the first such complete overview. Traditionally the different constituencies have moved along very narrow lines of self-interest. Fragile and temporary coalitions have had mixed success and raised questions of the need for a different amalgam at the national level. The resource shortages of the 1980s will make the need for reassessment even more critical. Ross himself has spent many years on Capitol Hill, presiding over organizational squabbles, both large and small. His words ring of truth gleaned through personal involvement and commitment. He is a participant/observer historian. The future of lobbying efforts of national associations is in question. Whichever direction is taken, Ross's analysis will provide an invaluable historical guide to understanding future developments.

William Copeland, who authored Chapter 4 with the help of Iver Iverson, is associated with the Hubert H. Humphrey Institute of Public Affairs of the University of Minnesota. He has conducted numerous studies in the financing of human services and has served as policy consultant for a number of states as well as for the federal government. He has also worked as a private consultant in addition to his teaching activities. The chapter is included because it presents a series of strategies cutting across narrow definitions of individual disabilities. It also is an interesting complement to both Chapter 1 and Chapter 2 as well as a foil for Reagan administration policy shifts in managing and funding human services.

Valerie Bradley, author of Chapter 5, is president of her own private consulting firm, and has studied extensively both organizational and programmatic issues in mental disabilities practice, examining governmental activities at the local, state, and federal levels. She has analyzed the process in several major class action suits in the United States courts and has provided consultation to governmental agencies on implementation strategies for deinstitutionalization and community care. Her chapter focuses attention on the implications for shifting agency for service provision from the state to private providers. She identifies the trend toward entrepreneurial activity far removed from the locus of direct service, raising serious questions about the implications for maintaining standards and as well as questions about the potential value conflicts in profitmaking and not-for-profit operations. The most urgent questions she raises about policy outcome concern who will shape, plan, and assume ultimate responsibility for the mentally disabled.

The work of Robert M. Moroney in examining the family in human service practice is well established. His analysis (in Chapter 6) of the changing roles of families is neither predetermined nor static with regard to definition. He reminds us of the basic strength of families; they are a primary support often underestimated by human service providers. He views families as an important resource in which we must invest more vision and imagination. They are the cornerstone to providing care for many of the disabled.

Chapters 7 by Hilary Sandall and Chapter 8 by Robert Carl represent direct practice material and advocacy positions respectively. Dr. Sandall, a psychiatrist affiliated with community mental health programs, identifies successful application of community care programs where the institution does have a role. She stresses the concept of continuity. Dr. Carl, an educator and state mental health administrator, argues the dysfunction of the institution with the advocate's passion. Both views reflect the contemporary status of the mentally disabled and in their own way distinguish treatment patterns for the mentally ill and mentally retarded. Both authors see the significance of community capacity for provision of services to the mentally disabled.

It is not fifty years since Social Security was first established in the United States. State planning for the mentally disabled is not twenty years old. These two developments have had an important impact on the care of the mentally disabled through the broadening of benefits and through the greater visibility of the mentally disabled in our health and social service systems.

The seven chapters in this volume provide important commentaries on and interpretations of the ramifications of these developments. The payment for and the organization of services are not permanent arrangements. In the end these questions become settled and are arbitrated by our political process. John Fogarty was an excellent example of this reality. We are honored to dedicate these papers to his memory and to perpetuate his advocacy for and understanding of mentally disabled citizens.

## REFERENCES

The Comptroller General of the United States. *Returning the mentally disabled to the community: Government needs to do more.* HRD-76-152A. Washington, D.C.: U.S. General Accounting Office, January 7, 1977.

Office of Handicapped Individuals, U.S. Department of Education. *Summary of existing legislation relating to the handicapped.* Publication no. E-80-22014. Washington, D.C.: U.S. Government Printing Office, 1980.

# 1 NEW DIRECTIONS FOR PUBLIC POLICIES AFFECTING THE MENTALLY DISABLED

*John H. Noble*

The mentally disabled population of the United States, comprising mentally ill and mentally retarded and other developmentally disabled persons, like all other human beings, has need of food, shelter, clothing, social support in family networks and in the community and the opportunity to participate in the full range of economic, social, civic, and recreational activities that characterize every human society. The problems that the mentally disabled face in meeting their needs stem from their stigmatizing impairments and disabilities, which impede fulfillment of roles considered normal for persons of given sex and age. Their impairments involve specific losses of psychological, physiological, or anatomical structure or function and lead to disabilities that are restrictions in their abilities to perform in the manner or within the range considered normal for a human being (World Health Organization (WHO), 1980). The disadvantages they experience, including rejection and discrimination by other human beings, arise from the nature of their impairments and disabilities and limit their self-fulfillment and full participation in community life. Effective intervention to overcome the effects of impairments, disabilities, and handicaps requires normalization to the extent possible of the role functioning of the mentally disabled.

In this chapter I first sketch the nature of the problems faced by mentally disabled persons in the context of the public policies that impinge on their need for family support, income maintenance, housing, and assorted services. In the absence of adequate provision of certain essential goods and services, mentally disabled persons not only cannot participate fully in community life but also suffer deprivation of the freedom and entitlements guaranteed to all its citizens by the Constitution of the United States. Second, I look at the prospects for more adequate, equitable, and efficient allocation of society's resources to meet the special needs of the mentally disabled. In this view, demographic and economic trends are taken into account, as are pressures on the United States as a world power both to share its resources with the Third World and to act as defender of democratic and free enterprise values against the Communist bloc. Third, I review recent policy trends in the United States in light of the experience of several European countries and the recent changes in political ideology and power that have transformed the executive and legislative branches of the U.S. government.[a] Last, I explore the policy choices that face the United States in the 1980s and their implications for improving the adequacy, equity, and efficiency of the allocation of resources, emphasizing the high and increasing overhead costs imposed by the myriad categorical programs of county, state, and federal governments. I urge adoption of policies favoring development of cooperatives for the handicapped. These would give provider status to disabled persons capable of assuming responsibility for their own lives and to the families (or their surrogates) of disabled persons unable to do so.

## SPECIAL PROBLEMS

Mental disabilities often cause behaviors and dependency that place a burden on families and the community. For many years the response to serious mental disability was rejection and institutionalization in order to minimize the burden. The historical patterns of care of the mentally disabled in England are reflected in modern America.

a. The original presentation on which this chapter is based has been revised to reflect the changed prospects for policies affecting the mentally disabled stemming from the Republican Party's ascent to power in both the executive and legislative branches of the federal government. While the problems calling for reform remain largely the same, the feasibility of specific proposals is very much dependent on the prevailing philosophy of government, as well as the particular power relationships that exist at any time between the branches and levels of government. I have attempted to take the new political realities into account but recognize how ephemeral and unpredictable these realities are.

Throughout recorded English history, families and communities have vacillated between community care and institutionalization of the mentally disabled. Instances of very enlightened treatment are interspersed among the many examples of neglect and abuse. History has witnessed communal foster care of a mentally retarded person as ordered by the court in Warwickshire, England, in 1616 as well as confinement in workhouses, poorhouses, and houses of industry under the English "poor laws"; it has seen the earliest practice in England of providing psychiatric services in the general hospitals of time changed to treatment in private "madhouses" in the eighteenth and nineteenth centuries (Allderidge, 1979). Eventually, the county asylum became the favored repository for the mentally disabled in the belief that fresh air and outdoor work and exercise were therapeutic. How much this belief served as a rationalization for the desire of families and the community to rid themselves of undesirable persons is unknown but can be surmised.

The legacy of English history is with us in twentieth century America. The original policy questions are still unresolved: Who shall be placed in institutions? Who shall be allowed to leave? What authority shall have the power to make these decisions? According to what standard will care be provided? And perhaps the most important consideration of all, who shall bear the costs of providing care, whether in institutions or in the community?

Ironically, the issue of who shall pay for the care of the mentally disabled has become entangled with the issue of discrimination. As the federal government gradually developed special programs to subsidize a variety of services to various segments of the population, the mentally ill have not, it has been argued, received their fair share. Notwithstanding the desire of the U.S. Congress to have state and county governments maintain their traditional responsibility for the institutional care of the mentally ill (undoubtedly motivated by the wish to avoid the substantial costs involved), the states now argue that many federal programs discriminate against the mentally ill. They would have the federal government provide a "floor" or guaranteed minimum amount of funds to pay for the care of the mentally ill while preserving the right of the states to compete for the rest of the total available federal program funds for this purpose (National Association of State Mental Health Program Directors, 1980). The states would also like to see removed the Medicare exclusion in Section 1861 (j) of the Social Security Act, which prohibits reimbursement for skilled nursing services in "institutions primarily for the care and treatment of mental diseases."

In view of the entanglement of financing issues with just about every other aspect of policy affecting the welfare of the mentally disabled, there is reason to believe that the single most important threat to the welfare of mentally disabled people at this time is how public financing issues are resolved. We all know that family and professional judgments as well as political decisions at every level of government are influenced by considerations of who must bear the costs of care and treatment for handicapped persons. We have all witnessed at one time or another the operation of the "collocation principle": People will have their needs defined in relation to where the dollars lie. Alternatively stated: Bodies and dollars will be collocated in the absence of iron-tight sanctions against inappropriate collocation. All other problems of the mentally disabled pale in comparison with this dynamic.

If we can find the right combination of financial incentives, mentally disabled citizens of the United States will have a better chance than they have now of living in the least restrictive environments commensurate with their need for appropriate care and treatment. But serious resource constraints and the perverse incentives embedded in current policies will have to be overcome before this can happen. The right combination of incentives will encourage family support, whenever feasible, for mentally disabled persons, as well as sufficiency of income maintenance, decent housing, and services directed to sustaining mentally disabled persons in self-fulfilling and productive lives.

## DEMOGRAPHIC AND ECONOMIC TRENDS

Energy shortages and inflation will undoubtedly be the dominant concerns of the 1980s. In an earlier article (Noble 1980) I accepted the prediction that the want of a strong incomes policy (government imposed wage and price controls) would produce semiprotracted recession with its attendant ills of rising unemployment, fewer and smaller wage increases, more limited opportunities for advancement, and diminished purchasing power. Now the prediction must be hedged against the attempts of the Reagan administration to apply the untested theory of,"supply-side economics." If supply-side economics fails to stimulate healthy growth of the economy, it may well be that both the want of a strong incomes policy and the loss of consumer demand that Keynesian-inspired government spending formerly sustained, will cause even more serious ills.

In the 1980 article I also documented how budget trends since 1970 were shifting an increasing share of available resources into inpatient hospital services for the acutely ill and long-term care in nursing homes and chronic disease institutions and in the process starving the supply of social services that could be considered substitutes for care in more restrictive settings. These trends are occurring despite the statutory intent of Medicare, Medicaid, and Title XX of the Social Security Act that all citizens who become eligible for participation in these programs should receive care appropriate to their needs in settings that are the least restrictive of their personal liberties. I urged that mental health authorities establish effective linkages to Title XX and Medicaid agencies in their respective states in order to obtain reimbursement for as much as possible of the *community* mental health services needed by mentally ill people. This, I believe, is still good advice.

I am not so sure, however, that my advice about taking advantage of the open-ended character of the federal Medicaid budget to supplement the closed-ended social services programs was the best. The structural characteristics of Medicaid, its operational philosophy, and the considerable likelihood that Congress will "cap" Medicaid make it a less certain bet as a source of adequate support for the care and treatment of the mentally disabled. The combination of inappropriate standards, lax enforcement, out-of-control growth of expenditures for both the Intermediate Care Facility for the Mentally Retarded (ICF/MR)—Developmental Disability (DD) component and the program as a whole draw attention to Medicaid and invite drastic measures of curtailment. As the American economy is squeezed by the high costs of energy, low productivity, a diminished competitive position in world markets, increased spending for defense, and a rapidly growing national debt arising from both on- and off-budget programs, it is inevitable that the remaining open-ended federal programs will come under close scrutiny and be curtailed by whatever means appear possible. The Medicaid program serving the poor is more vulnerable than old age retirement, disability insurance,

Figure 1-1.   Real Gross National Product.

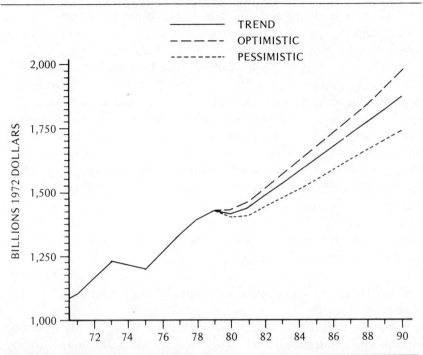

*Source*: Chase Econometrics, Inc. Long-term trend forecast of U.S. economy, Calendar year 1980, 1st quarter. Balacynwyd, Pa.: May 1980.

and the Medicare programs of the Social Security Act, although proposals to limit these programs have already been introduced for congressional action.

Chase Econometrics, Inc., offers three projections of economic conditions in the 1980s: the current trend and growth and decline under optimistic and pessimistic assumptions (Figures 1-1 through 1-4). If we accept the projection of the current trend as our forecast of the future, we can expect resumption of the real growth of the gross national product (GNP) in 1981. By 1990 the GNP will reach an estimated $1,780 billion in 1972 constant dollars, up from $1,385 billion in 1979. Under pessimistic assumptions, GNP growth in 1972 constant dollars will reach only $1,595 billion in 1990. The annual percentage change in real GNP is predicted to return to 3.5 percent in 1982 and reach 4 percent in 1983, and then drop to

Figure 1-2.  Unemployment Rate.

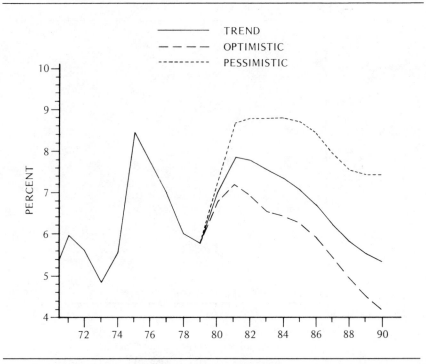

*Source:* Chase Econometrics, Inc. Long-term trend forecast of U.S. economy, Calendar year 1980, 1st quarter. Balacynwyd, Pa.: May 1980.

3.25 percent for the remainder of the decade. The trend for unemployment shows unemployment dropping from a high of close to 8 percent in 1981 to 7 percent in 1985, 6 percent in 1988, and 5.5 percent in 1990. The pessimistic assumptions are very discouraging— 8.8 percent unemployment in 1981 and continuing through 1985, and leveling off to 7.8 percent for the remainder of the decade. The same forecast sees total federal expenditures reaching a high of just over 24 percent of GNP in 1981 and declining to 21.5 percent by 1990. Defense expenditures are projected to remain at the 1980 level of about 5.5 percent through 1990.

At the time they were made, these projections of GNP growth, unemployment, and total federal and defense expenditures allowed little hope for greater expenditures in the 1980s for the mentally disabled. Countercyclical spending to alleviate the pain of unemploy-

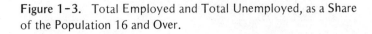

**Figure 1-3.** Total Employed and Total Unemployed, as a Share of the Population 16 and Over.

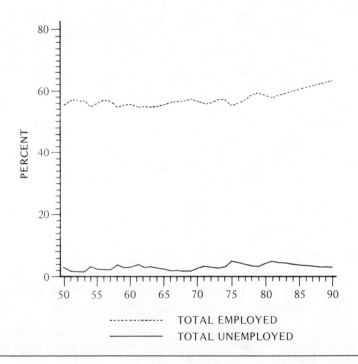

------------- TOTAL EMPLOYED

——————— TOTAL UNEMPLOYED

*Source*: Chase Econometrics, Inc. Long-term trend forecast of U.S. economy, Calendar year 1980, 1st quarter. Balacynwyd, Pa.: May 1980.

ment seemed likely to absorb whatever savings could be achieved through retrenchment and greater administrative efficiencies in selected federal programs. The Reagan administration's budget would drastically alter the picture. By 1984, total federal expenditures would be squeezed from 24 percent of GNP in 1981 to 19 percent. Nondefense spending, now constituting 17 percent of GNP, would be reduced to 12.5 percent in order to keep total federal expenditures within 19 percent of GNP while accommodating a substantial increase for defense spending. This means that after provisions are made for the social security entitlement programs, defense, and payment of interest on the national debt, the remainder of federal spending must be cut by 50 percent—from 6.7 percent to 3.4 percent of GNP (Schlesinger, 1981).

**Figure 1-4.** Total Federal and Defense Expenditures, as a Share of GNP, 1950-1990.

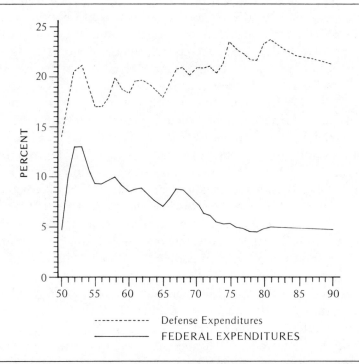

------------ Defense Expenditures

——————— FEDERAL EXPENDITURES

*Source:* Chase Econometrics, Inc. Long-term trend forecast of U.S. economy, Calendar year 1980, 1st quarter. Balacynwyd, Pa.: May 1980.

Even under a modified version of this scenario, it is quite apparent that the sector of federal spending upon which the mentally disabled largely depend for basic income, shelter, and services will sharply decline in the next few years. The competition for funds from the shrinking budget for social programs will intensify and constituencies will be pitted against one another. If the Congress also accepts the Reagan administration's program consolidation and block grant proposals, the competition between constituencies for the diminished social program budget will take place at the state and county levels of government. The power of national lobbies representing these constituencies will be diminished as they attempt to carry their causes to fifty state legislatures and to negotiate with fifty governors and hundreds of mayors and county executives.

Competing for a share of the GNP over the next twenty years will be the demand by the developing countries of the world for large-scale transfer of resources from the developed countries. It is difficult to envision how the United States as a world power can avoid playing a major role in averting what the Brandt Commission and other international experts see as an emerging world crisis (Independent Commission on International Development Issues, 1980). The Third World is in desperate straits because of escalating oil prices. Mayer (1976) claims that petroleum-poor countries have gone as far as they can in improving their crop yields by traditional methods of farming, and that the increase in oil prices has put the "green revolution" effectively beyond their reach. Thus far the United States and the other developed countries have ignored or denied the validity of the Brandt Commission report; but to the extent that the United States and other Western economies must depend on trade with the developing countries for both raw materials and a market for their products, they must respond—peacefully, one hopes. A peaceful response will mean providing the $10–12 billion (U.S. 1975 dollars and prices) that the World Bank estimates it will cost between now and the year 2000 to raise the standard of living of the world's poorest nations (Burki and Voorhoeve, 1971).[b]

The Brandt Commission argues that responding to the desperate needs of the Third World will make it possible for all the nations of the world to survive imminent economic crisis. Massive transfer of funds from the rich to the poor nations of the world is believed necessary to prime the pump of the world economy in order to break out of the current recession and to promote higher growth in the long run.

One way or another the United States will have to make its contribution to preserving the world order—either by increasing spending for aid to the developing countries or by increasing spending for defense. Either way the U.S. economy in the 1980s will feel the

---

b. Although outlays of this magnitude for the next twenty years may appear too great to sustain, some perspective can be had by comparing these costs with the size of the world's income. Burki and Voorhoeve (1971) noted that total investment cost of $377.4 to $381 billion for a twenty-year global basic needs program amounted in 1975 to only 6 percent of world income for that year, or 0.3 percent of world income if total investment costs are expressed as an annual rate. The total investment costs amount to slightly more than the estimated $375 billion spent in 1975 on defense by the nations of the world. Expressed in these terms, it is apparent that the seemingly enormous costs of a global basic needs program is affordable—if only the nations of the world give up a relatively small proportion of spending for defense.

strain, diminishing the availability of funds for improved services to the mentally disabled. This will force individuals and families to sustain a greater share than they now do of the burden of ill health, dysfunction, and dependency.

Many of the programs assisting the disabled population of the United States to achieve greater independence have felt the pinch of inflation. The federal–state vocational rehabilitation program, for example, has fallen behind in real growth at an annual rate of –3.76 percent since 1975 (Table 1-1). While total vocational rehabilitation expenditure grew at an annual rate of 4.12 percent in current dollars, from $1.021 billion to $1.2 billion, it declined in 1975 constant dollars to $0.876 billion in 1979. During the same period, the average expenditure per client rose at an annual rate of 6.72 percent in current dollars, from $821 to $1,065, but in constant 1975 dollars it declined at an average rate of –1.36 percent to $777 in 1979. The number of cases served by the vocational rehabilitation program declined by –0.71 percent for every percentage point reduction in its 1975 purchasing power, from 1.244 million persons served in 1975 to 1.128 million in 1979. Somewhat confounding this drop-off in the number of persons served was the higher priority given to serving the more severely handicapped as the result of the 1973 amendments to the Rehabilitation Act.

What seems clear is that programs with budgets eaten by inflation must place priority on serving those who are worst off and cut back on both the number of persons served and amount spent (in constant dollars per capita). But spreading fewer resources among fewer but more severely impaired people can lead to lower quality services, reduced staff morale and productivity, and diminished cost-effectiveness. The cost-effectiveness of employment oriented programs such as the federal–state vocational rehabilitation program depends on acceptance of persons who are capable with help of achieving legislatively imposed program goals. Staff of such programs are judged by the legislative standard; hence, they must taste success with a large proportion of their clients in order to function effectively.

Assuming nothing changes that would alter the estimate of the prevalence of disabilities in the world population at 10 percent, the projected growth of the world population to the year 2000 will increase the estimated number of disabled people by 193 million over the 1975 estimated number of 387 million (WHO, 1976; Noble, Note 1). The World Health Organization estimated that mental retardation and functional psychiatric disturbance each accounted for

Table 1–1. Impact of Inflation on Federal–State Rehabilitation Program, 1975–1979, and Projected Impact, 1980–1985.

| | 1975 | | | 1979 | | |
|---|---|---|---|---|---|---|
| | Total Expenditure, millions[a] | Cases Served, Thousands | $/Case | Total Expenditure, Millions | Cases Served, Thousands | $/Case |
| | $1,021.3 | 1,244.3 | $820.3 | $1,200.4 1975 $(876.2) | 1,127.6 | $1,064.6 1975 $(777.1) |

*Annual Growth Rates, Percent*

| | Actual, 1975–1979 | Projected, 1980–1985 |
|---|---|---|
| Total Expenditure | | |
| Actual | 4.12 | 4.12 |
| 1975$ | −3.76[b] | −3.85 |
| Cases Served | −2.43 | −2.73[c] |
| Expenditure per Case | | |
| Actual | 6.72 | 7.04 |
| 1975$ | −1.36 | −1.16 |

*Projected Total Expenditure, 1980–1985, $Million*

| | 1980 | 1981 | 1982 | 1983 | 1984 | 1985 |
|---|---|---|---|---|---|---|
| Actual | $1,249.9 | 1,301.4 | 1,355.0 | 1,410.8 | 1,468.9 | 1,529.4 |
| 1975$ | $ 838.9 | 798.4 | 762.2 | 734.8 | 709.6 | 692.1 |
| Cases Served, Thousands | 1,096.8 | 1,066.8 | 1,037.7 | 1,009.4 | 981.8 | 955.0 |
| Expenditure per Case | | | | | | |
| Actual | $1,140 | 1,220 | 1,306 | 1,398 | 1,496 | 1,602 |
| 1975$ | $ 765 | 748 | 734 | 728 | 723 | 725 |

a. Includes federal and state expenditures for Basic Support and Innovation and Expansion grants, as well as federal expenditures under the Social Security Disability Insurance and Supplemental Security Income programs. Source: U.S. Department of Education Rehabilitative Services Administration. "Benefit/Cost Ratios: the state federal program of vocational rehabilitation," Washington, D.C., April 1980; "The effect of inflation on the purchasing power of the vocational rehabilitation dollar, fiscal years 1967 to 1979," Washington, D.C., February 1980.

b. The state and local government purchases implicit price deflator increased by 36.6 percent, 1975–1979, or 8.1 percent annually, and was forecast by the Office of Management and Budget (OMB) in 1979 as likely to increase by 8.35 percent annually, 1979–1985. Executive Office of the President, Office of Management and Budget, "Economic assumptions for use in preparing budget estimates," Washington, D.C., August 1979 and February 1980.

c. Assuming the –0.71 percent decline in cases served, 1975–1979, associated with a 1 percent decrease in 1975$ value continues to hold for 1980–1985 in face of the OMB forecast of state and local government purchases price increases during the period.

7.7 percent of total disability in the world. There is evidence that the prevalence of disability is highly correlated with poverty and social disadvantage caused by the skewed distribution of society's available resources. In the United States, for example, recent survey data on the population of California show that the risk of disability for blacks and native Americans approaches twice the risk for whites, when the age and sex composition of the study sample is standardized to reflect that of all working-age adults in California; the risk of *severe* disability among blacks and native Americans is roughly twice the risk for whites (Table 1-2). These differentiated prevalence rates occur among the socially disadvantaged subpopulations of the United States in face of a 10.5 percent prevalence rate in the general population. Repeated surveys of the noninstitutionalized population of the United States provide estimates of the prevalence of disability of roughly between 10 and 15 percent.

Within broad limits, therefore, one can anticipate both higher rates of disability among the socially disadvantaged classes of society and an absolute increase in the number of disabled people in these classes if they grow at a proportionately higher rate than the general population. Such a growth pattern is projected for the 1980s and beyond in the United States (U.S. Department of Commerce, 1974). The minority populations are expected to grow at a higher rate than the general population; hence, the absolute number of functionally impaired persons as the result of mental illness and mental retardation and other developmental disabilities related to socioeconomic status can be expected to increase. This will occur as federal resources available to cope with disability problems diminish.

## RECENT POLICY TRENDS

The late 1970s saw the development of a number of small-scale initiatives to cope with various aspects of chronic illness and dependency. As the result of the combined efforts of the President's Commission on Mental Health and the U.S. Department of Health, Education, and Welfare (HEW) Secretarial Task Force on Deinstitutionalization, the U.S. Department of Housing and Urban Development (HUD)/Health and Human Services (HHS) Demonstration Program for the Chronically Mentally Ill was launched. Long-Term Care Channeling Demonstrations were subsequently initiated to improve

**Table 1-2.** Comparison of Working-age Disability and Severe Disability Rates, by Ethnic Group from Four Surveys.

| Ethnic Group | 1978 California Disability Survey | 1976 Survey of Income and Education in California | 1970 U.S. Census Public Use Tape | 1972 Nagi Survey (Continental United States) |
|---|---|---|---|---|
| Total sample of working-age adults | 56,332 | 6,825 | 114,937 | 5,331 |
| | | *Percentage Disabled* | | |
| All adults[a] | 10.5 | 12.5 | 10.5 | 10.6 |
| Native American | 18.9 | b | 15.0 | b |
| Black, non-Hispanic | 16.0 | 23.0 | 13.9 | 16.7 |
| White, non-Hispanic | 10.6 | 12.1 | 10.2 | 10.2 |
| Hispanic | 9.0 | 11.5 | 10.2 | 7.3 |
| Mexican-American | 8.7 | b | 10.3 | b |
| Other Hispanic | 9.5 | b | 10.1 | b |
| Asian-American | 4.5 | b | 6.3 | 0.0[c] |
| | | *Percentage Severely Disabled* | | |
| All adults[a] | 5.7 | 7.2 | 4.3 | 6.3 |
| Native American | 11.9 | b | 6.0 | b |
| Black, non-Hispanic | 9.9 | 15.5 | 7.3 | 12.1 |
| White, non-Hispanic | 5.5 | 6.6 | 3.9 | 5.8 |
| Hispanic | 5.5 | 8.2 | 4.4 | 3.1 |
| Mexican-American | 5.8 | b | 4.4 | b |
| Other Hispanic | 5.0 | b | 4.4 | b |
| Asian-American | 2.1 | b | 2.5 | 0.0[c] |

a. Includes other or unreported ethnic group not shown separately.

b. Not separately available.

c. No disabled persons were found in the small sample of Asian-Americans in the Nagi survey.

*Source*: Nicholls, W.L., Freeman, H.E., Shanks, J.M. and Kiecolt, K.J. Ethnic differences in work disability. Submitted to the Office of the Assistant Secretary for Planning and Evaluation, U.S. Department of Health, Education, and Welfare, March 20, 1980, p. 16a.

the distribution of existing resources, as well as to fill some resource gaps when they were evident, in order to maintain the elderly and severely disabled in their own homes. There was also an attempt to launch an independent living initiative during the waning months of the Carter administration. All three initiatives depended on the exercise by the secretary of the Department of Health and Human Services of the waiver authority of Section 1115 of the Social Security Act to pay for a portion of the costs of providing more generous than usual services to demonstration project clientele. After the service subsidies authorized by Section 1115 waiver are withdrawn, as they must be at the end of three or five years at most, either the states or the local communities that hosted the demonstration projects will have to assume responsibility for financing the services if they are to continue.

Obviously the magnitude of these demonstration activities is not commensurate with the scope of the problem of long-term care in the United States. Each of these efforts represents the temporizing that is necessary when budget constraints do not permit major change of either substantive law or the appropriations to accommodate the level of need.

The change in the definition of developmental disabilities by the 1979 amendments to the Developmental Disabilities Services and Bill of Rights Act represents a very great change of policy, albeit perhaps inadvertent, with potential for doing either great good or great harm to the expanded population of persons who fall within the scope of the new definition. Because of the regulatory linkage between the Medicaid ICF/MR–DD program and the Developmental Disabilities Services and Bill of Rights Act, it appears that the Medicaid ICF/MR–DD program now covers all persons with a mental or physical impairment or some combination thereof that is manifested before the person attains 22 years of age, is likely to continue indefinitely, and results in substantial functional limitations in three or more of seven areas of major life activity (self-care, receptive and expressive language, learning, mobility, self-direction, capacity for independent living, and economic self-sufficiency), if the person needs a combination or sequence of "special, interdisciplinary, or generic care, treatment, or other services which are individually planned and coordinated" (Health Care Financing Administration (HCFA), Note 3).

Given the softness of most of the elements of the redefinition of developmental disabilities, onset of the chronically disabling condition prior to age 22 will most likely become the more robust test of the applicability of the definition to specific individuals. Some persons in the State of Texas, for example, see the new definition as very broad and interpretable to "include everyone admitted to a mental health treatment program," so much so that "the revised definition offers a 'pot of gold' for those mental health agencies able to overcome the limitations that may exist in their State Medicaid plans" (Texas Department of Mental Health and Mental Retardation, Note 2). In a word, following the collocation principle, enunciated earlier, the states could take advantage of the redefinition of developmental disabilities by amending their Medicaid plans to cover populations that are now entirely excluded from federal funding or only covered through closed-ended program authorities, which unlike Medicaid cannot exceed the annual budget set for them by the appropriation committees of the Congress.

Depending on how restrictive the ICF/MR-DD program defines the services and the conditions attached to their delivery, that is, on how "institutional" the setting must be to qualify for reimbursement, the problem of financing services for the mentally disabled in the least restrictive environment appropriate to meeting their needs has been solved in theory. Suffice it to say that federal Medicaid officials will undoubtedly move to attach very stringent conditions to the delivery of services in the ICF/MR-DD program, if not to decouple the program from the definition of developmental disabilities contained in the Developmental Disabilities Services and Bill of Rights Act, in order to curtail program costs. But the operation of the collocation principle will by one estimate (Copeland and Iversen, 1980) cost the federal treasury an additional $2.5 billion annually by 1983 unless definitional decoupling occurs. (See also Chapter 4 of this book).

We may well become the victims of our opportunism if reform of currently deficient policies continues along the emerging line of development, reform, namely, by launching periodic minimally funded initiatives and hoping that they will catch on or by changing definitions to capture open-ended funds. It is all too easy and tempting to try different combinations of the available patent medicines in the attempt to suppress the symptoms of a serious underlying disease.

Of course, the game as played by the states in relation to the different federal categorical programs will change radically under the Reagan administration's budget concepts and proposals to consolidate programs. The proposal to cap Medicaid by limiting annual growth to a certain percentage increase, although it would give greater flexibility to state officials in their determining of permissible uses of funds, would force the states to take a careful look at the cost-effectiveness of covered services in light of the total demand for services by assorted needy populations. The danger, of course, is that institutional care, because of the vested interests of its large provider constituency, will, under the guise of greater flexibility of use, bleed off even larger amounts of Medicaid funding than it now does. In a more perfect world, one would hope that the findings of the Touche Ross (1980) study of institutional and community-based program costs in Nebraska, together with more flexible use of Medicaid as well as other funds contained in the block grants being advanced by the Reagan administration, would lead to less institutional and more community care of the mentally disabled.

The problem of long-term care of the elderly and severely disabled imposes a heavy burden on the economically active segment of the population and creates a painful strain between the generations, especially in countries where the forces of industrialization and high labor force mobility have loosened the ties of family responsibility for dependent members. The experience of eight cities in seven different European countries parallels, with a single exception, that of the United States (Wiseman and Barnard, 1980). As their populations' age and the old-age dependency ratios increased, the eight cities faced significant problems relating to:

- Provision of adequate care facilities;
- Education of physicians concerning the needs of the elderly and severely disabled;
- Placement of patients into the appropriate kinds of facilities and/or hospital beds;
- Changing attitudes and practices in hospitals toward confused patients and how they should be treated;
- Staffing in face of the poor distribution of services;
- Complex organizational and financing systems for supporting the elderly and severely disabled.

Of the eight cities (Stockholm; Amsterdam; Copenhagen; Dublin; Edinburgh; Geneva; Nottingham, England; and Zagreb, Yugoslavia), only Zagreb with its cultural emphasis on having the elderly continue to live with their families, buttressed by a well-developed primary health care system, seemed able to cope with long-term care without undue stress. The contrast between Sagreb and the other cities per- mits statement of a hypothesis concerning the course that successful as compared to unsuccessful long-term care policy development is likely to take.

Countries that can provide financial and other incentives as well as service supports to the families of severely handicapped or debili- tated persons will minimize the burden of long-term care at least cost to the public treasury and win for this type of policy a greater measure of taxpayer support. Countries, on the other hand, that try to improve the effectiveness of their existing service systems by spending increasing amounts on coordination—the course of least political resistance—will achieve only marginal improvements at inordinate cost. They will succeed in adding layers of bureaucracy and regulatory controls and increase thereby not only friction be- tween government agencies and service providers but also between government and families. The already weakened ties that many families have with their elderly and severely disabled members may be loosened still further.

The United States presents an extreme example. The vested inter- ests that surround the very complex, often duplicative set of cate- gorical social programs tend to block basic reforms. So many forms of categorical government intervention have gradually eroded family responsibility for severely disabled members. Some programs, be- cause of the strong financial disincentives they provide to continuing responsibility, may even encourage families to jettison their handi- capped into nursing homes, institutions, or board and care arrange- ments. The Supplemental Security Income (SSI) program, which pro- vides income support for the elderly, blind, and disabled who can meet a means test reduces by one-third the amount of benefits if the beneficiary lives in or takes up residence in the household of a related other.

The United States is not removing these disincentives to family responsibility. The cost of higher near-term budgetary outlays (which might conceivably lead to lower future costs) and the demand for adoption of costly competing policies that often favor providers of nursing home and institutional care prevent it from happening. Instead, the United States continues to pursue the temporizing, cost-avoidance strategy of mounting serially duplicative and overlapping low-cost demonstrations to prove how better coordination and packaging of resources can improve service delivery to the chronically ill and disabled populations. To the extent that critics of U.S. long-term care and disability policies accept the bone that is tossed to them to gnaw on, these efforts, by one standard, succeed. They fail as valid demonstrations, however, to the extent that they succumb to compromises in scientific method or accommodate to the institutional care bias of the providers within the communities in which they are launched.

## NEW DIRECTIONS

How can we improve the adequacy, equity, and efficiency of the allocation of resources for the welfare of mentally disabled persons in need of long-term care and treatment? Are there any viable ways to proceed in face of the severe financial constraints facing the nation in the 1980s? There are some ways to proceed, but I hesitate to predict how traditional service providers may react. The majority of handicapped people and their families, or the surrogate families that could be found for them, I believe, will respond favorably to what I propose. The Reagan administration's decision to consolidate categorical programs and to allow state and local governments greater flexibility in determining how to use federal funds may actually enhance possible acceptance of my proposals.

### Formation of Cooperatives

Perhaps the only way of reducing the increasingly high administrative and overhead costs of the many categorical programs that characterize the American welfare state is to organize handicapped consumers and their families or family surrogates into cooperatives. Only by eliminating at least some of  the middlemen can handicapped consumers stretch the value of the available service dollar and at the same time preserve some semblance of acceptable quality. In the 1980s the economy will undoubtedly force all consumers either to do without or to engage in barter to obtain desired goods and services. There is no reason why members of cooperatives for the handicapped could not do likewise. The cooperative structure is well suited as a framework and a medium through which the exchange of needed goods and services can take place among handicapped individuals and their families or family surrogates.

Smith (1979) provides support for greater reliance on informal social networks, either in themselves or in conjunction with the formal intervention system, to promote greater independence among handicapped persons. Summarizing the results of his study of 950 chronically disabled adults living in a metropolitan community, which unexpectedly found no statistically significant relationship between utilization of rehabilitation services and recovery status,[c] Smith concluded that

> the evidence suggests that informal social networks play an important role in the rehabilitation of the disabled. Reliance on informal resources is enhanced in the absence of formal rehabilitation intervention, suggesting alternative modes of social support are actively sought and utilized by the disabled. Furthermore, lay-initiative may constitute another effective resource in the process of recovery. (p. 63)

Family, friends, and nonrehabilitation agency sources of help such as unions, employers, and fraternal and religious organizations constituted the informal social network in question. Smith's study does not stand alone in pointing to the vital role played by family and informal social networks in face of acute or chronic illness and dysfunction. Others (WHO, 1976; Martin, 1978; Croog and Levine, 1977; Kaplan, Cassel, and Gore, 1977) have remarked on the importance of this resource for impaired individuals.

In suggesting that handicapped consumers and their families or family surrogates organize themselves into cooperatives to stretch the value of the available service dollar while preserving some semblance of acceptable quality, I have in mind a concept broader than a housing cooperative, although some cooperatives for the handicapped may involve creation of a housing cooperative or even a nonprofit housing development corporation in order to qualify for financial and technical assistance from the National Consumer Cooperative Bank. A cooperative for handicapped persons, in order to meet the full range of needs of its membership, might have to acquire provider

---

c. Recovery status was measured by a four-factor index of independence. Changes toward greater work activity, unrestricted mobility, self-derived income, and not being under a physician's care were deemed indicative of greater independence.

status under a variety of social programs — most notably under the ICF/MR – DD authority of Medicaid and Title XX Social Services (or the block grant program that has been proposed as its successor). Within the constraints of budget afforded by such provider arrangements with state and local governments, handicapped persons and their families or surrogate families might begin to exercise a greater measure of responsibility for their own lives. They could contract, according to their needs, with a variety of organizations and individuals for whatever goods and services they might require, or they could make purchases on a fee-for-service basis.

The concept of a cooperative for the handicapped differs from that of the Centers for Independent Living, now authorized by Title VII, Part B, of the Rehabilitation Act of 1973, as amended. The handicapped and their families or surrogate families would be provided with something more than a service supplement because of the provider status the cooperatives for the handicapped would have to obtain. A cooperative would thus be defined as a nonprofit entity existing for the purpose of providing on a cooperative basis goods, services, or facilities primarily for the benefit of its members or voting consumer stockholders. Such status would confer eligibility for loans at below-market rates of interest from the National Consumer Cooperative Bank, as well as eligibility for assistance under the HUD Sections 202, 213, and 265/235 and Home Ownership programs (Schwarzentraub, 1980).

## Realigning Financing Incentives

The single most important threat to the welfare of mentally disabled people is how services are financed by public authorities, not necessarily how much is spent on services. This issue intrudes into the everyday decisions of individuals and families, service providers, and politicians who attempt to cope with the functional limitations of chronically ill or developmentally impaired persons. The very existence of so many categorical programs — each offering often only a fraction of what is needed and governed by many complicated rules and regulations that serve to ration the limited categorical resource — creates perverse incentives with attendant distortions in service delivery and high administrative costs. Copeland (1979) seemingly accepts the inevitability of categoricalism and advises social service professionals on how to obtain inflation-adjusted increases in social services funding of up to 30 percent in the next five years. His advice is "to use available funds, in part at least, on a program developmental and organizational basis, in order to attract funds from income-maintenance, health, housing, and food and nutrition programs, and to package total *sets* of services which will be identifiably social services" (p. 62). (See also Chapter 4 of this book).

Pursuit of Copeland's strategy has the good effect of permitting successful social service entrepreneurs to capture sufficient funds now and then with which to develop a program package that makes sense in meeting the needs of at least some of those who require care and treatment. It has the bad effect of promoting inequitable resource distribution among persons with equally valid service needs. Moreover, the strategy fosters gimmick solutions, game-playing among actors located in different parts of the interacting service provider and governmental systems, and a general disregard for the principles of efficient resource allocation. With everybody trying to use their available funds as leverage against other limited funding sources, there comes a point of diminishing returns. Not unlike people who join pyramid clubs, latecomers will end up losers.

Last, Copeland's strategy does not address the larger dynamic of the budget shifting that is occurring among the social programs as well as among the major sectors of the economy. It can do nothing to stop the squeeze on community health care and the social services that results from accelerated federal spending for hospital and nursing home care under Medicare and Medicaid. The trend, if it continues unabated, will reduce the share of total federal spending going for community health care and social services, which was 37 percent in 1970, to 21 percent in 1985, while increasing the share going for acute inpatient hospital and long-term care (including that in mental hospitals), which was 63 percent in 1970, to 79 percent in 1985 (Noble, 1980). It is important to note in this regard that nothing in the Reagan administration's Medicaid reform and block grant proposals will reverse this trend. Medicaid growth is to be limited to no more than 5 percent annually; the budgets of the programs being consolidated into the social services block grant will be reduced by 20–25 percent in 1982, and the resultant block grant budget held level for the three succeeding years.

There is no way of combatting these trends except by adopting an explicit countervailing budget strategy with built-in incentives to promote community care of the mentally disabled. Unless such a budget strategy is adopted, the current trends seem likely to curtail needed community-based programs and services, making a mockery of the ideal of providing care appropriate to client needs that is least restrictive of personal liberties.

Two models for constraining the growth of Medicaid in favor of increased spending for community health care and the social services were outlined by the HEW Secretarial Task Force on Deinstitutionalization (1978). Neither was adopted because of the incrementalist philosophy of the Carter administration and the seeming impossibility of getting the Congress to adopt a budget strategy that would require disciplined implementation over six or more years to achieve the desired reversal of trend. It was also recognized that, even if community health care and social services spending was expanded at the expense of the inpatient hospital care and long-term care, several important but as yet unanswered questions remained: On whom should the expanded community spending be targeted? What mix of income support, direct services, and advocacy would provide the greatest benefit?

Admittedly, the remaining questions are vexing, but probably less so to the state and local government officials who are directly responsible for administering programs than they are to the farther removed federal officials. Under the Reagan administration's budget and program consolidation policies, it will be state and local government officials who must fashion answers to these questions and, in doing so, translate their answers into specific allocations of commingled federal block grant and state and local funds. The repeal of state matching requirements as a condition for receipt of federal funds may correct the uneven valuation of program dollars by state and local governments and thus promote use of the criteria of cost-effectiveness and economic efficiency as guides to action. No longer will the federal matching rate determine the relative values of different categories of program expenditures—the less costly being defined by the relative generosity of the federal matching rate and/or by the open-ended as compared to closed-ended character of the federal funding stream. If the states maintain overall program effort in face of the temptation to cut back in favor of taxpayer relief, less regulatory encumbrance and greater flexibility in use of federal block grant funds might well free state and local governments to pursue a coherent budget strategy in support of community care of the mentally disabled.

In the event that this does not happen, state and local governments will no longer have the federal government to blame for program failures. The intent of the Reagan administration is clearly to return as much control as possible over the social programs to state and local government officials. Public accountability goes with the territory, and so does the "heat" when things go wrong or when some constituencies remain dissatisfied despite best efforts.

## Income Maintenance and Health Care Reforms

Among the many changes of current policies that could ease the burden of disability on individuals and families, improvements in income support and health care coverage are basic. Bringing about constructive change in these areas is difficult at best however; even greater challenges must be faced during a period of fiscal austerity and retrenchment. Definitional problems in setting eligibility criteria, the worrisome work disincentive effects that sometimes ensue, and the high costs of changing welfare and health care policies present formidable obstacles to would-be reformers.

The HEW Secretarial Task Force on Deinstitutionalization (1978) identified three income maintenance policies that impede deinstitutionalization and community care of the mentally disabled: long delays at the point of hospital discharge in determining the eligibility of mentally ill persons for SSI benefits; the one-third reduction of the SSI award of persons living and receiving in-kind support and maintenance in others' huseholds; and the $25 per month limitation on SSI payments to institutionalized persons. Evidence of the harmful effects of these policies was not sufficient to overcome arguments that it would cost too much to make corrective policy changes (Noble and Conley, 1981).

It seems unlikely that anything can be done to change these policies, unless in the realignment of federal, state, and local government roles and responsibilities being proposed by the Reagan administration an acceptable tradeoff can be found to induce the federal government to make the requisite changes. Many governors and mayors would like to see the federal government take over completely responsibility for income maintenance and health care coverage of the poor. If the suitable *quid pro quo* presents itself, the governors and mayors would be far wiser to put aside the incrementalist reforms identified by the HEW Secretarial Task Force on Deinstitutionalization and to seek instead adoption of the recommendation by Elizabeth Boggs (in the next chapter) that the policies of SSI be aligned more closely with those of Social Security Disability Insurance, making the federal payment contingent only on disability or old age and financial need rather than on place of residence or site of care. Such basic reform would in one sweep correct several of the flawed income maintenance policies adversely affecting handicapped persons, as well as remove the incentive that now exists to place people in overly restrictive case settings in order to secure the combination of income maintenance and services support. In effect, the reform would provide an income floor paying for food, shelter, and other basic living necessities, to which state and local governments or private philanthropy could add services support as needed.

Finally, more cost-effective vehicles must be found for delivering health services to all kinds of handicapped persons. Noninstitutionalized handicapped persons have greater health care needs than the rest of the population, and they spend more on medical care both through Medicare and Medicaid and out-of-pocket expenses (Stanley and Swisher, 1969; Brehm and Cormier, 1970; Jones and Jones, 1976). There is also evidence showing that acceptance of community-based care by the families of institutionalized retarded persons is more dependent on their perceptions of the medical needs of their retarded members than on any other factor (Keating, Conroy, and Walker, 1980). Families generally believe that their institutionalized members require greater amounts of medical supervision than do the medical staff actually providing care and so resist their placement into less restrictive care settings (Conroy, Feinstein, and Lemanowicz, 1981).

In view of these facts, it is important to assure mentally disabled persons—whether or not they belong to cooperatives for the handicapped—of membership in health maintenance organizations (HMOs), the American equivalent of the primary health care system that, as was mentioned earlier, so successfully meets the long-term care needs of handicapped and elderly people in Zagreb, Yugoslavia. The HMO seems particularly well suited to meeting the health care needs of mentally disabled persons because it strongly emphasizes preventive medicine and instruction of families in self-care. To the extent that the HMO philosophy and practice actually results in cost-savings through reduced use of more expensive medical facilities, the savings will be passed along to handicapped persons and their families, enabling them to spend less on medical care and more on other, more preferred kinds of consumption. But perhaps even more important than the possible savings involved is the likely positive influence that HMO care will have on family perceptions of the medical needs of their handicapped members. More accurate perceptions of medical need can be expected to promote greater reliance on community-based alternatives to institutional care.

In closing, it is worth noting that HMO membership is not only important to the mentally disabled but also to the majority of Americans as perhaps the only viable way to contain the spiraling costs of health care. These costs are squeezing the budgets of the community-based programs and services needed by mentally disabled persons in order to enjoy normalized living, as well as the budgets of each and every taxpayer. This reality makes adoption of policies that encourage expansion of HMOs offering coverage to all people—handicapped and nonhandicapped alike—a high priority item for the agenda of the 1980s. Such expansion might well free resources for alternative uses, including that of providing more humane and beneficial care of mentally disabled persons.

## REFERENCES

Allderidge, P. Hospitals, madhouses and asylums: Cycles in the care of the insane. *British Journal of Psychiatry*, 1979, *134*, 321–334.

Brehm, H.P., and Cormier, R.H. Medical care costs for the disabled, *Social Security survey of the disabled, 1966*, Report no. 8. Baltimore: U.S. Department of Health, Education, and Welfare, Social Security Administration, Office of Research and Statistics, January 1970.

Burki, S.J., and Voorhoeve, J.J.C. *Global estimates for meeting basic needs: Background paper.* Washington, D.C.: World Bank, August 10, 1971.

Chase Econometrics, Inc. *Long-term trend forecast of U.S. economy, calendar year 1980, 1st quarter.* Balacynwyd, Pa.: May 1980.

Conroy, J.W., Feinstein, C.S., and Lemanowicz, J. *Medical needs of clients: Perceptions of relatives and of staff.* Philadelphia: Temple University Developmental Disabilities Center, Evaluation and Research Group, February 17, 1981.

Copeland, W. C. Financing social services for the developmental continuum. In *The Social Welfare Forum, 1979.* New York: Columbia University Press, 1980, pp. 62–75.

Copeland, W. C., and Iversen, I. A. *The new DD definition—Should it be decoupled from Title XIX?* Minneapolis: University of Minnesota, Hubert H. Humphrey Institute of Public Affairs, July 8, 1980.

Croog, S. H., and Levine, S. *The heart patient recovers.* New York: Human Sciences Press, 1977.

HEW Secretarial Task Force on Deinstitutionalization for the Mentally Disabled. *Interim report of the Task Force on Deinstitutionalization of the Mentally Disabled—Decision memorandum for Secretary of Health, Education and Welfare.* Washington, D.C., Annex pp. 10–4–10–11 and Annex 2.

Independent Commission on International Development Issues. *North-South: A programme for survival.* Cambridge, Mass.: MIT Press, 1980.

Jones, P. P., and Jones, K. J. *Costs of ideal services to the developmentally disabled under varying levels of adequacy.* Interim report no. 4. Waltham, Mass.: Brandeis University, Florence Heller Graduate School for Advanced Studies in Social Welfare, July 1976.

Kaplan, B. H., Cassel, J. C., and Gore, S. Social support and health. *Medical Care Supplement,* 1977, *15,* 47–58.

Keating, D., Conroy, J. W., and Walker, S. *Family impacts baseline: A survey of the families of residents of Pennhurst.* Philadelphia: Temple University Development Disabilities Center, Evaluation and Research Group, October 30, 1980.

Martin, J. F. The active patient: A necessary development. *WHO Chronicle,* 1978, *32,* 51–57.

Mayer, J. The dimensions of human hunger. *Scientific American,* September 1976, 40–49.

National Association of State Mental Health Program Directors. *A blueprint for a national plan for the chronically mentally ill.* Washington, D.C.: National Association of State Mental Health Program Directors, June 12, 1980.

Nicholls, W. L., Freeman, H. E., Shanks, J. M., and Kiecolt, K. J. Ethnic differences in work disability. Prepared for the Office of the Assistant Secretary for Planning and Evaluation, U. S. Department of Health, Education, and Welfare, Washington, D.C., March 20, 1980.

Noble, J. H., Jr. Mental health services delivery: Problems and opportunities in the '80s. *Rhode Island MHRH Journal,* 1980, *2,* 24–34.

Noble, J. H., Jr., and Conley, R. W. Fact and conjecture in the policy of deinstitutionalization. *Health Policy Quarterly,* 1981, in press.

Schlesinger, J. R. Balance-of-government. *Washington Post,* March 4, 1981, A-21.

Schwarzentraub, K. *Cooperatives and its implications to individuals who have special needs.* Sacramento: California Department of Housing and Community Development, June 18, 1980.

Smith, R.T. Rehabilitation of the disabled: The role of social networks in the recovery process. *International Rehabilitation Medicine*, 1979, *1*, 63–72.

Stanley, G.L., and Swisher, I.G. Medical care utilization by the disabled: 1966. In *Social Security survey of the disabled, 1966*. Report no. 5. Baltimore: U.S. Department of Health, Education, and Welfare, Social Security Administration, Office of Research and Statistics, January 1969.

Touche Ross and Company. *Cost study of the community based mental retardation regions and the Beatrice State Development Center*. Report to Directors of the Departments of Public Institutions and Public Welfare, Nebraska. Kansas City, Mo., August 15, 1980.

U.S. Department of Commerce, Bureau of the Census. *Projections of the population of the United States: 1975–2050*. Series P-25, no. 601. Washington, D.C.: Government Printing Office, October 1975.

Wiseman, C., and Barnard, K. *Information for planning: Services for the elderly*. Final report of workshop, Stockholm, 1979. University of Leeds, Nuffield Centre for Health Services Studies, United Kingdom, 1980.

World Health Organization. *Reports on specific technical matters—disability, prevention and rehabilitation*. A29/INF. DOC/1. Geneva, April 28, 1976.

World Health Organization. *International classification of impairments, disabilities and handicaps*. Geneva, 1980.

## REFERENCE NOTES

1. Noble, J.H., Jr. *Population and development problems relating to disability prevention and rehabilitation*. Background paper submitted June 30, 1980, for meeting of the Expert Committee on Disability Prevention and Rehabilitation in Geneva in February 1981.

2. Letter from the Texas Department of Mental Health and Mental Retardation, April 23, 1980.

3. Health Care Financing Administration. *Redefinition of developmental disabilities*. HCFA regional letter, no. 80-3, Baltimore: U.S. Department of Health, Education and Welfare, HCFA, February 1980.

# 2 BEHAVIORAL FISICS

*Elizabeth M. Boggs*

We live in a time when new scientific specialties frequently emerge at the interfaces between traditional disciplines in response to new challenges. For example, in the past five years behavioral medicine has emerged as a new branch of science. It's credentials include a professional society, a journal, and a focal point in the federal research and development establishment, specifically a branch in the National Heart, Lung, and Blood Institute of the National Institutes of Health (Holden, 1980). Like many scientific specialties this one did not spring full fledged from the head of Zeus but, rather, evolved synergisticly, drawing on several disciplines not previously seen as complementary. Behavioral medicine has roots in psychosomatic medicine, behavior modification, and psychoneuroimmunology, among other fields. It also draws on anthropology, sociology, and basic biology.

Similarly it is time to define and endow another new science: *behavioral fisics*, the study of the ways in which the behavior of individuals, in both their personal and organizational capacities, influences and is influenced by the uses of the public fisc. There is nothing new about dollars being dangled with intent to influence politicians, bureaucrats, voters, workers, patients and clients in a variety of legitimate ways. However, the burgeoning of intergovernmental transfer systems and personal benefit entitlements in the past quarter century concurrent with advances in behavioral psychology suggests that the time is ripe for a new synthesis. Behavioral fisics draws upon political science, economics, social psychology, marketing, demography, and ethics. This chapter is concerned with applications of behavioral fisics to incentives and disincentives associated with allocations of public and semipublic resources on behalf of vulnerable citizens in general and specifically persons who, as a result of a mental impairment, are unequal contenders in the economic and social marketplaces.

People with significant chronic mental disabilities are unequal contenders on three counts: (1) They need more and usually produce less than the "average" citizen of the same age. (2) They are deficient in competitive competence in a competitive culture. And (3) they are more limited in their ability to cope, to manage their lives and the resources they have, in a way that is satisfying to themselves and at the same time elicits from others the intangible goods and psychic satisfactions associated with affirmative interpersonal interactions.

## PSYCHIC VERSUS MATERIAL RESOURCES

Although most books on traditional economics deal with "hard" and measurable resources such as barrels of oil, acres of real estate, pounds of food, gold, manganese, grain, and so on, along with manhours of workers' productive time, doctors' visits, episodes of care, TV rights, and the like, there are some who also recognize psychic benefits and costs as goods in the economic sense. Man does not live by bread alone, and he may trade some of his bread for a concert ticket (Boggs, 1979). The concept of psychic benefits and costs is especially important in a conference on changing governmental policies for the mentally disabled for several reasons:

1. Human service workers, both professionals and nonprofessionals, place a special value on psychic benefits such as satisfaction in helping others, a sense of accomplishment on the job, and enhanced self-esteem. If these benefits are not enjoyed, there is likely to be high employee turnover, a costly phenomenon (Lakin and Bruininks, 1981; Zaharia and Baumeister, 1978) and

frequent organized demands for wage increases, perhaps a form of sublimation.[a]

2. The willingness of the public to allocate some portion of charitable and tax dollars to alleviating the ills of "the less fortunate" depends on the psychic benefits the taxpayer or contributor derive from a sense of altruism or good citizenship, as distinct from willingness to pay for what is seen as personal security (Rubin, 1978).

3. The product—better mental health and functioning for mentally disabled people—is itself a psychic benefit.

It is hard to put a monetary value on psychic benefits (Sharfstein, Turner, and Clark, 1978). This is a major reason why coverage for mental health services is so limited in public and private third-party health care programs.

Papers on financing human services often explore the fiscal incentives and tradeoffs, that may be at work among such actors as employees of local, county, state, and federal executive agencies, legislators, the private providers, and, in some instances, consumers. It is generally posited that the behavior exhibited is explainable by the expectation that each agency maximizes its apparent productivity or profit while minimizing its net costs. State rehabilitation agencies, for example, use state employees to carry out much of their mission; they tend to play down the fact that 80 percent of their funding is federal, except when impressing the state legislators with the fine return the state gets on its state matching dollars. It is assumed that a state generally deploys its own controllable dollars so as to maximize its federal reimbursements. Closer inspection reveals, however, that not all incentives and disincentives are fiscal or even political in the eye-to-reelection sense. Moreover, it is the movers and shakers, the *individuals* within agencies who are affected by incentives, more than the agencies as entities. We speak of incentives to the state, but within a state a governor, various different agency heads, and the minority whip in the legislature may respond differently to different incentives.

a. In a recent panel discussion involving four individuals rendering direct care to retarded persons, with a participating audience of about 100, wages were mentioned only once, in passing.

At least two forms of psychic benefits or costs enter into these fiscal phenomena. First and foremost is the sense of power, not merely the power to spend, give, or grant, but the power to channel, direct, or guide. The person who controls the sluices may not drink a glassful or divert a single gallon to irrigation, and he certainly cannot impound the waters more than temporarily (as Richard Nixon found out), but the timing of his releases have influence downstream, as anyone who has run the rapids on the Colorado below Glen Canyon Dam can attest. It is this kind of power—control—not the total volume of dollars allotted to a state, that led to intense negotiations over the role of the state mental health agencies under the Mental Health Systems Act (PL 96–398) enacted late in 1980.

The second and more subtle form of psychic benefit (or cost) has to do with what George Stevenson many years ago called "administrative ease." Most change is disruptive of administrative ease; this fact accounts for much of the resistance encountered when changes are proposed.

Administrative ease is fostered when responsibilities are focused, risk is reduced, or at least contained, and resources are channeled and relatively reliable. These are the conditions sought by insurance companies when they design and sell group policies; they are also the conditions that can make large state universities, large public housing projects, and larger residential institutions for retarded persons comfortable and convenient for administrators who are in charge of the missions that these facilities have been devised to serve. Administrative ease is also enhanced by packaging and by standardization. Thus, when large enterprises are dispersed and services decentralized, there remain unstated incentives that motivate administrators to standardize units of service and reduce the number and variety of categories. Discrete payment levels are established accordingly, with the result that the client or patient comes to be labeled with the level of care he is deemed to require. Moreover, from the administrator's point of view (whether regional program director, budget officer, information system specialist, or comptroller) the idea of an "all-in" capitation or per diem rate is very appealing. This is one reason why the model embodied in the small intermediate care facility for the mentally retarded (ICF/MR) has been attractive to program managers. The board, lodging, and services are paid for in a single accounting. Since these incentives produce relatively few pigeon holes, a wide variety of people can end up identified as, for example, "Skilled

Nursing Facility (SNF) level II." Providers in turn respond to the incentive to fill as many "beds" as possible with persons who fall at the least troublesome (or least costly) end of the spectrum included in a particular category. This is an example of "creaming."

When Bruininks and his colleagues initiated their multipurpose project to document the "community" models of living arrangements for persons with developmental disabilities, they attempted to develop a taxonomy of such living arrangements. The states' own descriptions were highly idiosyncratic. Categories ranged in number from one to thirteen per state with the model value running around five to seven. Bruininks, Thurlow, Thurman, and Fiorelli (1980) found that the forty or more different terms could be accommodated into ten types including the traditional "institution" as one. Increasingly program planners are finding that, with small facilities, external professional expertise must be brought to bear along with selective out-of-home programming. With this comes the question of out-of-home sponsorship with separate funding for the residential component and for each of several day programs or therapies or activities. Under these circumstances, total costs attributable to particular clients are somewhat harder to trace unless a sophisticated client information system is maintained.

## SYSTEMS AND OTHER INVISIBLE INSTITUTIONS

Institutions are most visible when they are embodied in bricks and mortar and contained at a particular place. However, as a social structure, prone to homeostatis that maximizes administrative ease, an institution is no less an institution just because it is physically dispersed. Moreover, physical dispersion does not protect against social isolation. It has been estimated that one-third of the 1.3 million nursing home beds in this country are now controlled by only twenty chains, a phenomenon of aggregation that has developed rapidly in the past five years (*U.S. News and World Report*, 1980), yet the average size of individual homes is still well under 100 beds. In Chapter 5 of this volume, Valerie Bradley discusses the evidence for similar clustering of group homes, including ownership by interstate corporations. The phenomenon of group home aggregate ownership was reported earlier by Bruininks et al. (1979). There are cogent economic and administrative reasons why the country inn has been displaced by Ramada and Howard Johnson's and the locally owned country bank by Bankamerica, but at least in the latter cases, the customers maintain some autonomy and have some choices. There is less evidence that societal institutions serving the mentally disabled, whether centrally located or "scatter sited," are as responsive to consumer needs and interests as are motel chains and banks.

Public human service systems, like water and power companies, tend to view themselves as highly structured natural monopolies (social institutions) each with its own established distribution system and catchment area or special population of customers. The map that delineates the respective catchment areas of various utilities can appear very gerrymandered to an observer unacquainted with their prior history. These apparently independent entrepreneurs are interconnected in ways that become obvious only in times of stress, such as a major power outage when a larger grid is activated. The human service analogy here is to intersystem fungibility of funding streams, such as was practiced most conspicuously in the midseventies between social services funding under Title IV A and XVI (and later Title XX) of the Social Security Act, and other systems such as personal health care, income maintenance and even education. Such responses require administrators with some degree of initiative and sense of reciprocal interests, as well as an acquiescent public.

The Medicaid component of the health care financing system is still used fungibly to pay for income maintenance and social services for some populations, especially for persons needing long-term care. History has shown that when the press, budget offices, or legislators perceive abuses of fungibility provisions, efforts are made to constrain them. The constraining regulations may well be somewhat arbitrary and are likely to limit the legitimate uses of the program being regulated. The classic example is the "capping" of federal social services funds in 1973 and of social service training funds in 1980. Both were preceded by several years of deliberate overregulation aimed at containment.

It is also instructive to look at what is happening to another historical monopoly, the U.S. Postal Service. It is now being forced to share the package and express mail market with such private entrepreneurs as United Parcel, Federal Express, Purolator, the airlines, Greyhound, and even Quip. Here, some customers from the private sector are willing to pay for speed, convenience, reliability of scheduling, and security, in addition to transportation. The providers are not bound by rules of equity but may elect to serve only profitable destinations. They do not have to provide a universal service; they need not maintain offices in rural areas; they set their own conditions. These entrepreneurs segregate the most manageable or most lucrative components of the market, a practice known in the human service field as "creaming." As a result, the public service (in this case the U.S. Postal Service) that was constructed as a natural or public monopoly to serve everyone becomes instead the resource of last resort, and hence, is likely to have the highest unit cost. As mentioned earlier, creaming by private providers is a major factor in the delivery of mental health services. This phenomenon is likely to become even stronger with the trend away from direct public operation of facilities and toward reliance on the private sector. The public agency is likely to find itself responsible for the least attractive client, after the public resource capable of serving them has been dismantled.

The administrator faced with immediate demands to find "community alternatives" to public institutional care, is induced by the incentive of administrative ease in the short run to let the consumer do his own brokering in the private sector or to purchase private care or services on behalf of clients, using a public employee as agent. Additional incentives for these practices are found in federal biases against public, nonmedical institutions, and against all facilities defined as "institutions for mental diseases." However, downriver one may expect considerable disease for the public administrator as well as "fragmentation," "duplication," and "discontinuities," as this new, largely unplanned, uncontrolled, and untidy system expands. Given the job life expectancy of state commissioners and even supervisors, the short-term incentives are more powerful than the long-term incentives, unfortunately.

The process is referred to as "dumping," a term which has attained new currency in the human services field in the last decade and is now familiar to readers of the *Wall Street Journal* as well as more popular papers. It refers to the indiscriminate discharge of mental patients who have been evaluated as not dangerous but whose coping skills are marginal; more particularly, "dumping" is used to describe the resulting concentration of such patients in converted hotels and blighted areas, and their visible presence in doorways of public buildings and the benches of public waiting rooms. This is the seamy side of liberating the still vulnerable patient to be his own broker. Leaders at the National Institute of Mental Health and in-state mental health agencies have recognized this phenomenon as a continuing problem and have formulated criteria for community support programs; the fiscal incentives for an appropriately prescriptive, dispersed, and less visible system have not yet been put in place (Sharfstein, Turner, and Clark, 1978).

## WHO AND WHERE ARE THE CONSUMERS?

Behavioral fisics has multiple manifestations in the consumer sector as in other sectors, and these took on some new colorations in the 1970s. During the late seventies, the U.S. Congress gave important attention to the issue of work disincentives among persons under age 65 eligible for disability benefits under Social Security, Supplementary Security Income, and Medicaid. Although the test of "substantial gainful activity" as an index of work disability has been maintained as a requirement for initial eligibility, a number of provisions were enacted in 1980 to mitigate the notch effect (sudden loss of important benefits as earnings increase) for those whose physical or mental impairments persist but who, with rehabilitation, ongoing supportive services (such as attendant care) and strong motivation, can reenter the job market in a productive capacity. The principal proponents and beneficiaries of these changes in Titles II and XVI of the Social Security Act were younger adults with physical disabilities. For the most part, the new rules assure that once such a person has qualified for benefits, he or she will usually be better off going back to work (if possible) than not working. However, most observers agree that, for those beneficiaries who will take advantage of the new rules, the cash and health care incentives are only part of the tradeoff. At least as important for many are the psychic benefits of meeting the expectations of age peers by participating in the work force. When net costs to the public of the necessary subsidies are computed, these psychic benefits may have to be included along with the marketplace value of the disabled worker's product in order to show a net benefit.

The same motivations clearly energize this same constituency in its twenty-year pursuit of "independent-living" legislation finally enacted in 1978. The psychic benefits of being a head of household or at least not a dependent son or daughter in the parental home have obviously influenced the behavior of this group (De Jong, 1979). Many mentally disabled persons could participate in the independent-living movement, but often someone else must advocate their right to share in the benefits of the new legislation.

Similar motivations are apparent in the constituency of elderly Americans who wish to maintain their independence in living arrangements as well as in income. We are all aware of the relatively greater longevity of women and hence the plight of widows, but it is not widely recognized that as longevity has increased for both sexes, a larger proportion of the elderly have spouses and can live with them in a mutually supportive relationship. Even at age 85 a man is about twice as likely to be living as the head of a household as to be in a nursing home; for women at age 85 the likelihood of living with spouse or living in a nursing home are about equal (Soldo, Note 1) even though about 20 percent of this age group (both sexes) is institutionalized.

Overall among those over age 65, only 5 percent are in nursing homes (skilled, intermediate, and personal care facilities taken together). Nevertheless this elderly institutionalized population accounts for well over one million people, among whom some 200,000 have a primary diagnosis of mental disorder, including those considered senile. Most have physical ills as well (National Center for Health Statistics (NCHS), 1979). When secondary conditions are taken into account, about two-thirds (700,000) are found to have a significant mental disability, many being aggressive or hyperactive. An additional 50,000 elders are in psychiatric hospitals, state and county (National Institute of Mental Health (NIMH), 1978).

Considerable attention has been given by the appropriate committees in both houses of Congress to the proposition that many older people who enter nursing homes do so as much because of the falling away of natural support systems as because of intrinsic frailty. With or without familial or social aid, an estimated 14 percent or approximately three million elderly persons who are "greatly" or "extremely" impaired by physical or mental disorders are living in the community (Federal Council on Aging (FCA), 1979). It is generally assumed that the behavioral fiscal incentives impinging on this population favor institutional care because of limits on Medicaid and Medicare funding for noninstitutional health care. This proposition will be examined later.

Minkoff (1978) has estimated the number of severely mentally disabled adults under age 65 and outside of institutions for mental diseases. There are few hard data. Using Minkoff's estimates (p. 15), we can estimate that there are now at least 800,000, or 1.5 million if the "partially" disabled (those who can do some work) are taken into account. This is a widely quoted figure. Of patients in state and county mental hospitals 70,000 to 80,000 of working age are believed to be "chronic." Aggregating these figures suggests that nationally there are some four to five million chronically mentally ill persons over 18.

Although there are 8,000 to 10,000 children in public psychiatric hospitals, the majority of seriously disturbed children in out-of-home care are found in the child welfare system. Mayer et al. (1977) estimated the number of such children in group care to be over 100,000. It is not clear how many of these might be properly projected as chronic mental patients.

Age at onset of disability is an important determinant of the outcome. Although the majority of people who are considered disabled at any moment become disabled after mid life, mental disability is relatively more important among the causes of disability of early onset. Mental retardation is by definition a condition manifesting itself in childhood, with the more severe forms usually originating at birth or in early childhood. Cerebral palsy, epilepsy, and spina bifida are other examples of chronic disorders typically first manifest in early years. Because they impinge on the developmental process in a way that differentiates those affected from persons disabled in middle or later life, persons of all ages who have severe, pervasive chronic disabilities originating before age 18 were singled out for special attention by the Federal Developmental Disabilities Act of 1970 (PL 95–602).

Information on age at onset of disability is difficult to obtain for older disabled persons, partly because it is not routinely recorded in client records. (See, for example, the Minimum Long-Term Care Data Set, NCHS, 1980.) In a survey of adults in institutions other than nursing homes conducted in 1967, however, Frohlich (1974) found that of those in psychiatric hospitals for whom data were available, between 20 and 25 percent had been disabled prior to age 18. Making allowances for the 8.5 percent of those hospitalized who had a primary diagnosis of mental retardation (NIMH, 1969), one can estimate that about 15 percent of adults hospitalized at that time for disorders other than retardation had been disabled since childhood.

Another indirect indicator of the relative importance of mental disorders among adults with disabilities originating in childhood can be found in records of the Social Security program. The "adult disabled child" program allows benefits to flow to certain adults who have been continuously disabled since childhood. More than two-thirds have primary diagnoses of mental disorder, with another 20 percent to 25 percent accounted for by neurological and sensory disorders (mostly cerebral palsy and epilepsy), among whom a secondary mental impairment is common. Even this total may be an underestimate inasmuch as such disorders as Down's syndrome are classified as congenital malformations and not always included in these compilations.[b] The total number of adult disabled child beneficiaries in 1981 exceeded 425,000. Such persons may be in the community or in institutions.

It is also worth noting that schizophrenia and other mental disorders play an important role in adult disability originating after the adult has entered the work force. Mental disorder accounts for between 11 and 12 percent of those workers found eligible for Social Security on the basis of inability to continue working (work disability). Among workers who become disabled before age 40, the rate is over 35 percent. (Social Security Bulletin Annual Supplement, 1977–1979). On the assumption that the overall rate of "allowances" is a conservative index of the prevalence of mental disorder among the beneficiaries in current payment status at any one time, one concludes that there were more than 300,000 adults receiving benefits due to such disability in 1976, about two-thirds of them men. When disabled workers and adult disabled child beneficiaries are combined, the number of persons of working age out of the work force and receiving Social Security benefits because of mental disability is found to exceed 500,000. To the extent that any of these persons may be admitted to mental institutions or institutions for

b. These data are derived from Social Security Administration's figures for applications processed in 1970, the last year for which data were published. It is understood that since then "allowances" for epilepsy without other impairments have been declining as a result of better control of seizures in persons of normal intelligence, who thus are considered as not "work disabled" within the meaning of the Social Security program. It is also believed that the incidence of cerebral palsy is declining, but this has not yet affected the adult population significantly.

the retarded, this personal income is available to pay toward the cost of their care or that of their dependents.[c]

During 1976 the U.S. Bureau of the Census, at the request of the U.S. Department of Health, Education, and Welfare (HEW), conducted a detailed household interview survey, one objective of which was to ascertain the extent of functional disability among noninstitutionalized persons of various ages. With respect to disability, the data reflect the willingness of the respondent to identify himself or herself or a member of the same household as having a limiting health condition that interferes with his or her major life activity—play, schooling, work, and so on, depending on age. Persons who made that identification were then asked to point to the type of limiting condition, selecting a condition from a list where mental retardation was the first item. The survey shows that approximately 866,000 people over age 5 who are not living in institutions or "group quarters for five or more" (thus excluding, for example, dormitories, convents, and congregate housing) are identified by their families or themselves as mentally retarded. Similarly some 700,000 persons of various ages were identified as "seriously emotionally disturbed." Although there is reason to conclude that they are underestimates, these figures have some validity for service planners, since persons who neither identify themselves nor are identified by the other members of their households are unlikely to come forward looking for specialized services.

Adding to these figures are 150,000 in state residential facilities for the retarded (as of July 1977); 18,000 retarded persons in public mental hospitals (of whom about 10,000 were in "distinct part" units); over 60,000 retarded children and adults in various nonpublic community residences (including some larger private facilities but excluding nursing homes); and some 80,000 in nursing homes of various levels (Scheerenberger, 1978; Bruininks, Hauber, and Kudla, 1979; NCHS, 1979; NIMH, 1978) for a total of 1.16 million.[d] Thus,

c. A little noted set of amendments to the Social Security Act (PL 96–473) signed in October 1980, rescinded the eligibility of prisoners for Title II benefits. During his debate with President Carter, then candidate Ronald Reagan also advocated a similar denial to patients in mental hospitals on the mistaken notion that such patients are also not charged for care even if they have income.

d. Bruininks Hill and Thorsheim (1980) also identified 5,000 retarded persons in state-approved foster family care. However, Rymer et al. (1980) found an estimated 13,000 retarded children on SSI in foster care. Some of these foster care facilities may have been counted by Bruininks as "community residences."

it can be said that of those retarded persons who are *identified* candidates for direct service consequent to mental retardation, about three-fourths are living in their own homes or foster families, about one-eighth in designated public residential facilities, about 1.5 percent in public mental hospitals and the remainder (slightly less than one-eighth) in various recognized private facilities. Since 1976–1977, another 10,000 to 20,000 have left public facilities for the private sector or are no longer receiving residential care (Bruininks, Thurlow, Thurman, and Fiorelli, 1980).

## LONG–TERM CARE: AN EMERGENT COMMON AGENDA

John Iglehart (1977) quoted Robert Derzon, then administrator of the Health Care Financing Administration (HCFA): "Long term care will be government's health-financing dilemma of the 1980s." Iglehart then went on to observe:

> The phrase "long-term care" is used commonly to refer to the care of the elderly in nursing homes. But it also applies to services for the mentally ill, the mentally retarded and the young, physically handicapped. Moreover, the needs of this vulnerable population range far beyond care in nursing homes to include income, personal care, social services and housing.
>
> Although the needs relate to one segment of the population, they are so diverse that it would be impossible for the Department of Health, Education and Welfare (HEW) or any other government agency to place responsibility for them under a single administrative roof without skewing the priorities of other client groups. Thus, coordination among a number of programs becomes critically important. (p. 1725)

The past five years have indeed seen a growing consensus that long-term care must, first, be viewed from the perspective of those in need of it, rather than in terms of types of providers, and, second, be free of arbitrary age boundaries yet recognize that both current age and age at onset are relevant to specific needs (Boggs, in Knee, ed., 1977). In support of this assertion, one can cite the convergence of views of traditionally distinct constituencies. For example, the Federal Council on Aging (1979), under the leadership of Monsignor Charles Fahey, has abandoned territoriality by age. It defines long-term care primarily in terms of:

- The individual who needs long-term care;

- The need for intervention by others for a long period of time rather than for a temporary condition (it is unclear what the length of time should be);

- The functional ability of the individual as the basis for intervention rather than the physical and/or mental diagnosis. (p. 5)

From another quarter, the National Center on Health Statistics (1980), comes the following:

> Long-term health care refers to the professional or personal services required on a recurring or continuous basis by an individual because of chronic or permanent physical or mental impairment. These services may be provided in a variety of settings, including the client's own home. (p. 3)

These definitions should suffice to indicate that the chronically mentally ill, the developmentally disabled, and certain additional persons with mental retardation certainly belong to the long-term care population. A particularly insightful elaboration of these themes can be found in a report developed over two years by a task force led by Ruth Knee (1977). The group of twenty-two worked under the auspices of the National Conference on Social Welfare with financial support from the Division of Long Term Care of the Health Resources Administration of the U.S. Public Health Service.

One significant exception to this trend is found in the report of the Congressional Budget Office entitled *Long Term Care for the Elderly and Disabled* (1977). Having defined long-term care as "a series of services provided to chronically ill and disabled persons over an extended period of time" (p. 1), the report subsequently qualifies this for its own purposes as "services to persons with chronic physical disease or disability." While admitting that long-term needs of the mentally retarded and mentally ill involve "considerations similar to those involved in the care of the physically disabled, including the lifetime nature and treatment and the appropriateness of institutional versus non institutional treatment," it stakes its case for limiting its study on a preference for "administrative simplicity" rather than "conceptual purity." A classic case of the incentive effect of administrative ease as a behavioral influence!

Considerable policy research has been done in the field of long-term care of the elderly, the results of which can be readily translated to the broader field. For example, the staff of the Older Americans Resource and Service Project (OARS) at Duke University has developed a list of twenty-five services "not specifically tied to any single type of service provider or service setting, but which would be appropriately provided in different selections and combinations according to the varying needs and functional statuses found among persons in need of long-term care" (Goodman and LeBlanc, 1977). They fall into three groups as follows:

1. *Basic Maintenance Services* are those services required by all persons, healthy or impaired. They include the need for food stuffs (i.e., groceries), living quarters and transportation. It is never a question of whether these services are to be provided but only by whom they are to be provided, i.e., the healthy individual residing in his own home provides these services for himself. However, for the individual who has multiple impairments and who has become institutionalized, these basic maintenance services become part of the total service package which must be provided for the individual.

2. *Supportive Services* are those services which are provided to impaired individuals which of themselves do not improve the basic functional capacity of the individual but which serve to maintain his functioning. In this category are personal care services, homemaker-household services, checking or continuous supervision, meal preparation, and administrative, legal and protective services.

3. *Remedial or Rehabilitative Services* are those services which are designed or which can improve the basic functional capacity of an impaired individual. This includes all the remaining services. The criterion which has been used for labelling a service as *remedial* is that the service has a chance or a probability of improving the functional rating of an individual on one of the five dimensions. (adapted from Pfeiffer, 1976 by Goodman and LeBlanc, 1977)

The specific elements assigned to each group of services are listed in Table 2-1. Although differing slightly in format, this taxonomy is similar to that cited by Bruininks, Thurlow, Thurman, and Fiorelli, (1980, Table I) as "essential services for retarded and other handicapped persons."

An attempt was made by Goodman and LeBlanc (1977) to define certain clusters of these services as being sufficiently characteristic of certain classes of providers to permit the collapsing of the list for statistical purposes. This did not prove feasible.

Table 2-1.    OARS Service Definitions, by Category.

---

A.  Basic maintenance services
    1.  Transportation
    19.  Food stuffs (unprepared)
    21.  Living quarters

B.  Supportive services
    10.  Personal care services
    15.  Continuous supervision
    16.  Checking
    18.  Meal preparation
    20.  Homemaker-household services
    24.  Administrative/legal/protective services

C.  Remedial services
    2.  Social/recreational services
    3.  Employment services
    4.  Sheltered employment
    5.  Educational service, employment related
    6.  Educational service, nonemployment related
    7.  Psychiatric services
    8.  Counseling
    9.  Psychotropic drugs
    11.  Nursing services
    12.  Medical services
    22.  Systematic multidimensional evaluation
    23.  Financial assistance
    25.  Coordination of services

---

*Source*:  Pfeiffer (1975) as adapted by Goodman and Le Blanc (1977).

For the array of services listed, the bulk of public funding comes from such major federal programs as Supplementary Security Income, Social Security benefits, Medicaid (not much Medicare), housing for the elderly and handicapped (including congregate housing services), social services, the Comprehensive Employment and Training Act (CETA), and the generic employment services, along with state and local funds that match or augment federal funds or support public schools (Boggs, 1977, 1978). The categorical service programs managed by the National Institute of Mental Health, the Rehabilitation Services Administration, the Administration on Developmental Disabilities, the Administration on Aging, the Maternal and Child

Health programs, the Office of Child Development, and even the Office of Special Education in the new Department of Education, while complementing the generic money streams somewhat, serve mainly as focal points and loci of systems advocacy for their respective constituencies, as defined by such factors as age and type of impairment.

The various "categorical" constituencies are not mutually exclusive. Hence certain linkages and deliberate "duplications" are called for.

## THE CHANGING SHAPE OF THE HUMAN SERVICES DELIVERY SYSTEMS

Several years ago I postulated (Boggs, 1975) that

trends in financing in the field of services to the retarded will be dominated by two kinds of pressure: (a) the general trends in financing patterns for other health, education, welfare and social objectives, and (b) the directions evident in respect to *programs* for the retarded and the *organization* thereof. Table [2-2] reflects the parallelism we may anticipate in the latter dimension. (p. 50)

In the intervening years most of these trends have become even more evident. The three components, *program, concepts, organization* (system structure), and *financing* sources and modes are cyclically related in a kind of feedback loop. We often complain that the funding streams are driving the programs rather than vice versa. This suggests that we should modify the funding mechanisms. However, the funding mechanisms and allocations are also a product of the content and structure of programs and systems. As long as we permit the psychic benefits of administrative ease to weigh in favor of single-line financing for package programs (*neatness*), we can expect self-contained systems that tend to be de facto "restrictive" even if clients are technically living "in the community."

I remember once hearing a prominent psychiatrist describe in vivid terms the culture shock he had experienced in moving from the superintendency of a state hospital (where he had been an autocrat in a small domain—a closed system) to the position of director of a community mental health center in an urban area, where his access to resources for patients depended to a large extent on his ability to collaborate with his peers or counterparts in other systems (health

Table 2-2.    Program Organization Trends.

| | Away From | Toward |
|---|---|---|
| Programs | Packaged | Individualized |
| | Few options | Many options |
| | Discipline-dominated | Interdisciplinary, collaborative |
| | Well-defined | Readily modified |
| | Isolating | Normalizing |
| Organization | Self-contained systems | Interlocking open systems |
| | Hierarchical | "Democratic" |
| | Defined by preset criteria | Defined by capacity to serve |
| | Static constituency | Dynamic, changing constituencies |
| Financing | Single-line | Multisource |
| | All public or all private | Mixed money streams |
| | Intracategorical | Transcategorical |
| | Single-mode | Multi-mode[a] |
| | Federal supplementation of specific state roles | Federal assumption of some roles: greater devolution in others |

a. "Modes" include individual entitlements, tax credits, vendor payments, formula grants-in-aid, project grants, in-kind benefits, "staffing" grants (start-up costs), fixed subsidies, percentage reimbursements, and so forth, as well as loans, interest subsidies, and loan guarantees for capital costs.

care, corrections, rehabilitation). He had entered a world of interlocking open systems; this particular fellow accepted the challenge and its attendant frustration, but not all bureaucrats have been able to relinquish the power inherent in the closed system, and to accept the messiness of normal life in the real world. If we want the program options listed on the right of Table 2-2, we must accept and even promote their fiscal counterparts.

Former patients face the same challenge with fewer personal and social resources. Less restriction means more (perhaps bewildering) choices. Normal living is messy. Normal people normally do not have comprehensive support systems. Okin (1978) and also Bachrach

(1980) have pointed to the failures of professionals to appreciate fully that the "help of a few friends," although it might keep Kenneth Donaldson alive outside the hospital, would not suffice for many others. As Okin puts it,

> many states failed to appreciate the extent to which the institution was for many patients an integrated human service system that provided medical, nutritional, vocational, residential, legal, and economic services, albeit very inadequately. Many states did not recognize the importance of replacing this system of services once the patient had left the institution. . . . The provision of a range of human services to the disabled client has been and will continue to be more difficult in the community than it is in the institution . . . the role of the state mental health authority must shift from one of direct service to one of planning, integrating, sanctioning, monitoring, priority setting, and funding. It is the integrative role that I am focusing on here, for unless the state mental health authority can influence those systems it does not directly control, the disabled patient will not have access to the range of human services he requires (p. 1357)

This view clearly assigns a "system advocacy" role to the categorical agency. Moreover, as Pollack (1979) has pointed out,

> Extended coverage of a spectrum of non-institutional long-term care services would virtually require new organizational arrangements, both to coordinate a more complex service array and to control equitably and efficiently utilization of services that are considerably more attractive than those now provided (p. 64).

Lacking any such spectrum, many former hospital patients have found refuge in reinstitutionalization in nursing homes, usually general intermediate care facilities rather than skilled nursing facilities. These are visible institutions, defined by the discrete "levels of care" they are supposed to provide and for which they are paid. Like the mental hospital, they offer a package of board, lodging, supervision, protection, personal care, recreation, and some "treatment." The public's concern about fire hazards and other conditions within these facilities, the majority of which are proprietary, has led to increasing public (and hence federal) demands for more rigorous "conditions of participation," with more programming along with sprinklers.

With the enactment in 1965 of Titles XVIII (Medicare) and XIX (Medicaid) of the Social Security Act, coverage of care became available under certain conditions to persons over 65 in institutions for mental diseases (IMD). An IMD is defined as an institution "primarily engaged in providing diagnosis, treatment, or care of individuals with mental diseases, including medical care, nursing care, and related services." In 1965, and since, only one level of IMD care has been recognized under Medicare, the inpatient psychiatric hospital. In general such a facility must meet the standards of the Joint Commission on Accreditation of Hospitals (JCAH). There is a lifetime limitation of 190 days of covered care per person over 65. Under Title XIX two levels were originally recognized: hospital and skilled nursing. After 1971 intermediate care services in an IMD were also recognized under Medicaid but again only for the elderly. Inpatient psychiatric hospital care was recognized for persons under age 21 beginning in 1973. Persons under 65 and over 22 are not recognized, even if disabled, for Medicaid coverage or for SSI while in a public or private IMD.

Since 1965, however, facilities for mentally retarded persons have been excluded from the IMD definition. Thus, persons who are disabled by mental retardation may receive full SSI while residing in almost any type of private, nonmedical facility and can be covered by Medicaid on an inpatient basis in a public or private facility that is certified as an ICF/MR. These entitlements are not age-specific.

Despite the restriction on federal financing of care for the mentally ill, nearly 25 percent of the Medicaid dollar goes for mental health services of various kinds (in this case including intermediate care for the retarded; see Table 2-3).

During the 1970s, as many formerly hospitalized chronic mental patients under age 65 found their way into nursing homes, including general intermediate care facilities after discharge from mental hospitals, the proportion of clients or patients with mental disorders in such facilities steadily increased. Recently the HCFA began auditing the practices of certain states (notably California, Illinois, and Wisconsin). The HCFA averred that making Medicaid payments to private skilled nursing facilities (SNFs) and ICFs on behalf of such patients is illegal because those facilities have become de facto "institutions for mental diseases." The issue was brought to a head by HCFA in an issuance of new "proposed conditions of participation" in the *Federal Register* of July 14, 1980. The Mental Health Liaison Group responded by opposing the development of separate categories of IMD/SNFs and IMD/ICFs on the grounds that mental health services are needed by many nursing home patients whose primary diagnosis is not mental illness, and vice versa, and that standards for

Table 2-3. Medicaid Expenditures for Mental Health Services, FY 1977.[a]

| Type of Care or Service | Estimated Expenditures, $ Millions |
|---|---|
| State, county, and private mental institutions and psychiatric hospitals | 558 |
| General hospital, inpatient, outpatient, and emergency care related to mental health | 185 |
| Community mental health centers | 100 |
| Private free-standing clinics | 25 |
| Physicians and other practitioners | 82 |
| Nursing homes | 2,189 |
| ICF/MRs | 702 |
| Residential treatment facilities, rehabilitation and children's programs | 110 |
| Drugs | 110 |
| TOTAL | $4,091 for mental/retardation |
| Total | $17,102 for all medicaid |
| Federal Share 57% | |

a. Estimates include direct costs to Medicaid for mental illness and retardation.

Source: President's Commission on Mental Health (1978).

SNFs and ICFs should require staffing and other patterns of service appropriate to the residents' needs on a prescriptive basis (Alexander, Note 2).

## THE EVOLUTION OF THE INTERMEDIATE CARE FACILITY AS LEGALLY DEFINED

From the inception of the welfare titles of the Social Security Act in 1935, Congress prohibited federal financial participation (FFP) in the public assistance paid to or on behalf of otherwise eligible persons (1) while they were "inmates" of any public institution other than a medical institution or (2) while they were patients or residents of an institution for mental diseases, public or private. Up until

1965 these two prohibitions excluded FFP in any part of the cost of care of mentally retarded or mentally ill persons in specialized residential facilities. The law did not prohibit FFP in public assistance for persons disabled by mental disorders who were cared for in either general hospitals (including their psychiatric wards) or in private non-specialized, nonmedical facilities such as boarding homes or child care facilities, or in public or private genetic nursing homes. It should be noted that prior to 1965 there was no formal federal program of medical assistance except for the aged.

With the enactment of Medicaid in 1965 Congress for the first time permitted FFP in the costs of care of mentally disabled persons over age 65 in "institutions for mental diseases." The definition of that term, which had up to that point been broad and inclusive of facilities for the retarded, was immediately narrowed by regulation so as to encompass primarily the mental hospital offering active treatment, public or private.

The 1965 act also permitted inpatient Medicaid coverage of persons otherwise eligible for categorical public assistance who entered skilled nursing facilities meeting federal standards. Care in skilled nursing facilities was and is a service states could opt to offer to persons under 21 but were mandated to offer to adults in need of it, although not without limit.

The net effect of these provisions as of 1967 was to provide federal coverage for low-income elderly persons disabled by mental illness as inpatients in specialized psychiatric or general medical facilities, public or private, but no coverage for younger persons even if clearly disabled. Facilities for the mentally retarded were no longer included as institutions for mental diseases and were considered nonmedical unless they could meet the standards either for specialized hospitals or for skilled nursing homes. Thus persons in *private* nonmedical institutions for the retarded could qualify for public assistance and for outpatient medical assistance as needed. The same persons in *public* institutions (other than Medicaid institutions) were disqualified, both as recipients of income maintenance and for inpatient coverage under Medicaid. However, indigent elderly and disabled persons who required personal care and were in private congregate care facilities classed as domiciliary, and were eligible for aid to the permanently and totally disabled, could earn federal reimbursement for the supporting state agency only at matching rates significantly lower than could patients in nursing homes certified as "skilled" under Title XIX.

The first-year student of behavioral fisics could have predicted the consequences of these provisions. Categorically eligible elderly and disabled adults began to move from facilities not certified for Medicaid into facilities certified as skilled, and some public agencies began to convert their institutions for the retarded into "skilled" nursing facilities. In addition, other public institutions began moving their residents laterally into private boarding facilities where they could pick up at least the income maintenance under Aid to the Permanently and Totally Disabled (APTD) and Old Age Assistance (OAA).

The overuse of skilled nursing facilities for impaired elderly persons who did not need this level of service came quickly to the attention of Congress as a spending overrun; the result was the prompt enactment in 1967 of a provision authorizing payments to states at their respective Medicaid percentages for the assistance costs under OAA or APTD for adults eligible for these programs who needed care beyond room and board but not at the skilled nursing level. Thus was born the very broadly defined concept of intermediate care.

The basic concept of an intermediate care facility as authorized by Congress in 1967, was that of a place that provided board, lodging, laundry, and "some other service," to a group of persons who needed "institutional" care but were otherwise responsible for themselves, or had family members or welfare workers as advocates. The purpose was simple: to authorize federal pro rata participation at Medicaid rates in the higher public assistance costs of disabled and elderly persons who needed domiciliary care. It was only after the transfer of the ICF program to Medicaid in 1972, that increased emphasis was placed on standards that required "health-related" care to be provided. For the first time, ICF residents acquired the status of being in a "medical institution," a status having both advantages and disadvantages.

Under the 1967 amendments, ICFs were required to meet the same life safety codes as nursing homes but remained otherwise "nonmedical." As such, no public facility could qualify. In the period from 1967 to 1972 the schema shown in Table 2–4 prevailed with respect to nonelderly adults needing some form of protective or personal care. Table 2–5 shows the same schema with arrows drawn

**Table 2-4.** The Basis for Federal Financial Contributions to the Cost of Care of Disabled Adults under 65, by Locus of Care.[a]

|  | *Public* | *Private* |
| --- | --- | --- |
| IMD | None | None |
| SNF | Title XIX | Title XIX |
| Other "medical" | APTD | APTD |
| ICF | — | Title XI[b] |
| Boardinghouse | None | APTD |
| Institution for the mentally retarded (IMR) not otherwise classified | None | APTD |
| Family home | — | APTD |

a. After 1967 but before 1972.

b. Title XI of the Social Security Act, which then permitted federal reimbursement of public assistance payments for intermediate care at the same state percentage as in Title XIX (Medicaid).

**Table 2-5.** Direction of Fiscal Pressures to Move Clients from One Locus to Another or to Convert Facilities from One Classification to Another.

|  | *Public* | *Private* |
| --- | --- | --- |
| IMD | None | None |
| SNF | Title XIX | Title XIX |
| Other "medical" | APTD | APTD |
| ICF |  | Title XI |
| Boardinghouse | None | APTD |
| IMR | None | APTD |
| Family home |  | APTD |

to indicate the behavioral fiscal forces engendered by this state of affairs. The pressures indicated are of two kinds: pressures to move individual clients from one milieu to another, either vertically or laterally and pressures to convert a facility or distinct part thereof to a different status. States such as California and Wisconsin began to reorganize their public institutions for the retarded as skilled nursing facilities, emphasizing the "medical model." States such as Illinois and Oklahoma began moving APTD–eligible adults from public to private facilities, leaving behind the nonindigent and the children. Both mildly retarded and chronically mentally ill adults were placed on APTD in their own homes or in private foster homes and discharged to the mercies of the welfare agencies.

These developments were viewed with alarm by leaders of the National Association for Retarded Children (now the Association for Retarded Citizens) (ARC). In 1970 they engaged the attention of key actors in public welfare in an attempt to show that policies that might be working to the advantage of the elderly needing health care were inadvertently working to the disadvantage of children and adults who were mentally retarded. Positive actions were urged that reflected the following points:

1. The premiums paid for nursing care under federal programs were displacing needed incentives for improved programming in a "social rehabilitation" mode, reflecting the "developmental model."

2. There was nothing in the track record of the private proprietary nursing home industry that suggested that publicly purchased private care was intrinsically superior to publicly administered care for impaired persons.

3. The fiscal pressures then being felt by many states to put state "front money" into upgrading their mental hospitals to meet the standards required to draw down Medicaid for their eligible populations in the over-age-65 and under-age-22 categories was diverting funds from needed improvements in the state-sponsored facilities for the retarded.

The ARC leadership envisioned a modification of the then existing "old" nonmedical ICF legislation that would authorize federal cost sharing at Medicaid rates for residential services and developmental programming in public as well as private facilities, with emphasis on social and rehabilitation services. As things turned out the legislation that created the ICF/MR coincided with a transfer of the entire ICF authorization to Title XIX. The ICF-general is described in Title XIX Section 1905 (c) and the (CF/MR in Section 1905 (d). This brought both the ICF-general and the ICF/MR under the general rules applicable to Medicaid, including various forms of medical review. An incidental but by no means negligible corollary was the inclusion of children and medically indigent persons among those eligible.

Section 1905 (d) covers services in a "public institution (or distinct part thereof) for the mentally retarded or persons with related conditions" whose "primary purpose is to provide health or rehabilitative services for mentally retarded individuals." At the time this provision was written public residential care was in some states still being provided for persons with epilepsy, usually by the same agency as served the retarded. Most, but not all of those served were in fact also retarded; the more capable and younger persons with epilepsy by that time were being maintained on the anticonvulsant medication outside institutions.

The language of the provision was first drafted in late 1970 for insertion in a Senate bill that never went to conference. It is doubtful that anyone on the Senate Finance Committee gave a second thought to the definition of "developmental disability" contained in the newly enacted developmental disabilities legislation (PL 91–517). By the time the regulations were written by DHEW, however, the new Division of Developmental Disabilities was providing substantive input, and "related conditions" was interpreted by the rules to be equivalent to the conditions included along with mental retardation in PL 91–517—namely, cerebral palsy, epilepsy, and later autism. The Senate Finance Committee and the House Ways and Means Committee doubtless had no intention of aligning Section 1905 definitions with those in the developmental disabilities legislation. The developmental disabilities legislation was and is under the jurisdiction of different committees in both houses. Moreover, individual for whom FFP was to be claimed under Section 1905 (d) was required to be residing in an institution whose *primary purpose* was service to retarded persons. This proviso applies today. It seems clear therefore that claims on behalf of persons of whatever diagnosis who are in institutions other than institutions *for the retarded* are not justified under this section.

Section 1905 (c), defining the "new" ICF–general, specifies that such a facility "provides, on a regular basis, health-related care and services" to persons to whom this care can be made available "only through institutional facilities." (The generic DHEW definition of an institution is a facility that provides board, lodging, laundry, and some other services to four or more unrelated persons.) Section 1905 (c) does not require that an ICF "provide" all or even most health-related services required by residents, individually or collectively, but only services that by their nature must be delivered in-house. State and, to some extent, federal regulations often do go beyond this statutory mandate to require that the management of an ICF be responsible for procuring medical care and other services needed by residents. Such requirements have the effect of pushing up the size of ICFs because they tend to involve a degree of professional staffing to which economies of scale must be applied. This factor can be offset when professional services (including case management) are provided to residents of several small facilities by an external agency, or by common management.

Section 1905 (d) specifies that eligible persons in a public institution for the retarded claiming reimbursement under ICF/MR must be receiving "active treatment." The requirement is peculiar to this category of ICF. The ICF/MR standards subsequently developed were applied also to specialized facilities in the private sector because the standards for what the *facility itself should provide* were considered higher and more appropriate to the target population than were the standards then and now put forward for the so-called general ICF. The latter standards, while not expressly age-limited, are at present targeted on images of care needed by older adults who manifest the impairments of aging, including senility. Data on all nursing homes (SNF, ICF–general, and personal care homes not certified for Medicaid) indicate that not more than 11 percent of the residents are under age 65 (NCHS, 1979). By contrast, in intermediate care facilities for the retarded, persons over 65 seldom constitute more than 10 percent of the residents; on the average at least one-third are children.

An ICF/MR is by definition an *institution* that is able to meet the treatment and other needs of its residents, either by direct provision or through contracts with external providers. Federal financial participation is available in both the basic maintenance and the treatment costs, on a means-tested basis, but not for costs of education for school-age children or vocational rehabilitation service. These services are to be provided under other funding streams, at no cost to residents. Case management is an internal responsibility requiring the services of a "qualified mental retardation professional" (QMRP) and health care must be supervised by a physician who reviews medications and other treatment modalities at least quarterly. Like an ICF–general, an ICF/MR may admit as residents only persons who need service that can as a practical matter be provided only in an institution. Nighttime supervision is one such service. A typical ICF can be expected to have responsible staff on duty and awake twenty-four hours a day. Nothing in the law or regulations places any upper or lower limit on the size (number or residents) of an ICF except that DHHS does not consider a facility for three or fewer to be an institution.

This legislation still precluded any federal support either under the Social Security Act's Title XVI or under its Title XIX for care of retarded persons in "public institutions" not meeting the foregoing rather elaborate requirement. In order to reduce the disincentives to public agencies to become sponsors of small group residences not invoking the ICF model, Congress enacted a proviso in 1976 (under PL 94–506) that added to Title XVI a subparagraph 1611 (e) (i) (c) which said in effect that a publicly operated community residence serving no more than sixteen residents shall not be considered a "public institution" for purposes of determining eligibility for SSI under Title XVI. This option has been relatively little exploited to date. It is available for any classification of disabled person, including the chronically mentally ill.

According to fire safety engineers evacuation of a small facility, whether a school, a theater, a day care center, or a residence, is easier than evacuation of a large facility of the same type even when multiple exits are provided for the latter. It is partly for this reason that the original ICF/MR proposed regulations issued in 1974 permitted the use of the "residential" life safety code as an alternative to the institution life safety code in ICF/MRs for less than sixteen residents if the individual residents were considered capable of self-preservation. This exception does not apply to small facilities housing non-ambulatory persons or persons who are mentally incapable of responding to a fire emergency. Such persons may be housed in small facilities under the ICF model, but the buildings must meet the institutional life safety code.

The apparent administrative ease of package funding that has elicited development of community-based ICFs for persons with mental retardation of all ages has led some leaders in the mental health field to propose a comparable model for the nonelderly chronically mentally ill. Others have tried to redefine chronic mental illness not as a "mental disease" but rather as a chronic brain syndrome, an organic disorder to be treated by internists, or, alternatively, as a developmental disability, and hence a disorder "related to mental retardation." These maneuvers were, in part, the result of fiscal behaviors triggered by the residue of arbitrary rules designed to keep federal aid out of "institutions for mental diseases." So far the semantic ploy has not succeeded.

## THE HOME-BASED MODEL

The Association for Retarded Citizens, nationally and in many states, has vehemently opposed the placement of retarded children or adults in nursing homes, whether ICF, or skilled facilities, or "personal care" homes, because the standards for these facilities are not seen as meeting the probable developmental needs of persons with mental retardation. Those needs can be analyzed according to a taxonomy such as that used by OARS (Table 2-1): (1) basic maintenance (food, shelter, clothing); (2) in-house support, including emotional support, personal assistance, and supervision or protection during the time the person would normally be at home but that may be needed in extraordinary degree because of the person's mental or physical condition and is hence health related; and (3) "active treatment" or rehabilitation or developmental enhancement, including formal therapies and training mediated by skilled personnel and provided either out-of-home on a group basis or individual (ambulatory) basis or by a practitioner making a house visit. The ICF/MR and SNF models address all three aspects under one management; the ICF–general model was intended and can be interpreted to address primarily the basic maintenance and supportive functions. The services of an ICF–general, perceived as a supportive living arrangement, can, of course, be complemented ad hoc with prescriptive programs of health, education, rehabilitation, and social services which are externally supplied, managed and funded through noninstitutional providers.

For the past five years or more, many state administrators and private providers have been advocating the modification of the ICF/MR rules so as to accommodate almost any kind of living arrangement appropriate for retarded and developmentally disabled persons that involves more than family care. However, in the states that have made greatest progress in developing small community alternative housing arrangements (for example, Washington, Michigan, Minnesota), state agency personnel are recognizing the desirability of retaining in the agency some responsibility for case management and for securing on an individual basis the various professional services required by the individualized habilitation plan. Dividing responsibility for night care and day programming is a logical step following the dispersion of congregate facilities, by which the living quarters of the residents are physically separated from the offices and classrooms of the associated professional staff.

Nevertheless, many people continue to maintain that all components of the required services, including board and lodging, should be fundable under Title XIX as a single packaged personal entitlement and that any living arrangement calling for on-site staff should be certifiable as an ICF no matter how small it is. Carried to its logical conclusion, this thesis calls, on the one hand, for Medicaid funding to cover board and lodging, and "awake and on duty" staff for night care facilities accommodating four to eight residents at night staffing ratios comparable to those in acute care hospitals. On the other hand, many small community facilities under private auspices are in fact staffed at night (and appropriately so, given the specific needs of the particular residents) with sleep-in staff. Most such facilities are frankly domiciliary, since the residents attend day programs in other places.

Why is there pressure to maintain the "Medicaid model" for this component of care? It is another example of behavioral fisics at work. First, the income eligibility cut-off point is higher for persons in inpatient facilities certified for Title XIX than it is under federal SSI. Second, the cost, whatever it is, for the board, lodging, and night supervision is split pro rata with the federal government using the state's federal Medicaid percentage (which ranges from 50 percent to something like 78 percent. And, finally, it is easy to cover handicapped children in this type of out-of-home placement. For adults, this fiscal arrangement constitutes a return to the situation prevailing between 1967 and 1971, when domiciliary care for persons eligible for public assistance in the "adult categories" enjoyed the same kind of dually open-ended funding, dual because there is not only no preset limit on the number of eligible beneficiaries but also because almost any documentable figure for annualized capital costs and for services provided in the facility can be claimed for federal reimbursement on a pro rata basis. Under SSI, the Federal Share is a predetermined dollar amount.

With SSI public assistance for the "adult categories" (aged, blind, and disabled) has been reformed. Instead of reimbursing states for a percentage of their expenditures according to many options open to the states, the federal agency now delivers the benefit directly to the eligible recipient, defined by federal standards of disability (or age) and income, or to a designated representative payee. Even without state supplements, the flow of dollars directly to consumers or their personal representatives through the SSI mechanism is considerable, as illustrated in Table 2-6. Each year the benefit levels are increased in proportion to the growth in the consumer price index, some 14.3 percent. The 1980-81 level for an individual living independently (or in a group home) was $238 per month; the 1981-82 level rose to $269.70. The amount is not intended to cover needed social services, personal assistance, or medical expenses, all of which can be made available to the client in kind (through Titles XIX or XX or through state funding) or in cash through variable state supplementation of SSI. Cash supplements may be federally administered on behalf of the state and can reflect the nature of the client's living arrangement. States' use of this supplementation mechanism for support of eligible persons is illustrated in Table 2-7.

In a crude sense, a state makes money on a client by using SSI instead of Medicaid to pay for night care or domiciliary care as long as the ratio of its supplement to the federal SSI maximum does not exceed the ratio of its state share under Medicaid to its federal share. From 1965 to 1981 this ratio for a high-income state was 1 to 1, since high-income states have been entitled to 50 percent matching under Medicaid. For an "average" state, the ratio is about 0.8 to 1. The advantages that accrue to states using SSI to support a component of their array of residential services include greater flexibility in meeting individual clients' needs and control over licensing of the residential component. States are required to have standards for and

**Table 2-6.** Developmentally Disabled Beneficiaries Receiving Payments under the Supplemental Security Income Program, 1977-1979.

| Disability | 1977 | | 1978 | | 1979 | |
|---|---|---|---|---|---|---|
| | Estimated Number of Beneficiaries[a] | Estimated Benefits, $000[b] | Estimated Number of Beneficiaries[a] | Estimated Benefits, $000[b] | Estimated Number of Beneficiaries[a] | Estimated Benefits, $000[b] |
| Mental retardation | 388,131 | $667,563 | 399,628 | $714,202 | 404,912 | $788,543 |
| Cerebral palsy | 33,750 | 58,049 | 34,750 | 62,104 | 35,210 | 68,569 |
| Epilepsy | 42,188 | 72,561 | 43,438 | 77,631 | 44,012 | 85,711 |
| Autism | n.a.[c] | n.a. | n.a. | n.a. | n.a. | n.a. |

a. Estimated number of persons receiving payments in December of specified year.
b. Estimated total payments during the year (federal only).
c. Not available (n.a.).

Source: Social Security Administration, Office of Research and Statistics.

**Table 2-7.** State SSI Monthly Payment Levels for Disabled People as of December 1979.

| | Payment for[a] Individual Living Independently | Amount of State Supplement | Maximum Payment in Nonmedical Residential Facility | Maximum State Supplement |
|---|---|---|---|---|
| Alabama | $208.20 | 0 | Same | 0 |
| Alaska | 331.00 | $126.80 | $414.00 | $201.80 |
| Arizona | 208.20 | 0 | 288.20 | 80.00 |
| Arkansas | 208.20 | 0 | Same | 0 |
| California | 329.00 | 120.80 | 402.00 | 193.80 |
| Colorado | 221.00 | 12.80 | Same | 0 |
| Connecticut | 297.00 | 89.00 | 297.00 | 89.00 |
| Delaware | 208.20 | 0 | 301.10 | 93.30 |
| District of Columbia | 223.20 | 11.00 | 441.40 | 237.20 |
| Florida | 208.20 | 0 | 362.00 | 113.80 |
| Georgia | 208.20 | 0 | 240.00 | 31.80 |
| Hawaii | 223.40 | 11.20 | 410.40 | 202.20 |
| Idaho | 262.00 | 73.80 | 376.00 | 187.80 |
| Illinois | State budgets each case individually regardless of living arrangement. | | | |
| Indiana | 208.20 | 0 | 403.10 | 191.30 |
| Iowa | 208.20 | 0 | 413.10 | 241.30 |
| Kansas | 208.20 | 0 | Payments vary. | |
| Kentucky | 208.20 | 0 | 379.00 | 170.80 |
| Louisiana | 208.20 | 0 | Same | 0 |

*(Table 2-7. continued overleaf)*

Table 2-7.  continued

| | Payment for[a] Individual Living Independently | Amount of State Supplement | Maximum Payment in Nonmedical Residential Facility | Maximum State Supplement |
|---|---|---|---|---|
| Maine | 218.20 | 10.00 | 300.00 | 91.80 |
| Maryland | 208.20 | 0 | 691.00 | 486.80 |
| Massachusetts | 323.08 | 114.88 | 310.21 | 142.01 |
| Michigan | 242.29 | 34.09 | 442.60 | 234.40 |
| Minnesota | 242.00 | 33.80 | 272.00 | 63.80 |
| Mississippi | 208.20 | 0 | Same | 0 |
| Missouri | 208.20 | 0 | 108.20 | 300.00 |
| Montana | 208.20 | 0 | 312.20 | 104.00 |
| Nebraska | 291.00 | 86.80 | 302.00 | 93.80 |
| Nevada | 208.20 | 0 | 398.60 | 190.40 |
| New Hampshire | 237.00 | 41.80 | 347.00 | 111.80 |
| New Jersey | 208.20 | 0 | 339.00 | 130.80 |
| New Mexico | 208.20 | 0 | 213.20 | 41.00 |
| New York | 271.41 | 63.21 | 693.46 | 481.26 |
| North Carolina | 208.20 | 0 | 420.00 | 211.80 |
| North Dakota | 208.20 | 0 | Optional with counties | |
| Ohio | 208.20 | 0 | Same | 0 |
| Oklahoma | 287.20 | 79.00 | 287.20 | 79.00 |
| Oregon | 220.20 | 12.00 | b | b |

| | | | |
|---|---|---|---|
| Pennsylvania | 240.60 | 32.40 | 311.10 | 147.30 |
| Rhode Island | 244.99 | 36.79 | 244.99 | 36.79 |
| South Carolina | 208.20 | 0 | 321.00 | 116.80 |
| South Dakota | 223.20 | 11.00 | 310.00 | 167.00 |
| Tennessee | 208.20 | 0 | Same | 0 |
| Texas | 208.20 | 0 | Same | 0 |
| Utah | 218.20 | 10.00 | 218.20 | 10.00 |
| Vermont | 247.00 | 38.80 | 347.00 | 138.80 |
| Virginia | 208.20 | 0 | 397.00 | 188.80 |
| Washington | 233.10/213.30 | 41.10/21.30 | 213.30 | 41.10 |
| West Virginia | 208.20 | 0 | Same | 0 |
| Wisconsin | 300.90 | 92.70 | 378.80 | 170.60 |
| Wyoming | 228.20 | 20.00 | 228.20 | 20.00 |

a. In December 1979 the federal SSI level for an individual living "alone" was $208.20. Because SSI levels are automatically indexed to the cost of living, the rate rose on July 1, 1980, to $238, and on July 1, 1981 to $269.70.

b. Additional costs are paid through special service funds.

*Source:* Compiled by Joni Fritz from Social Security Administration Report no. 1–SJB–31 revised November 1, 1979 (Supplemental Security Income for the Aged, Blind, and Disabled: summary of state payment levels, state supplementation and Medicaid decisions.) Originally published in *Links*, the newsletter of the National Association of Private Residential Facilities for the Mentally Retarded, February 1980.

inspections of premises where SSI recipients are likely to live, but the federal government does not set the standards.

SSI is not the only federal assistance that can be factored into the basic maintenance. A combination of HUD Section 8, federal rental subsidy, and food stamps can reasonably augment the basic SSI by 50 percent (Copeland and Iverson, 1980; and Chapter 4 of this book). The "average" state can then "afford" to use state dollars to pay "nonmedical" staff for supervision on a live-in or night shift basis at the rate of approximately $280 per month per resident. Several part-time staff members will be called for. If any of them qualify as homemakers or home health aides (giving personal care), their salaries can also be subsidized through Title XIX.

Day programming (schools, workshops, day activities, recreation) can be financed and administered separately on the same basis as for persons living in their own homes. Hence, this model can be appropriately referred to as the home-based model (Lazar and Mueller, 1974). It encourages "homelike" residential environments (by relying mostly on local domestic building codes instead of institution building codes) and puts persons who are in identifiably special residential settings on more nearly the same footing as similar persons living with families. Thus the house-based model comes closer to the ideal of normalization. It is not a household model however.

Administrative ease favors the comprehensive model for funding day programming as adjunctive to night care (or vice versa), using the inpatient rubric. All needed services are subsumed as health related as long as some "health" services are provided under medical supervision. However, as Robert Gettings (Note 3) has so succinctly put it: "As long as we continue to force under the rug of health care a whole range of support services that are needed by persons with chronic conditions, such services will not be rendered in an efficient and economical manner." It is therefore necessary to further examine the availability of alternative funding mechanisms for the needed services when they are delivered outside an institutional (inpatient or residential) setting or by a provider other than the sponsor or landlord.

Under the mandates of the Education for All Handicapped Children Act (PL 94–142) day programming for school-age children, consisting of education and "related services," can be developed as a fairly secure universal entitlement. Assuring the severely disabled adult of adequate social rehabilitative care is more problematical with existing funding streams, because support under Title XX is now tightly capped and support under Title XIX has been subject to conflicting policy directives and may also be capped.

The home-based model supports normalization. Its viability will depend, not on forcing funds through a modified ICF/MR entitlement, but on generating appropriate support for components of service available without reference to living arrangements.

## THE ROLE OF SOCIAL SERVICES

Those who fashioned Title XX to authorize funding for social services had the foregoing considerations strongly in mind. Of its five major goals, the fourth could not be more explicit [Section 202 (a) (1)(D)]: "preventing or reducing inappropriate institutional care by providing community based care or other forms of less intensive care." Led by Georgia, Nebraska, and Florida, a number of enterprising states had attempted to do just that for the retarded prior to 1975 under the old Titles IV and XVI. Despite the "cap," on Title XX funds the Office of Human Development Services was able to identify more than $122 million in 1979 expenditures under Title XX targeted for persons with developmental disabilities in twenty-one states. A total of $67 million could be similarly identified under mental health. A substantial portion of the latter has been captured by community mental health centers. (Both figures are clearly gross underestimates because expenditures are reported by service type rather than target group.)

Title XX became effective October 1, 1975; the full effect of capping federal reimbursement was not felt for several years, because not all states were spending their full allotments in fiscal year 1976. The immediate effect was a loss of individual entitlements to (not to be confused with eligibility for) social services, on the part of recipients of SSI because states were no longer required to provide needed social services to all welfare recipients who applied. Before stasis set in completely in the late 1970s, many states were able to develop a variety of effective models for apportioning the service dollars among the different groups of eligible people (generally anyone whose income fell below 80 percent of the median in the state). The states also devised ways of channeling those funds through state and local agencies with some expertise in dealing with the recognizable target groups, such as the frail elderly, working mothers, battered women, the mentally retarded or developmentally disabled, or former mental hospital patients. In general, the state-level interagency contracting process under Title XX worked more smoothly than the lateral interagency transfers under Medicaid.

These days, almost any argument that a certain service (homemaker, chore services, case management, protective supervision, personal care, day care, to name a few) should be fundable under Title XX is immediately brushed off as irrelevant because service allocations within each state are to all intents and purposes frozen at the level in effect when that particular state reached its cap on federal spending. Recent modifications of the ceiling have not kept up with inflation. Nevertheless it is important for federal policymakers to bear in mind that much of the pressure to find a way to use Title XIX for health-related social and support services arises because the more appropriate resource for funding social services has been bottled up. Even the most elementary student of behavioral fisics knows that when you turn off the spigot at one point, more people line up to get more out of some other hydrant, drawing from the same underlying reservoir. It is no more possible to design a totally unfungible funding stream in human services than it is to keep kids from opening any hydrants anywhere in New York City on a hot day.

In the meantime, unhappy with the inflexibility of Medicaid, cut off from further access to social service dollars, and desperate for "interstitial" funding to glue the components of health, income maintenance, and categorical grants together, a newly emerging constituency for long-term care, as earlier defined, appears to be making headway toward legislative reform. What is sought is an alternative funding stream for noninstitutional support services in which it will not be necessary to differentiate between homemakers or personal care givers by whether they earn "health" dollars or "social service" dollars. This strategy appears to have bipartisan support. If successfully carried to eligible consumers as an individual entitlement, it will still be a semigeneric program requiring mediation between consumers and providers. If providers are categorized by their discipline cluster or system identity, then consumers need individual guidance and advocacy by persons with categorical competence across systems. Enter the case manager, the man or woman who can meet the need for individual advocacy based on expertise in working with members of one or another special populations.

## SPECIALIZED INDIVIDUAL
## CASE MANAGEMENT —
## A REVISED COMPONENT

No matter how the client may be identified categorically, he or she should have access (according to need) to a prescriptive selection of services drawn from a buffet more versatile than the table d'hote of the traditional institution or single agency. Whether because of the unusual complexity of the choices or because of personal impairment in capacity for self-advocacy, many persons needing long-term care (especially those who are mentally impaired) will require assistance in selecting and balancing their choices from this menu with an eye to good "nutrition" as well as personal satisfaction.

Assuring the consumer living in the community a chance to choose among reasonable alternatives requires that there be both an array of services and, for those intrinsically disadvantaged, effective individual case management or service coordination. The developmental disabilities amendments of 1978 (PL 95–602) put priority on such case management services; a conference on this topic conducted by the National Conference on Social Welfare (NCSW) under a grant from the federal Administration on Developmental Disabilities late in 1980 revealed that a number of states are already well along the road to establishing systems for managing clients residing in the community, whether in community residences or elsewhere (NCSW, 1981).

Where an individual is in a "total" institution such as a public or private mental hospital or intermediate care facility for the retarded (which by definition has program responsibility), responsibility for case management has usually been assumed internally and paid for as a (small) part of the health care. This has been called "mural casework" (American Association of Social Workers (AASW), 1929). In open systems, however, the practical and policy options are less open and shut. There are strong arguments for putting some distance between the case manager and any one of the several service providers with whom the manager should be negotiating on behalf of any particular client. This is one conclusion to be drawn from an extended analysis by Aiken et al. (1975) of five demonstration projects designed to promote coordination of services for retarded persons at the local (metropolitan) level.

In any case, it seems highly preferable that case management be a universal service, that is, available without charge regardless of income. Information and referral as well as protective services have been recognized as universal services under the Title XX social services schema. One reason for this is the low cost per capita relative to the cost of determining eligibility and liability on a sliding scale and then billing per capita per hour as needed.

About 250,000 persons annually receive services categorized as case management under the much more liberal income eligibility rules of Title XX, at a cost of about $60 million federal, state, and local dollars (Office of Human Development Services (OHDS), 1980). The global average of about $240 per person, per year conceals a wide dispersion. During the fiscal years 1978, 1979, and 1980, some twenty-three states elected to focus developmental disabilities formula grant funds on case management projects. Nearly 30,000 persons were served in more than 140 projects at an average per capita annual cost of $169. The range (by state) was from less than $30 to more than $800 (Henney and Alldredge, 1981; NCSW 1981).

Sharon Landesman–Dwyer of the University of Washington (Note 5) has made two cognate studies for the Washington State Division of Developmental Disabilities on the workload experienced in its six regional offices serving nearly 8,000 clients. Time spent in thirteen common activities was measued; this study also confirmed the great variability in time spent per case.

It is worth recalling that case management is not new as a federally supported social service. In 1961–62, the architects of the amendments liberalizing the welfare titles of the Social Security Act persuaded Congress that making social services more widely available to current, former, and potential recipients of public assistance would reduce the need for such cash assistance in the long run. By the end of the 1960s a revolt had developed among both recipients and private providers of social services (who were potential bidders for purchase of service contracts). These groups claimed that the states were continuing to stress state delivered "soft services" (counseling, placement, case management) at the expense of "hard services" such as child day care and homemaker services, which are often purchased from private sources. This revolt was one factor in the move toward "separation of services" from cash assistance and eventually to enactment of Title XX in 1974.

Although it can be well argued that a "dependent" child's need for public assistance does not justify making his mother the target of gratuitous advice on child rearing or how to get to the free clinic, the resultant generalized deemphasis on casework did deprive some truly vulnerable elderly and disabled people of caseworkers' assistance just as deinstitutionalization was occurring. Now twenty years later, it appears that we should restore case management as a social service directed to persons who are actual or potential users of the SSI/Medicaid systems because of their need for long-term care. Some states may consider reemphasizing generic casework services.

Recognizing case management as a "universal" service under Title XX would permit states who wish to use this structure to do so with less bookkeeping and also to combine the universal functions of protective services, information, and referral with case management in freestanding community resource centers.

On the other hand, a state may prefer to identify a need for categorical case management, assigned *ab initio* to the appropriate categorical agency, whether for the chronically mentally ill, the mentally retarded, the severely physically disabled, the elderly, or any other group. In either case, categorizing case management by target group while maintaining access for members of the group to the full range of discipline-defined generic or quasi-generic services (health, mental health social services, rehabilitation, education) and the life support resource systems (income maintenance, housing, transportation, communication) is a viable model compatible with the expected and desired directions of change toward pluralistic patterns of service delivery.

If the recommendation of the DHHS task force that drafted the National Plan for the Chronically Mentally Ill (July 1980) is heeded, we would have separate funding for case management services for this group at a high federal reimbursement rate under Title XIX–Medicaid. This would entail means testing for mentally disabled persons, who might well be disqualified on the basis of income and assets but unwilling to pay for needed case management services that are in fact protective. Under these circumstances the Title XIX paradigm fails; it is open ended but only for a limited group of eligibles.

Although the DHHS task group on the chronically mentally ill claimed that there is precedent for paying for case management under Medicaid, this is misleading, since (as pointed out earlier) this service in general is paid for only when it is incidental to the receipt of health services in an organized health care setting. The precedent for inclusion as an identifiable or freestanding service is much clearer in the social service systems. Moreover, if we recognize as inevitable the prospective decline in total federal dollars flowing to states, it scarcely seems justified to go upstream of Medicaid regulations and accounting in order to fund a relatively inexpensive activity in which it is particularly desirable to keep flexibility. Thus, from a state perspective, the DHHS suggestion seems like a red herring, and from a consumer perspective, it risks overregulation as well as exclusion.

A hard-nosed appraisal from a federal budgetary perspective seems scarcely more favorable. Here principles from behavioral fisics clearly apply. The only reason for recommending Medicaid funding is its open endedness. Federal policymakers are increasingly wary of putting "soft" services into an open-ended money stream. In this case, there could be a real risk that states with more ingenious gamesmen would find ways to refinance case management services already in place.

If case coordination itself is not (or should not be) very costly, that which is mediated by the case manager will, when summed up, represent the cost of long-term care. Again the distinction between mural and extramural case management are important.


## COSTS

The complexity of true cost accounting for total institutional care, even within that closed system, is effectively concealed by the common practice of reporting one annual per diem cost for a facility housing 50 to 1,000 individuals of different ages and relevant characteristics. Occasionally, such per diems are reported only as averages for an entire state. Different residents are housed in different units with different staffing patterns. There is still a lack of uniformity in the way capital costs are allocated to annual costs. Central office and other administrative costs of state operations are not reflected in appropriations or vendor payments to particular public or private facilities and the costs of licensing and inspection of private facilities are not reported by them. Enthusiasts for one form or another are wont to claim that, for example, community care is less expensive than institutional care. Such broad unqualified statements are scarcely justified. Serious studies that control as many variables as possible suggest that, given comparable services to comparable clients, the differences are within the margin of error of the assumptions, which are often crude, or at any rate inconsequential from a public policy perspective. (See Allard and Toff, 1980; Pollak, 1979; Jones and Jones, 1976; Wieck and Bruininks, 1980; Touche Ross, 1980.)

What is very apparent in any detailed analysis is that dispersion of the functions formerly performed by state institutions (mental hospitals and facilities for the retarded) redistributes the cost among various actors. It does so in automatic ways, both noticeable and unnoticeable; but redistribution of costs can also be planned. Considerable attention is naturally paid by public administrators at state and federal levels to the visible and calculated redistribution of amounts to be appropriated by line item at federal, state, and county levels, respectively (Copeland and Iversen, 1980; Touche Ross, 1980). Occasionally, someone remembers to look at the impact on local school systems (Touche Ross). However, these calculations do not include comparisons of the relative costs of transporting dispersed clients or the impact (positive or negative) on local tax bases when real estate shifts from taxable to tax exempt or vice versa; nor do they include the costs of administering a vendor system, or the opportunity and social costs (and conversely the tax costs) of imposing responsibility for dependent care on a family.

Students of the economics of long-term care generally recognize that relative costs of in-home care versus institutional care depend on the severity and complexity of need. If the impairment demands only intermittent attention or informal care under professional guidance, home care is usually less expensive as well as less burdensome to family members, if any. (See Figure 2-1.) If continuous care is needed, especially at night, or frequent visits to or by a variety of therapists are called for, then a congregate or inpatient setting is indicated by economic considerations. These considerations take into account not only the dollar costs per patient but the appropriate use of professional time and resources. It is also recognized that the unavailability of intermittent or informal supports in the home can force admission to a congregate care facility when the condition of

**Figure 2-1.**  Cost of Care as a Function of Degree of Disability for Care in Own Home Compared to Care in a Congregate Facility Offering Health-Related Care on Site  (*schematic representation*).

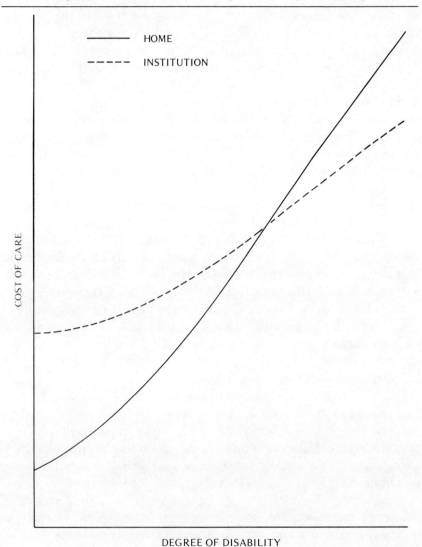

the client alone would not require it in the presence of community-based homemaker, attendant care, chore or "sitter" services.

Requirements for physical care of the physically impaired are much easier to explain to legislators and citizen groups and much easier to sell to health care intermediaries than are the extraordinary components of home care for the mentally disabled. Anyone who has reared a child, and even those who have not, should be able to understand that just as children require different amounts of supervision from infancy to maturity, there are different degrees of impairment among the mentally disabled, requiring different degrees of supervision. Persons with impaired ability to care for themselves may (1) need frequent attention day and night, in the case of the most severe impairment; or (2) need daily presence of a responsible adult, especially overnight, to supervise or assist; or (3) need only occasional counsel and direction in managing major decisions and spending money; or (4) be self-sufficient, able to take responsibility for themselves day or night and able to live alone. Anyone who has reared a child can remember the first weeks or months of life with the newborn, a time of stress made bearable by the prospect of its ending soon and by the fact that usually it was shared with the child's other parent. Even with this two-to-one "staff ratio" the stress for the two generally youthful parents would have been very hard to bear if interminably long, yet this is just the situation faced by parents of children and adults whose organic brain damage has resulted in very erratic patterns of sleep as a chronic condition. For parents whose children also lack the mental capacity to act rationally and cooperatively when they are awake or the capacity for self-preservation in an emergency, the term "24-hour care" takes on a new meaning. Providing such care in the natural home or very small group home is costly.

In out-of-home care for the mentally disabled, level (3) of care is represented by the supervised apartment, level (2) by the group home with sleep-in staff, and level (1) by the ICF/MR or large general ICF, providing staff present and on duty whenever clients are present in the facility. Each of these levels entails progressively higher cost.

The National Association of Private Residential Facilities for the Mentally Retarded has been conducting a running battle with the U.S. Department of Labor concerning fair wages for "sleep time" of live-in staff (level 2, above). The association claims that having to pay regular minimum wages for sleep time would be economically disastrous. Public institutions do not have this option. They are staffed in shifts around the clock (level 1). Comparisons of cost of public versus private care do not always recognize this factor.

In an especially relevant study Weick and Bruininks (1980) applied multivariate regression analysis to data in the University of Minnesota data bank on retarded clients in public and private facilities. Not to anyone's surprise, they found staff/resident ratio to be an important factor in cost. In analyzing "community" facility costs, it is therefore important to distinguish facilities responsible for the full-service needs of their residents from those operating on a home-based model, which does not include much day programming. Weick and Bruininks also found that there are significant regional differences in cost, with the Northeast high and the South low; high staff turnover is associated with lower costs; care of children is more costly than care of adults; and a high proportion of severe and profoundly retarded residents increases costs in community facilities. These results can be quite heuristic. The limitations are that the cost data cover only what is reported by the facility and do not necessarily reflect the true source of funding or total costs per resident of services not paid by the sponsor.

In some studies comparisons are made between public and private to the advantage of the latter; however, one factor little noted in this dichotomy is wage differentials between these sectors, especially for direct care personnel. In one state where a significant purchase of care program is in effect, there is now a strong push by employees for "parity" with state employees. The effects have yet to be measured. Lack of comparable employment opportunities in the private sector for state employees who are displaced by deinstitutionalization can be a serious barrier to this movement.

From the perspective of a behavioral fisician, it is, of course, the way in which perceptions of incentives influence the behavior of those who are in a position to bring about planned change that is of most interest. It is clear that the exploitation by states of the small ICF/MR model is gaining momentum as a way of approximating good practice while passing more of the cost along to the federal fisc. Most of the data used to support these moves by states are aggregated and macroscopic.

Little has been done to date to study systems models based on permutations for combining the various living arrangements with the service alternatives, using some set of components such as the OARS list. Those who see "least restriction," not in its original meaning of minimal government interference in private lives, but as prescriptive optimization of interventions, will not settle for simplistic solutions based on a limited number of prepackaged alternatives. Sufficient diversity must be supplied to avoid both overservice and underservice. Overservice is a factor in the high costs of institutional care of individuals who do not need the level of services maintained for their benefit—such as cooked meals for people who can cook themselves or escort service for those who can travel alone. Estimating the costs of various mixes requires a multivariate approach in which all costs to all actors are adequately represented.

## THE DIASPORA: IMPLICATIONS FOR FINANCING AND SERVICE DELIVERY

The foregoing recital has been developed in considerable detail in order to provide background for several postulates:

1. Members of the mentally disabled population at risk are not the "property of" and in many cases are not even known to the official public mental health and mental retardation delivery systems.

2. Persons with severe chronic mental disabilities frequently have other illnesses or impairments for the prescriptive treatment of which they should have access to services at least equal to those offered to persons not considered to be mentally handicapped.

3. Current emphasis on individualizing services through individual habilitation or rehabilitation planning is resulting in removing simplistic labels and substituting more sophisticated and personalized profiles.

4. Thanks in part to electronic data processing technology as well as more sophistication in diagnosis and evaluation, it is now possible to retrieve more complex information about clients in respect to concurrent functional deficiencies, secondary diagnoses, and chronic conditions.

5. Persons with mental disabilities can, do, and should draw on any other service delivery systems to which they are eligible or

entitled by virtue of age, handicap, economic status, residence, or ethnic identity.

6.  The majority of persons with mental disabilities sufficient to put them at risk can and do receive some services that are delivered other than through the sponsor of their place of residence, whether that sponsor be a family member or a proprietor.

7.  The population considered mentally disabled is intermingled in many service settings with other impaired persons or persons with special needs; this finding is compatible with a trend toward integration and is likely to be accentuated by further depopulation of specialized institutions for the mentally ill and retarded. It is already apparent in schools, sheltered workshops, and child welfare services (including a new and promising thrust toward adoption of handicapped children) and is becoming more apparent in nursing homes and also in adult day programs and senior centers.

8.  Between the nucleus of highly specialized comprehensive services for the most severely disabled mental patients (epitomized by the mental hospital) and the array of totally "generic" services used extensively by persons who are typically without significant chronic impairment lies a vast penumbra of programs for the elderly, dependent children, persons with limited incomes, handicapped children and adults, persons lacking job skills, one-parent families, and the like, to any combination of which categories a person with a mental disability may belong.

9.  The contingencies of behavioral fisics should be managed so as to recognize that integration of least restriction is not so much a matter of scatter site housing as of access by the client to multiple systems, multiple choices, and relative freedom of personal life-styles.

10. It is desirable to recognize that the population at risk as a result of mental impairment is appropriately viewed within the larger and admittedly heterogeneous population of those who need long-term care as currently defined.

11. The field of human services is undergoing what Alvin Toffler (1980) called "demassification," or disaggregation. As the stone shatters, however, there are several different possible cleavage

planes. The most obvious cleavage disperses an institution into smaller groups that are internally more homogeneous. Another cleavage will aggregate people by service provider category, thus bringing together individuals who may have similar functional or developmental needs but who were previously grouped by different diagnostic labels. A third cleavage and form of reaggregation or relabeling can arise from funding packages predicated on administrative ease.

Specific to funding issues are the following postulates:

1.  Changes in funding arrangements should be proactive, reflecting and anticipating social changes attendant on value-driven movements such as deinstitutionalization.

2.  In view of the differences in state and local systems and the diversity of needs in the populations at risk, incremental changes at the federal level are preferable to massive displacements or rearrangements. Such increments should be planned to move consistently and cumulatively toward important goals, however.

3.  Macroaveraging over a heterogeneous group (whether of consumers or providers or states) should not be used to conceal the diversity within the groups or the wide dispersion around the mean or the number of variables involved.

4.  Arguments for change based on relative costs should distinguish between and among component costs to particular segments or sectors as well as total costs to all parties affected. Unloading costs (by shifting the burden from "mental health" to "education," or from federal to state budgets, or from taxpayers generally to individuals or families) should be analyzed and recognized for what it is, an exercise conducted according to the rules of behavioral fisics.

5.  The incomplete data and analyses available on overall costs suggests that using economic arguments to drive change is risky at best. The first question should be "What is socially desirable and equitable?" Distributive justice is never easy.

6.  Long-term care is already a major industry in the United States. It is labor-intensive. The local economic and political consequences of closing down an institution may be comparable to the

consequences of closing a major automobile assembly plant, with similar ripple effects. This observation is not limited to traditional institutions but can apply to an agency providing community-based services, like Upjohn's home health care network. Conversely the contribution of this industry to full employment is and can be an economic plus. It can be argued that in the long run dissagregation and dispersion can spread the economic impact of this industry. With the growth and spread of new forms of long-term care will come new aggregations, new constellations of power, new owners of capital investments, and new configurations of labor unions. The projection of the long-range costs and political consequences of these developments has not as yet attracted much attention among administrators or legislators.

7. The post-World II War era of expanding federal aid to states and municipalities for health, education, and social services is rapidly winding down.

## RECOMMENDATIONS

The following recommendations reflect views that were altered through exchange with the other participants in the Fogarty Conference at the time and subsequently. They also incorporate some recommendations from *The National Plan for the Chronically Mentally Ill.*

### Recommendation 1

States should resume and reassert their statutory and constitutional leadership roles and responsibilities in assuring availability of essential and appropriate human services; this requires cross-system structuring of those health, mental health, education, rehabilitation, employment, housing, and social services needed and wanted by the citizens within each particular state. States should recognize and use federal aid for what it is—assistance in meeting goals of quality, equity, and adequacy. No state administrator should be embarrassed to ask a legislature for a justifiable state dollar for which there is no federal match. Even before the events of 1981 many legislators were already convinced that chasing the federal dollar had reached the point of diminishing returns; the ratio of federal to nonfederal funds in state budgets reached a peak in 1978 and is now declining (Advisory Commission on Intergovernmental Relations (ACIR), 1979).

### Recommendation 2

Congress should reaffirm and make still more rational and equitable the existing system of basic individual entitlements for elderly persons and disabled individuals of all ages, including the mentally disabled, under Titles II, XVI and XVIII of the Social Security Act. As an entitlement for disabled persons with limited or no income, SSI (under Title XVI) should be aligned more nearly with Social Security benefits (under Title II) in that the federal payment should depend only on disability (or age) and financial need, not on place of residence or site of care. One effect would be to continue full benefits to an eligible person entering a medical institution of any kind. These benefits would then become part of the personal income available to be tapped (in part) for the cost of care and treatment just as is currently the case with benefits received under Title II. Since about one-third of persons receiving SSI also receive Social Security, this step would simplify administration. The change would obviate the current demand for a special presumptive disability status for patients about to leave an "institution for mental diseases." Another effect would be to reduce the sometimes arbitrary distinctions among smaller boarding facilities, some of which are defined for administrative or financial reasons as institutions, as are ICFs, and some of which are defined as noninstitutional community residences, although both house very similar clients.

### Recommendation 3

Medicaid should no longer be available to pay the basic "hotel" costs for long-term residents in any institution, medical or nonmedical. A stay of less than three months would be considered short term; a stay of more than six months would be considered long term. In the period three to six months, increases in copayment (out of SSI, if necessary) could be scheduled to avoid notch effects. Medicaid, Title XX, or any special long-term care benefits would be focused on those additional personal services and professional care components needed and provided by licensed providers external to the living unit or by the same management but separately accounted for, using a home-based or ambulatory-care model. An accounting system to separate "hotel" costs from costs of such added services would be devised along lines already developed for colleges and universities.

## Recommendation 4

As at present states should be free to supplement SSI at different levels for persons in specified circumstances. This option permits states to adjust supplements to meet variations in cost of living by geographical region, as well as for the amount of food preparation needed and for other domiciliary services where justified, but it would relieve the federal Medicaid program of the elastic burden of paying unreasonable amortization costs of real estate that is frequently turned over.

## Recommendation 5

SSI state supplementation should also be permitted (with the state being able to opt for federal administration) for certain elderly or disabled persons with very severe, functionally limiting handicaps that interfere with personal self-care and self-management. As under recommendation 2, the payments would be payable regardless of setting. Such supplements could be used to compensate recipients living in their own homes or with their families for the costs of "informal" assistance, extraordinary transportation, "sitter" or diaper services, adapted clothing, and other incidental expenses accounting for which in detail would not be cost-effective.

The net effect of recommendations 2–4 could be to reduce slightly the effective federal Medicaid percentage in the cost of care of persons now in Medicaid institutions while providing a minimal and dollar-limited participation in the costs for adults under age 65 in state mental hospitals (a relatively small population) and decreasing the incentives to select the Medicaid inpatient long-term care option except where such care is truly cost-effective. It could also be used to tip the scales slightly away from capital outlays in cases where a state may be contemplating dubious renovations under the ICF incentive, since pro rata FFP in amortization costs of housing would not be assured even though adequate life safety would still be mandatory.

### Recommendation 6

States should have the option, not now permitted, to include as medically indigent under Medicaid, persons meeting SSI age and disability criteria whose incomes do not exceed 133–1/3 percent of the applicable SSI supplemental level in the state. This provision would, among other things, permit access to certain forms of medical care not covered by Medicare for persons whose social security benefits put them just beyond the line for SSI. It would permit noninstitutionalized disabled persons in this income stratum to carry a Medicaid card rather than requiring them to pay out their own money ("spend down") before they can apply; it would create greater equity in access to needed components as between people in the community and people in Medicaid-certified inpatient facilities.

### Recommendation 7

Recognizing that the ICF/MR is by design a comprehensive, live-in, active treatment model appropriate for some persons with multiple needs, but that trying to make it fit too wide a spectrum of domiciliary needs or using it as a basis for small residences for mentally ill persons may be self-defeating, I recommend that the trend to convert many community residences to an emasculated ICF/MR standard be averted. In its place, I envision new and appropriate variations of a small home-based care model with essential age-appropriate in-home services. This can be developed under the rubric of the general (noncomprehensive) ICF, with a caveat that mentally disabled persons may be admitted to such facilities only after independent assessment and only if they have external case managers, and if appropriate day programming is separately available out of the home.

### Recommendation 8

States should provide case management services (resource mobilization assistance) for any mentally disabled person for whom it is requested by self, guardian, or immediate kin. Such services should be essentially freestanding and universal—that is, not means tested.

These services should be categorical in the sense that individual case managers would specialize in serving specific target populations such as the older chronically mentally ill, psychotic adolescents, deaf children, developmentally disabled preschoolers, or aging retarded, but without rigid boundaries. This model has been successfully used by the vocational rehabilitation agencies for whom case management on a short-term basis is a key component of service delivery. A centralized human services model (as for rehabilitation) or a "categorical" model, which distributes both funds and responsibilities to categorical agencies, can be considered. Funding should be derived from state dollars or possibly Title XX or XXI dollars.

### Recommendation 9

Individualized remedial program components, including day care, identified for a client by his or her case manager should be funded from one or more generic sources (including Medicaid), with interstitial state dollars if necessary; however, all should be funded independently of the cash entitlements that underwrite basic maintenance or "hotel" costs in the setting considered most appropriate.

### Recommendation 10

Resource limitations set for SSI eligibility in 1973 (Sections 1611, 1613) should be updated. A flat increase of 60 percent would serve, but a preferable method would be to allow the equivalent of one year's basic benefit for the 1980–81, say, an individual would have a resource limitation of $238 × 12, or $2,856. States should be permitted and encouraged to permit reservation of resources above these limits for "Medicaid only" recipients over a reasonable period of time (not less than six months but preferably up to two years) during which a long-term-care candidate might be expected to achieve greater capacity for independent living. The present practice of requiring inpatients to pay out their own funds until their assets are reduced to a very low figure (even below the SSI assets test) before Medicaid is applied puts the person who is trying to return to work or to get started in a more independent living arrangement at a considerable disadvantage relative to persons who command other third-party payment modalities.

Large families should be allowed a resource increment (of the order of half that for an independent disabled adult) for each non-disabled child. Data on incomes of families with SSI children at home indicate that they cluster at the very low end of the permissible income scale (Rymer et al., 1980). This seems to reflect a disproportionately severe limitation on assets. Also, the application of the assets test to farm and ranch families should be reviewed for SSI as well as Medicaid.

### Recommendation 11

States should as a matter of policy retain a pluralistic array of services and residential options. A range of living arrangements recognizing twelve to fifteen types as alternatives for mentally disabled persons should not be considered excessive. Under channeling concepts, we also need pluralism in types of gatekeepers at the community level.

### Recommendation 12

State governments should begin now to plan and implement a policy of assuring a mix of public and privately sponsored facilities, with public participation in operation of exemplary facilities of all those types requiring some full-time employees. In particular, states should take greater advantage of the 1976 amendment to Title XVI, Section 1611 (e) (1) (C), which made clear that a publicly administered community residence housing no more than fifteen persons is not a public institution and is therefore a place whose residents may receive full SSI benefits, any noninstitutional Medicaid services, and so on.

## Recommendation 13

A national technical assistance project should be mounted to analyze the feasibility, advantages, and disadvantages of various ways of combining public and private resources for initial investment (capital assets, equipment, start-up costs) for particular projects, and to document actual experience with innovative ideas.

## Recommendation 14

Inasmuch as the natural environment of the family is usually the most cost-effective in human terms for children and since out-of-home care for retarded children has been found more expensive than care for adults, states should address themselves more vigorously as a matter of policy to providing active and meaningful supportive services to natural, adoptive, and foster families with disabled children; various federal agencies should also encourage this policy and the district offices of the Social Security Administration should increase their information and referral competence and practice.

## Recommendation 15

The limit on outpatient psychiatric benefits under Title XVIII (Medicare) should be raised to $750 per year.

## Recommendation 16

Federal agencies with responsibility for operating or supporting data gathering and management information systems should encourage and financially support inclusion of data that identifies client variables that are important to planning for long-term care and to policymaking. The Minimum Long Term Care Data Set developed by the National Center for Health Statistics (1980) should be adopted by HCFA and used by states, with expanded modules appropriate to the respective major categorical groups. In the meantime, the Social Security Administration should enhance its already impressive research and statistics capacity so as to identify more readily for other agencies (and make more readily available to scholars) variables significant for policy analysis. For example, a recent sampling survey based on personal interviews revealed that about 13 percent of SSI children are in foster care and that half of these (or about 13,000) are mentally retarded (Rymer et al., 1980). About 14 percent of children receiving SSI are in Medicaid-certified institutions, but data has not been published showing what portion are in specialized hospitals for the orthopedically handicapped, in mental hospitals, or in ICF/MRs. Data on categorical groups of this kind are needed in order to apportion resources and develop incentives appropriately within the long-term-care framework.

### Recommendation 17

In view of the possibility that, even in the current climate of retrenchment, Congress will consider legislation liberalizing support for certain noninstitutional health-related social and instrumental services for persons in need of long-term care, consumers and providers of services mentally disabled persons of all ages should rally support to assure an appropriate place under this umbrella for mentally disabled persons, lest they find themselves once again counted as covered by an umbrella with holes in it.

### REFERENCES

Advisory Commission on Intergovernmental Relations. *Significant features of fiscal federalism*, 1978–79 ed. Washington, D.C. 1979.

Aiken, M., Dewar, R., DiTomaso, N., Hage, J., and Zeitz, G. *Coordinating human services.* San Francisco: Jossey–Bass, 1975.

Allard, M.A., and Toff, G.E. *Current and future development of intermediate care facilities for the mentally retarded: A survey of state officials.* Washington, D.C.: Intergovernmental Health Policy Institute, 1980.

American Association of Social Workers (AASW). *Social case work –generic and specific, A report of the Milford Conference.* New York, AASW, 1929. Reprinted by the National Association of Social Workers, New York, 1974.

Bachrach, Leona L. Overview: Model programs for chronic mental patients. *American Journal Psychiatry*, 1980, *137*, no. 9, 1023.

Boggs, Elizabeth M. The financing of mental retardation programs. *Association of University Programs in Health Administration—Program notes.* No. 63, February 1975, pp. 49–65.

Boggs, Elizabeth M. Income maintenance: Federal income resources for persons with long-term disabilities originating early in life. *Mental retardation and developmental disabilities,* vol. IX. New York: Brunner/Mazel, 1977.

Boggs, Elizabeth M. A taxonomy of federal programs affecting developmental disabilities. In J. Wortis (ed.) *Mental retardation and developmental disabilities,* vol. X. New York: Brunner/Mazel, 1978.

Boggs, Elizabeth M. Economic factors in family care. *Family care of developmentally disabled members: Conference proceedings.* Minneapolis: University of Minnesota, 1979.

Boggs, Elizabeth M. Toward a national policy for prevention of developmental disabilities. In McCormack, Michael K. (ed.). *Prevention of mental retardation and other developmental disabilities.* New York: Marcel Dekker, 1980.

Bradley, Valerie J. *Deinstitutionalization of developmentally disabled persons. A conceptual analysis and guide.* Baltimore: University Park Press, 1978.

Bruininks, R.H., Hauber, F.A., and Kudla, M.J. *National survey of community residential facilities: A profile of facilities and residents in 1977.* Minneapolis: University of Minnesota, 1979.

Bruininks, R.H., Hill, B.K., and Thorsheim, M.J. *A profile of specially licensed foster homes for mentally retarded people in 1977.* Minneapolis: University of Minnesota, 1980.

Bruininks, R.H., and Krantz, G.C. (eds.). *Family care of developmentally disabled members: Conference proceedings.* Minneapolis: University of Minnesota, 1979.

Bruininks, R.H., Thurlow, M.L., Thurman, S.K., and Fiorelli, J.S. Deinstitutionalization and community services. *Mental retardation and developmental disabilities, vol. XI.* New York: Brunner/Mazel, 1980.

Copeland, W.C., and Iversen, I.A. *Medicaid funding for the continuum of care for MR/DD persons—A policy memo.* Mimeo. Minneapolis: Hubert J. Humphrey Institute of Public Affairs, March 11, 1980.

De Jong, Gerben. *The movement for independent living: Origins, ideology, and implications for disability research.* East Lansing, Mich.: University Centers for International Rehabilitation—USA, 1979.

Federal Council on Aging. Public policy and the frail elderly. DHEW Publication No. (OHDS) 79-20959. Washington, D.C., 1978.

Federal Council on Aging. *Key issues in long term care: A progress report.* Mimeo. Washington, D.C.: December 1979.

Frohlich, Philip. *The 1967 survey of institutionalized adults—residents of long-term care medical care institutions.* DHEW Publication No. (SSA) 11803. Washington, D.C.: U.S. Government Printing Office, 1974.

Goodman, Carolyn, and LeBlanc, Linda. *Feasibility of defining typical packages and services for long-term care providers.* Publication G-105. Applied Management Sciences, Silver Spring, Md., 1977.

*HCFA Forum.* Supermarket of services allows dependent adults to avoid institutions. November 1978, p. 17.

Henney, R. Lee, and Alldredge, Carol. *State councils/administrative agencies fill gaps in the service system—A report.* Washington, D.C.: Institute for Comprehensive Planning, 1981.

Holden, Constance. Behavioral medicine: An emergent field. *Science, 1980, 209,* 479.

Iglehart, John K. Long-term health care—The problem that won't go away. *National Journal,* 1977, *11,* no. 5, 1,725.

Jones, P.P., and Jones, K.J. *The measurement of community placement success and its associated costs.* Mimeo. Heller School, Brandeis University, Waltham, Mass., 1976.

Knee, Ruth, ed. *The future of long term care in the United States: The report of the task force.* Washington, D.C.: National Conference on Social Welfare, 1977.

Lakin, K.C. and Bruininks, R.H. *Occupational stability of direct care staff of residential facilities for mentally retarded people.* Minneapolis, Mn. University of Minnesota, 1981.

LaPorte, Valerie, and Rubin, Jeffrey. *Reform and regulation in long-term care.* New York: Praeger, 1979.

Lazar, I., and Mueller, J. *Cornell studies of P.L. 92-603.* Ithaca, N.Y.: Cornell University, 1974.

Mayer, M.F., Richman, L.H., and Balcerzak, E.A. *Group care of children—crossroads and transitions.* New York: Child Welfare League of America, 1978.

Medicaid/Medicare Management Institute. *Data on the Medicaid program: eligibility, services, expenditures,* 1979 ed. (rev.). Baltimore, Md.: Health Care Financing Administration, 1979.

Merrit, R.E., and Gale, G. (eds.) *Some state and federal perspectives on Medicaid—Selected papers on the Medicaid program, 1976-78.* Special Report, DHEW Publication no. (HCFA) 20001. Baltimore, Md.: Medicaid/Medicare Management Institute, Health Care Financing Administration, 1978.

Minkoff, Kenneth. A Map of the chronic mental patient. In Talbot, J.A. (ed.). *The chronic mental patient—problems, solutions and recommendations for a public policy.* Washington, D.C.: American Psychiatric Association Ad Hoc Committee on the Chronic Mental Patient, 1978.

National Association of State Mental Retardation Program Directors. *Trends in capital expenditures for mental retardation facilities: A state by state survey.* Arlington, Va., 1980.

National Center for Health Statistics (NCHS). *The national nursing home survey, 1977: Summary for the United States.* DHEW Publication no. (PHS) 79-1794. Hyattsville, Md., 1979.

National Center for Health Statistics. *Long term health care—minimum data set.* DHHS Publication no. (PHS) 80-1158, Hyattsville, Md., 1980.

National Conference on Social Welfare. *Case Management: State of the Art.* Report submitted to Administration on Developmental Disabilities. Washington, April 16, 1981.

National Institute of Mental Health. *Patients in state and county mental hospitals 1967.* Series A, No. 2, Public Health Service Publication no. 1921. Chevy Chase, Md., 1969.

National Institute of Mental Health. *Additions and resident patients at end of year—State and county mental hospitals, by age and diagnosis, by state, United States 1976.* Mimeo. Rockville, Md., 1978.

Office of Human Development Services. *Annual report to the Congress on Title XX of the Social Security Act, fiscal year 1979.* Washington, D.C., 1980.

Okin, Robert L. The future of state mental health programs for the chronic psychiatric patient in the community. *American Journal of Psychiatry,* 1978, *135,* no. 11, 1355.

Pfeiffer, Eric (ed.). *Multidimensional functional assessment: the OARS method.* Durham, N.C.: Center for the Study of Aging and Human Development, Duke University, 1975.

Platman, Stanley R. *How do we achieve integrated services in the community for the chronic mentally ill?* Address, Conference of the Southern Regional Education Board, June 12, 1978. Text available as a mimeo from National Association of State Mental Health Program Directors, Washington, D.C.

Pollak, William. *Expanding health benefits for the elderly. Volume 1: Long term care.* Washington, D.C.: Urban Institute, 1979.

President's Commission on Mental Health. *Report to the president.* Washington, D.C.: U.S. Government Printing Office, 1978.

Rubin, Jeffrey. Public Attitudes and the Financing of Community mental health services. In Baron, R., Rutman, I.D., and Klaczinska, B. (eds.) *The community imperative; proceedings of a national conference on overcoming public opposition to community care for the mentally ill.* Philadelphia, Horizon House Institute for Research and Development, 1980.

Rymer, M., Reither, M., Goldman, R., and Van De Vanter, M. Urban Systems Research and Engineering, Inc. *Survey of blind and disabled children receiving supplemental security income benefits.* SSA Publication no. 13: 11728, January 1980 (see also *Social Security Bulletin,* January 1980, *43,* no. 1, 9).

Scheerenberger, R.C. *Public residential services for the mentally retarded 1976.* Madison, Wis.: National Association of Superintendents of Public Residential Facilities for the Mentally Retarded, 1976.

Scheerenberger, R.C. *Public residential facilities for the mentally retarded, 1977.* Madison, Wis.: National Association of Superintendents of Public Residential Facilities for the Mentally Retarded, 1978.

Sharfstein, S.S., Turner, J.E. and Clark, H.W. Financing issues in providing services for the chronically mentally ill and disabled. In Talbot, J.A. (ed.). *The chronic mental patient—problems, solutions and recommendations for a public policy.* Washington, D.C.: American Psychiatric Association Ad Hoc Committee on the Chronic Mental Patient, 1978.

*Social Security Bulletin, Annual Statistical Supplement,* 1977–1979. Social Security Administration, Baltimore.

Talbot, John A. (ed.). *The chronic mental patient—problems, solutions and recommendations for a public policy.* Washington, D.C.: American Psychiatric Association Ad Hoc Committee on the Chronic Mental Patient, 1978.

Task Force on the National Plan for the Chronically Mentally Ill, U.S. Department of Health and Human Services, draft manuscript, June 1980.

Toffler, Alvin. *The Third Wave.* New York: Morrow, 1980.

Touche Ross & Company. Cost study of the community based mental retardation regions and the Beatrice State Developmental Center. *Report to directors of the Department of Public Institutions and Public Welfare, Nebraska.* Kansas City, Mo., August 15, 1980.

Trager, Brahna. Home health care and national health policy. *Home Health Care Services Quarterly* 1980, *1,* no. 2, 1.

U.S. Bureau of the Census, *1976 survey of institutionalized persons: A study of persons receiving long term care.* Washington, D.C.: U.S. Government Printing Office, 1978.

U.S. Bureau of the Census. Survey of income and education. Offset unpublished data, Washington, D.C. 1978.

U.S. Congressional Budget Office. *Long term care for the elderly and disabled.* Washington, D.C.: U.S. Government Printing Office, 1977.

*U.S. News and World Report.* Big business moves into nursing homes. June 2, 1980, 60.

Vischi, T.R., Jones, K.R., Shank, E.L., and Lima, L.H. *The alcohol, drug abuse and mental health national data book.* DHHS Publication no. (ADM) 80–938, Washington, D.C., 1980.

Wieck, Colleen A., and Bruininks, Robert H. *The cost of public and community care for mentally retarded people in the United States.* Project Report no. 9. Department of Psychoeducational Studies, University of Minnesota, Minneapolis, 1980.

Wolins, M., and Piliavin, I. *Institution or foster family—A century of debate.* New York: Child Welfare League of America, 1964.

Zaharia, E.S., and Baumeister, A.A. Technician turnover and absenteeism in public residential facilities. *American Journal of Mental Deficiency,* 1978, *82,* no. 6, 580.

## REFERENCE NOTES

1. Soldo, Beth J. *Living arrangements of the elderly: Future trends and implications.* Statement prepared for joint hearing of the House Select Subcommittee on Population and Aging, May 24, 1978.
2. Alexander, Chauncey, Executive Director, National Association of Social Workers. Letter to Administrator, Health Care Financing Administration, September 5, 1980.
3. Gettings, Robert M. *Federal financing of services to mentally retarded persons: Current issues and policy options.* Paper prepared for U.S. Office of Human Development Services, 1980.
4. Landesman–Dwyer, Sharon. *Case management study and workload study.* In-house draft report for Division of Developmental Disabilities, Washington Department of Social and Health Services, Olympia, Wash. 1980.

# 3 DEVELOPMENT OF CONSTITUENCIES AND THEIR ORGANIZATIONS
## Public Policy Formulation at the National Level

*E. Clark Ross*

Researching this topic has led me to one initial conclusion: scholarly research and writing on both development of constituencies in mental health and their role in public policy formulation is desperately needed. It is hoped that this chapter will promote further research. Because of the lack of good-quality background material, I have relied upon generally available resources, conversations with organizational leaders, and my own experience in the field. Finally, I have focused on constituency groups that are active in the federal public policy arena, thus omitting discussion of many worthy groups, among them the Mental Retardation Association of America, American Academy on Cerebral Palsy and Developmental Medicine, American Schizophrenia Association, and American Orthopsychiatric Association. Similarly, groups that from time to time have exerted influence on programs of interest to the developmental disabilities and mental health fields, including the American Physical Therapy Association, the American Occupational Therapy Association, and the National Association of Social Workers, are not discussed, for they do not have as their primary purpose developmental disabilities or mental health, although their influence cannot be underestimated.

## CONCEPTUAL FRAMEWORK

### The Group Basis of Society

Norman Ornstein and Shirley Elder observed in 1978 that the social and political history of the United States revolves around groups:

> from the eighteenth century onward, observers of America have noted its group orientation. America, more than most, is a society of joiners and of groups . . . Americans are encouraged to join and to identify with organizations and associations. It is not surprising, then, that American politics would have a significant group dimension. (p. 7)

To Arthur Bentley, the founder of American group theory, the essence of a group was that it provides a benefit to its members; "there is not a group without its interest" (quoted in Olson, 1971, pp. 8 and 119).

The voluntary association is a prominent subject of sociological and political analysis; examples include Alexis de Tocqueville's 1835 *Democracy in America*, James Bryce's 1891 *The American Commonwealth*, Arthur Bentley's 1908 *The Process of Government*, and Earl Latham's 1965 *The Group Basis of Politics: A Study in Basing-Point Legislation*.

David Truman has defined an interest group as: "a shared-attitude group that makes certain claims upon other groups in society. . . . If and when the group makes claims through or upon any of the institutions of government, it becomes a political interest group" (Ornstein and Elder, 1978, p. x). There are two theories of the origin of interest groups: David Truman's "disturbance theory" and Robert Salisbury's "entrepreneur theory."

David Truman, in his 1971 version of *The Governmental Process* (originally published in 1955), maintains that interest groups arise from two interrelated societal processes. First is the increasingly complex nature of society with its diversity of groups and differentiation in the division of labor. Second, specific catalytic factors arise that cause individuals to organize into interest groups; they undergo a "disturbance" that alters their relationship with other groups or institutions. The disturbance changes the equilibrium of the group with other elements in society; they organize to stabilize their relations. Typical disturbances are wars, business cycles, and major changes in governmental activity (Ornstein and Elder, 1978).

Robert Salisbury, in a February 1969 *Midwest Journal of Political Science* article entitled "An exchange theory of interest groups," argued that individuals enter into interpersonal relationships because they derive some type of benefit from the relationship or exchange. To Salisbury it is the entrepreneur or political organizer, rather than the disturbing event, that is the determining factor in interest group formation. Entrepreneur success depends upon the organizational incentives offered, which can be material incentives (tangible goods); "solidary" incentives (socializing and friendship rewards); or "purposive" incentives (ideological satisfaction associated with group efforts) (Ornstein and Elder, 1978). In Jeffrey Berry's 1977 study of eighty-three public interest groups, he found that two-thirds were begun by "entrepreneurs" working without significant disturbances as additional stimuli (Barry, 1977).

In his 1957 study of voluntary associations David Sills emphasized that these organizations are not simply collectivities of individuals but social groupings that have a reality transcending the individuals who constitute them (Sills, 1957).

An expanded discussion of the entrepreneur and specialization explanations of group formation are necessary. Stephen Strickland, in his study of U.S. medical research policy, emphasizes the importance of the entrepreneur to voluntary agencies. Strickland focuses on the cancer movement as an example. In 1942 Mrs. Albert D. (Mary) Lasker persuaded her husband to join her in establishing a foundation to support medical research, the Lasker Foundation. Joined by Mrs. Daniel (Florence) Mahoney and Emerson Foote they formed the American Society for the Control of Cancer in 1945, which evolved into the American Cancer Society in 1946. The American Cancer Society, with its emphasis on the personal initiative of group formation, served as the model for many other voluntary organizations (Strickland, 1972). In his study of the National Foundation for Infantile Paralysis, David Sills emphasized Franklin Roosevelt's 1927 campaign to establish a treatment center at Warm Springs, Georgia, and the importance of the 1933 president's birthday ball as the stepping stone for organizing the foundation (Sills, 1957). The role of entrepreneurs will be repeated in explaining the development of most of the developmental disability and mental health associations.

To Earl Latham (1965), "self expression and security, ideology and interest, are sought by the group members through control of the physical and social environment which surrounds each group"

(p. 29). Every group must come to terms with its environment to survive and prosper; groups generally make the environment safe and predictable by (1) putting restraints upon it, (2) neutralizing it, or (3) conciliating it and making it friendly. The environment "changes every day," which means there is a "ceaseless struggle" by the groups to use one or more of the three methods (Latham, 1965, pp. 29–31). Coping with the environment relies upon the concept of *functionalism*, which assumes that human society is composed of many kinds of groups and many different parts of culture related to one another in some kind of system. These parts must be integrated by a functional arrangement of the parts. The emphasis is on the relationship of the functioning of the parts of the organization of society to each other (Ogburn and Nimkoff, 1964). Emile Durkheim defines functionalism as the situation when a division of labor becomes necessary to efficiently exploit scarce resources with this differentiation of society occurring along occupational lines. The division of labor results in society's solidarity or its "function" (Applebaum, 1970). Everett Hughes (1971) and Elton Rayack (1960) explain how professional societies attempt to standardize and thus control professional performance, for they are the "holders and guardians" of a specialized body of knowledge. Occupational control and specialization will reappear in this explanation of the developmental disabilities and mental health constituencies.

## The Economic Function of Voluntary Associations

Burton Weisbrod (1977) describes the voluntary nonprofit sector as America's third sector (government and private profit oriented being the other two). To Weisbrod, the voluntary nonprofit sector is a quasi-governmental response to the forces that constrain the ability of democratic governments, as political institutions, to satisfy consumer demands for collective goods. However, he believes "there is now no consensus among economists as to how to model, that is, describe and predict the behavior of voluntary non-profit firms" (p. 12). There have been studies of philanthropic giving but not of collective consumption.

Total 1973 revenue of U.S. nonprofit organizations was $530.9 billion; of this, sales and receipts accounted for $121.1 billion (23 percent), dues and assessments for $349.9 billion (66 percent), and contributions, gifts, and grants for $59.9 billion (11 percent). Total 1973 revenue for voluntary health organizations was $33.1 billion.

Constraints on government action restrict its ability to correct private market failures; one result is the establishment of voluntary groups to provide collective goods. The voluntary nonprofit sector appears to be a principle source of collective goods. Demands by all consumers do not generally develop simultaneously; thus, dissatisfied persons turn to nongovernment markets or organizations. These unsatisfied or undersatisfied demanders give rise to the voluntary sector. This explanation is particularly relevant to voluntary health agencies; David Sills (1957) and others emphasize the organizations that develop around specific diseases and disabilities. Weisbrod argues that the larger the quantity of collective good demand that is undersatisfied at the tax price scheme used by government, the larger the expected size of the voluntary sector. The size of the various developmental disability and mental health groups somewhat contradicts this statement. Weisbrod maintains that the larger the variance of demand, the greater the amount of voluntary sector output. This point will be discussed later.

Voluntary agencies produce both public and private consumer goods. The major distinction between the two is the greater individual control and consumer preference offered by private goods. Collective or public consumption goods require sharing. Many voluntary agencies sell their products only to their members; organizations that depend on donations, grants and gifts generally provide more public goods.

Weisbrod has described public versus private consumer goods. Paul Feldstein (1980) builds upon this by explaining that there is little incentive for public interest groups representing American citizens to provide financial and political support to legislators, for these citizens will benefit by the actions of the interest group whether or not they contribute. Thus public interest groups are difficult to form, lacking in resources, and frequently ineffective. The demands of voluntary health associations are more likely to prevail since their members will only benefit if they contribute.

Ornstein and Elder (1978) offer a second reason why disability or disease specific organizations are generally more successful in obtaining official or governmental recognition than larger citizen efforts:

> In many respects, groups and their representatives may have an even greater impact in moving issues toward implementation if the issues do not concern

a broad range of citizens. Such issues do not seriously disturb the status quo or activate opposition from other groups. (p. 225)

## Types of Organizations

Robert Alford (1975) describes the struggle between interest groups as inevitable because the groups are created and sustained by the technical and organizational requirements of a highly differentiated society and political system. He argues that there is a continuing struggle between major structural interests in the health care field and classifies these interests into three categories.

Alford's "dominant structural interests" are "those served by the structure of social, economic, and political institutions as they exist at any given time" (p. 13). An example of these interests is the professional monopolies, such as organized medicine, in which existing institutions protect and reinforce the logic and principle of professional monopoly over the production and distribution of health services. Conflicts occur within these groups, but none challenge the principle of professional monopoly; the groups all share an interest in maintaining autonomy and control over the conditions of their work. They are largely satisfied with the status quo. Their major weakness is the division of labor, which can fragment their unity; the problem is how to maintain a united political front while finding a viable method of dividing the resources among themselves.

Alford's "challenging structural interests" or "corporate rationalization" are "those being created by the changing structure of society" (p. 13). Alford maintains that the organization of health care has become more social than individual, is becoming increasingly dependent on technology, and involves a complex division of the labor of skilled specialists. The result is that bureaucratic organizations such as hospitals are principal agencies organizing and delivering these services. Examples of these interests are hospital administrators, health planners, public health agencies, and health researchers. They share an interest in maintaining and extending the control of their organizations over the work of the professionals, whose activities are key to achievement of organizational goals.

Alford's "repressed structural interests" (p. 13) are by nature organizations or institutions that will not be served unless extraordinary political energies are mobilized. Though the opposite of dominant interests, they are not necessarily in conflict with them. These interests contain the various minority population groups who require enormous political and organizational energies to offset the intrinsic disadvantages of their situation. These groups share an interest in maximizing the responsiveness of health professionals and organizations to their concerns for accessible high-quality health care. Alford maintains that these group efforts are likely to fail. If their demands are focused upon a particular program or need, the response is likely to be the establishment of a new program controlled by the professional monopolists. If their demands are directed toward the reorganization of the health system, new planning and coordinating committees will be established to rationalize the system and thus legitimize the activities of the corporate rationalizers.

Mancur Olson (1971) criticizes traditional group theory and political pluralism because there is no distinction between small and large groups except in degree, not kind. To Olson, groups with larger numbers of members generally perform less efficiently than groups with smaller numbers and tend to be exploited and/or defeated by small groups. Olson's standard for determining whether a group will have the capacity to act is whether the individual actions of any one or more members in a group are noticeable to any other individuals in the group. The larger the group, the more coordination, agreement, and organization is needed.

Olson outlines three factors that keep larger groups from furthering their own interests: First, the larger the group, the smaller the fraction of the total group benefit any person in the group receives. Second, the larger the number of members in the group, the greater the organizational costs. And third, the larger the group, the further it will fall short of providing an optimal supply of a collective good. Olson classifies groups into three types. The "privileged group" is one in which at least one member has an incentive to see that the collective good is provided and their effort is noticeable. The "intermediate group" is one where no single member gets a share of the benefit sufficient to give him an incentive to provide the good himself but their effort is noticeable. The "latent group" is one where if one member does or does not help provide the collective good, no other one member will be significantly affected and therefore no one has any reason to act. To Olson, only separate or selective incentives stimulate "a rational individual" in such a group to act in a group oriented way. His argument is that only when groups are small or when they are fortunate enough to have selective incentives do they organize or act to achieve their objectives. The "rational individual" in a large group is not willing to make any sacrifices to achieve group objectives.

Olson maintains one exception to this classification scheme—the "by-product theory" of pressure groups to explain why some "latent groups" are effective. These groups are organized for some other purpose than lobbying; lobbies are by-products of selective incentives that induce members to join and act. Olson's theory does not directly apply to "philanthropic groups" or the voluntary health agencies.

Paul Feldstein (1980) offers another classification system. Politically, the most important interest groups in the health field are those with "concentrated interests," the providers of care, third-party payers, and the educational institutions. These groups have a concentrated interest in government programs because of the impact these programs have on their jobs and incomes. "Diffuse" interest groups are interested in legislation that has little direct or immediate impact on their members' jobs and incomes. In general, constituencies with concentrated interests are willing to pay more than constituents whose interests are diffuse. A difficulty with any voluntary organization representing diffuse interests is that to be effective the organization must be able to provide political support to achieve its demands. This goes back to an earlier debate, the "free rider" problem: whether an individual constituent contributes or not, he or she shares in the legislative benefits. This, like the other classification schemes will be used in attempting to explain the performance of constituencies in the developmental disabilities and mental health fields.

## VOLUNTARY HEALTH SERVICES: AN OVERVIEW

Susan Ellis and Katherine Noyes (1978) argue that America's progressive movement (1900–1919) aroused the conscience of the middle class to the condition of the poor and introduced large-scale philanthropy and state and national organizations to the United States. These new organizations supplanted much of the spontaneous community volunteerism that had previously attempted to meet people's needs. To Ellis and Noyes, the first nationally oriented voluntary health agencies included the National Tuberculosis Association, established in 1904; American Conference for the Prevention of Infant Mortality, 1909; American Child Health Association, 1909; and the American Society for the Control of Cancer, 1913.

Other voluntary health organizations continued to develop with the greatest proliferation in the 1940s and 1950s (Ellis and Noyes, 1978; Carter, 1961): National Health Association, in 1946; National Multiple Sclerosis Society, 1946; Muscular Dystrophy Association of America, 1950; and National Cystic Fibrosis Research Foundation, 1955. These are just a few of the more prominent of the dozens of voluntary health agencies. When reviewing the developmental disabilities and mental health organizations, it is important to relate their evolution to these trends in voluntary health agency development.

## THE DEVELOPMENT DISABILITIES CONSTITUENCIES

### American Association of Mental Deficiency
(See Sloan, 1976.)

The 1876 Centennial Exposition at Philadelphia stimulated the management of the Pennsylvania Training School to invite all other administrators of existing institutions for "idiotic and feebleminded children" to meet in Media, Pennsylvania. To promote their special work these superintendents, all medical doctors, organized the Association of Medical Officers of American Institutions of Idiotic and Feebleminded Persons. The organization was to have three major concerns: development and organization of institutions, identification of the causes of idiocy and methods for its prevention, and methods used in educating idiots. In 1876, seven states had institutions; by 1885 twenty states had institutions. In 1896 the organization published its *Journal of Psycho-Asthenics. (Psycho-asthenics* was a new word focusing on the etiology of mental enfeeblement.) Philosophies of the nature and treatment of mental enfeeblement were the primary topic at annual organizational meetings. The focus remained on the institution; in his 1930 president's address, George L. Wallace, M.D., described the institution as "the rock and sheet anchor upon which so large a part of the work rests."

A major agenda item at the 1926 meeting was amalgamation with the American Psychiatric Association (APA). The American Association for the Study of Feebleminded, as the association was renamed, rejected this APA overture because of its interest and member involvement in education, criminology, sociology, and psychology as well as medicine and psychiatry. The 1930 meeting was held in conjunction with the First International Congress on Mental Hygiene. At the 1932 meeting, there were in-depth discussions of how to collaborate with the APA, National Education Association, National Committee for Mental Hygiene, and National Organization for Social Work. The decision was reached to stay a separate organization; mental deficiency was not a "symptom" but "a disease in itself."

In 1933, in a meeting held in conjunction with the APA, the organization changed its name to the American Association on Mental Deficiency (AAMD). Its president, Ransom A. Green, M.D., declared that "the problem of the mental defective is essentially a medical problem." However, the 1934 president, Mary M. Wolfe, M.D., Sc.D., argued that the psychological, sociological and educational aspects of the problem far exceeds its medical aspect. In 1940 the *Journal* was renamed the *American Journal of Mental Deficiency.*

At its 1950 meeting, the AAMD organized several sessions on parents, which led to the establishment of the Association for Retarded Citizens (ARC). Describing the relationship between ARC and AAMD between 1950 and 1955, William Sloan and Harvey Stevens (1976) stated, the relationship "was initially a rather tenuous one. Many people viewed this development with some skepticism. However, the work of a few individuals in both organizations led, by the end of the decade (1955), to a relatively safe and comfortable posture on the part of both groups. Because of the implied threat imposed by the growth of parents' associations, with respect to standards and a means of evaluating institutions, the AAMD reacted by starting work within its own organization in these areas to forestall such a development on the part of non-professionals" (p. 222).

The 1953 meeting concentrated on changing the organization's name to American Association on Mental Retardation, but this was defeated. Attention was given to the AAMD Parents Group Liaison Committee. In 1955, the AAMD revised its constitution to emphasize three objectives: to create and disseminate information, to facilitate cooperation among professional persons, and to encourage the highest standards of treatment. In 1959 the AAMD published its *Manual on Terminology and Classification of Mental Retardation.* In 1960 the AAMD hired a half-time executive director having earlier in 1956 received a $462,000 grant from the National Institute for Mental Health for a project on technical planning and standards. In 1963, a second journal, *Mental Retardation,* was launched. In 1968 the Columbus, Ohio, and Willimantic, Connecticut, offices were consolidated with the establishment of a new central office in Washington, D.C. In 1969, the University Affiliated Facilities were affiliated with AAMD and in 1971 a National Association of Superintendents of Residential Facilities for the Mentally Retarded was established within the framework of AAMD.

The AAMD focused its attention in the 1970s on deinstitutionalization, community-based services, accreditation, and public policy. The AAMD's involvement in public policy issues will be discussed subsequently. Today AAMD physically houses and chairs the Accreditation Council on Services for Mentally Retarded and Other Developmentally Disabled persons.

### Epilepsy Foundation of America (EFA)
(See Epilepsy Foundation of America, 1974.)

On May 24, 1898, a physician, Dr. Frederick Peterson, and a lawyer, William Pryor Letchworth, called a public meeting in the New York City Medical Library to discuss epilepsy. Before the meeting ended they had organized the National Association for the Study of Epilepsy and the Care and Treatment of the Epileptic, the first voluntary society for epilepsy. The association had 270 members, mostly physicians, led by Dr. William G. Lennox. The organization disbanded in 1914.

In 1935 32 physicians attending the Congress of Neurologists established the International League against Epilepsy and in 1939 the Laymen's League against Epilepsy was established in Boston. These efforts, led by Dr. Lennox, resulted in the renaming of the organization in 1944 as the American Epilepsy League. Shortly thereafter, a rival group, the National Association to Control Epilepsy, was founded by New York City physicians Jerry C. Price and Tracy J. Putnam. In 1949 these groups formed a new united group, the National Epilepsy League (NEL); however, in 1953 the United Epilepsy Association (UEA) was founded and in 1954 the Federal Association for Epilepsy was incorporated.

Faced in 1957 with three national epilepsy interest organizations and many other independent local epilepsy groups, the Epilepsy Organization Workshop was held to form a single national organization. A group of nine leaders was elected, and out of its discussions came the American Epilepsy Federation (AEF) in 1959. Now, rather than one organization, the nation had four! In 1961 the AEF requested the National Health Council's aid in unifying the epilepsy groups, and in 1962 the federal government Vocational Rehabilitation Administration awarded a federal grant to assist in these negotiations. As a result, the NEL, UEA, and AEF came together in 1965 to establish the Epilepsy Association of America, but the Epilepsy Foundation (which had renamed itself in 1956, changing from its previous title, the Federal Association for Epilepsy) refused to join. In January 1968 the Association and Foundation consolidated into the Epilepsy Foundation of America; "but as praise continued to pour in, the National Epilepsy League sent word from Chicago that it had decided to withdraw." In 1978 the league finally consolidated, and today we have one national epilepsy organization, the Epilepsy Foundation of America.

The history of the epilepsy movement is dominated by physicians, volunteers, parents, and business people competing for national attention in different organizations. The first EFA president in 1967 was Neal Gilliatt, a prominent New York advertising executive, followed in 1971 by Dr. A.B. Baker, regents' professor of neurology at the University of Minnesota. These individuals and organizations worked for increased governmental recognition of epilepsy, establishment of clinics to serve persons with epilepsy, and creation of generally available drugs and anticonvulsants to control seizures.

In its 1974 history EFA declared:

> So far, the record of state or federal legislation to help those with epilepsy, compared to the amount of legislation shoring up other rights, and aiding those with other handicaps, has been small. . . . There are some who would say that in 75 years the movement has made minimal progress. And in comparison with the cancer movement or the mental retardation movement they would be right. The price of disunity runs high.

With several years of unity behind it and with the addition of new professional staff and volunteers, EFA has begun to take its place as a leader in the voluntary health movement and an effective advocate for persons with epilepsy.

### National Easter Seal Society (NESS)
(See Ellis and Noyes, 1978; Carter, 1961;
Manchester, Note 1; NESS, Note 2;
Romer, Note 3.)

In 1907 in Elyria, Ohio, Edgar Allen's son died in a streetcar accident. Mr. Allen, a Rotarian, concluded that Elyria's facilities for the care of the injured were inadequate, and he launched a drive that resulted in the opening of the Elyria hospital in 1908. Shortly thereafter, having befriended a patient, the first "crippled" child he ever met, he became affectionately known as "Daddy" Allen. After surveying a three-county area and identifying 700 crippled children, he launched another campaign, which resulted in 1915 in the construction of a children's hospital specializing in "crippled conditions." In 1919 he launched the Ohio Society for Crippled Children, the first formal organization for helping physically handicapped children in the nation. By 1920 75 percent of Ohio's Rotary Clubs supported the state society. In 1921 the National Society for Crippled Children was founded to unify rehabilitation facilities; lay persons, orthopedic surgeons, and other physicians controlled the society. Rotarians nationwide took interest in launching community programs for crippled children, particularly hospitals and camps. The major function of the society, then and now, is the establishment and operation of rehabilitation programs.

In 1934 the first national seal campaign was conducted in Kentucky. In 1944, the organization added "adults" to its name. In 1967, the term "Easter Seal" was added to the name of the organization to strengthen the organizational identity and public awareness. In 1979, the organization became the National Easter Seal Society.

In a historical perspective, parents of disabled children have been critical of the Easter Seal Society for not providing a unique enough response to individual disabilities. As Richard Carter in 1961 explained: "Other troubles have derived intermittently from the under-standable feeling among victims of affliction 'A' that their needs are unique and should be accorded consideration as elaborate as that given to victims of affliction 'B'. This kind of thinking led, in fact, to the establishment of the United Cerebral Palsy Association." (p. 194)

As Joseph Romer has explained,

> Today, the Easter Seal Society is one of the largest and most diversified na-tional organizations providing services to the disabled. It has affiliates in forty-eight states, the District of Columbia and Puerto Rico which provide a wide range of services including physical therapy, vocational rehabilitation, camping, equipment loan and purchase, speech therapy and psychological counseling.

## United Cerebral Palsy Associations, Inc. (UCPA)
### (See Carter, 1961; UCPA Annual Reports; UCPA, 1974; Eaton, Note 4.)

The first known voluntary agency for cerebral palsy was the Los Angeles, California, Society for Cerebral Palsy founded in 1942. In 1945 a New York City Diagnostic and Evaluation Clinic desired to open an experimental school for ten children with cerebral palsy. The clinic ran an advertisement in the *New York Times* asking, "Do you have children with the following . . . ?" Over 300 parents an-swered the ad, which led to creation of the Association for Cerebral Palsy and parent-run schools opened in Buffalo and Nassau County.

In 1947, Alvin Boretz, a parent of a boy with cerebral palsy, wrote the script of "Love Is a Doctor," part of a national network radio show, "Exploring the Unknown"; in response, the radio network received thousands of letters. The New York City Cerebral Palsy Association financed a *Science Illustrated* pamphlet on cerebral palsy and sent copies to all those who had written. In 1948 the National Foundation for Cerebral Palsy was established and in February 1949, 12,000 people attended an international conference on cerebral palsy in New York City. Following this meeting, forty-five promi-nent women, led by Mrs. Leonard H. Goldenson and the Women's Division of the New York City Cerebral Palsy Association raised $50,000 and on August 12, 1949, the UCPA was officially organized.

These volunteers including Leonard H. Goldenson, Roger S. Firestone, and William Clay Ford were a unique group—parents of children with cerebral palsy who possessed significant socioeconomic standing. They wanted their own organization; as Richard Carter has explained, "The Easter Seal societies were as generously hospitable and helpful toward these patients (cerebral palsy) as toward all other physically handicapped persons but were unable to give the affliction the public emphasis required to inaugurate a full-dress program" (p. 207).

In its first full year, 1950, UCPA raised over $1 million; "perhaps never before had such legions of 'theatre people' entered so wholeheartedly in an effort to tell the world about a cause via radio, motion pictures, and personal appearances as did those who gave their support to cerebral palsy" (Eaton, Note 4, p. 1). With these funds, UCPA launched a research council, chaired by Dr. Sidney Farber, professor of pathology at Harvard Medical School, and a medical advisory committee, chaired by Dr. Winthrop Morgan Phelps of Yale University and director of the Children's Rehabilitation Institute in Cockeysville, Maryland. William F. Bleakley, an industrialist was the first chairman of the board and Leonard Goldenson served as the first president. In its 1950 mission statement UCPA declared as its second of eight objectives "to promote a normal outlook for the cerebral palsied."

In 1951, UCPA launched a new method of raising funds and educating the public about cerebral palsy—the Telethon. By 1952 affiliates had increased from the original eight to more than 100 and over $4 million was raised. From this point forward, the telethon became a prominent feature of UCPA. In 1955 UCPA established its UCP Research and Educational Foundation and $395,000 was granted for scientific investigation and training. Leading medical doctors and scientists were joined by industrialists such as Jack Hausman and social and philanthropic leaders such as Mary Lasker.

Though industrialists, theater people, doctors, scientists, and philanthropists have been a key to UCPA's success, UCPA also remains a strong parent and consumer organization. Many of its leaders are parents. In his 1961 study of voluntary organizations, Richard Carter recounted the firing of a UCPA affiliate executive director who had enlisted leadership from persons who did not have family members with cerebral palsy. As one parent told Carter, "We can't have this organization taken over by people who don't see CP as we do. We are the ones with the CP children." (p. 208). In 1975, UCPA institutionalized consumer involvement in the national organization by establishing a standing committee of the board of directors and a department staffed entirely by adults with cerebral palsy. In 1979 UCPA voted that at least one-third of the "members of the corporation" must be persons with cerebral palsy or their parents if the primary consumers are under age eighteen or cannot articulate their own interests.

### Association for Retarded Citizens (ARC)
(See Romanofsky, 1978; ARC, 1979;
NARC, Note 5; Boggs, Note 6.)

In 1933, the first parent group to help the mentally retarded was organized in Cuyahoga County, Ohio. At the May 1950 annual meeting of the AAMD parent sessions were offered to conference participants and some of these parents formed a steering committee. On September 28, 1950, forty-two parents and a handful of other concerned individuals representing thirteen states met in Minneapolis, Minnesota, and formed the National Association of Parents and Friends of Mentally Retarded Children. All of the initial officers were parents of retarded persons. There were five main reasons for the association's establishment: (1) the widespread exclusion of retarded children from schools, (2) acute lack of community services, (3) long waiting lists for admission to residential institutions, (4) parent leaders who believed that mutual assistance could bring major benefits, and (5) assistance of a few key professionals associated with AAMD. By 1951 when the constitution actually went into effect, fifty-seven local associations had joined the national association as charter members.

In 1952 the name was changed to the National Association for Retarded Children (NARC) and a research advisory board was established, chaired by Grover Powers, professor of pediatrics at Yale University. In 1954 the first executive director was hired when the headquarters was opened in New York City. In 1958 NARC made its first grants for research. By 1959 there were 700 local member units in forty-nine states with state federations in forty-six states.

In 1965 a national policy statement was published emphasizing that member units should expend their efforts to obtain services rather than provide them; however, as will be noted later, ARC affiliates are primary service providers. In 1970 the national headquarters was moved to Arlington, Texas, and in 1973 the name was changed to National Association for Retarded Citizens. It became prominent in the early 1970s litigating for its affiliates activities in the areas of education, right to treatment, and other protection of rights issues. In 1980 the name was modified to Association for Retarded Citizens.

### National Society for Autistic Children (NSAC)
(See NSAC, 1979; Note 7; Akerley, Note 8;
Benson, Note 9.)

In 1961, Rosalind Oppenheim wrote an article, "They said our son was hopeless," which was published by the *Saturday Evening Post.* In response, many letters from other parents of children with autism were generated. In 1964, Dr. Bernard Rimland, a psychologist and parent of a child with autism, published his book *Infantile Autism* and launched a series of meetings on the subject. In 1964 the NSAC was chartered in the District of Columbia. A volunteer office was opened to seek education, care, and cure of autism through legislation, research, and publicity. The chief function of the organization was to cultivate continuing contact with professionals who provide education and services to children with autism and related communications handicaps.

In 1968 the national office was moved to Albany, New York. In 1970 the Information and Referral Service was launched. In 1972 grants were obtained from the National Institute on Mental Health and Office of Child Development and in a 1976 Developmental Disabilities grant to expand these services into a National Information and Advocacy Project. In 1972 a part-time executive director was hired. In 1978, the national office was moved back to Washington with a full-time executive director and other staff.

### National Association of State Mental Retardation Program Directors (NASMRPD)  (See Boggs, Note 6; Gettings, Note 10; Schnibbe, Note 11.)

In 1970 a number of factors combined to result in the establishment of the National Association of State Mental Retardation Program

Directors. With the availability of federal grants for statewide planning in mental retardation beginning in the mid–1960s, each state was required to identify a state-level focal point for planning or coordinating services for the mentally retarded distinct from mental health. State mental retardation "coordinators" had been meeting for several years as a division on administration of AAMD. Dissatisfied with the academic and professional orientation of AAMD, with AAMD's general reluctance to become involved in the government sector, as well as with the dominance of institution superintendents, they desired a more appropriate forum. Federal funding programs were beginning to develop on a large scale, and these generally relied upon the states for implementation. Several state mental retardation programs had become independent state agencies in the late 1960s; in other states distinct subdivisions had been formed within mental health or human services agencies. Most of the state mental health directors, particularly those in larger states and most with a medical and psychiatric orientation, did not adequately represent mental retardation program interests in the National Association of State Mental Health Program Directors. Last, the federal Bureau of Mental Retardation provided grant funds for state mental retardation directors to conduct a conference, which led to the establishment of the National Association of Coordinators of State Programs for the Mentally Retarded, renamed in 1979, NASMRPD.

### National Association of Private Residential Facilities for the Mentally Retarded (NAPRFMR)
(See Fritz, Note 12.)

For several years providers of residential services for the mentally retarded, mostly the traditional private residential school, were a subdivision of AAMD. In 1970 these providers founded the National Association of Private Residential Facilities for the Mentally Retarded. More and more of these programs were community oriented, and some of these persons wished to be removed from what they perceived to be an institutional bias within AAMD. Many of these persons desired an organization that would be more active in working with the federal government and would supply continuing information in this area. Finally, facility providers desired a program of group insurance to specifically cover their needs and situations.

Today NAPRFMR represents 462 member agencies. Providing information on government and on insurance remain the chief objectives. The association has also become a major referral point for those seeking residential placement, and involvement in accreditation and quality programming has become a key objective. Lobbying and influencing public policy, particularly legislation, is secondary to the information role. NAPRFMR has continued its practice of conducting its annual meeting at the time of the AAMD annual meeting; additionally, for the first time, NAPRFMR conducted a meeting in conjunction with the ARC annual conference in the fall of 1980.

## THE MENTAL HEALTH CONSTITUENCIES

In order to limit the scope of this paper and to facilitate the bridge between similar service needs related to the developmental disabilities and mental health fields, alcoholism and drug abuse problems and organizations will not be discussed.

### American Psychiatric Association (APA)
(See Ridenouer, 1961; American Psychiatric
Association, 1963; Cutler, Note 13.)

In 1844 thirteen superintendents of psychiatric institutions founded the Association of Medical Superintendents of American Institutions for the Insane. In 1851 Dr. Thomas Story Kirkbridge, one of the "original thirteen," published *On the Construction and Organization of Hospitals for the Insane*; this was the standard text from 1851 to 1881 and is still used today. In 1892, the name of the organization was changed to the American Medico-Psychological Association. Since 1921 this oldest national medical association in North America has been known as the American Psychiatric Association.

As Jay Cutler (Note 13) has described it,

The APA today represents over 25,000 psychiatrists nationwide. Its objectives are (a) to improve the treatment, rehabilitation and care of the mentally ill, the mentally retarded and the emotionally disturbed; (b) to promote research and professional education in psychiatry and allied fields; (c) to advance the standards of all psychiatric services and facilities; (d) to foster the cooperation of all who are concerned with the medical, psychological, social and legal aspects of mental health and illness; (e) to make psychiatric knowledge available to other practitioners of medicine, to scientists in other fields of knowledge and to the public; and (f) to promote the best interest of patients and those actually or potentially making use of mental health services.

## American Psychological Association
(See Ridenour, 1961).

The American Psychological Association was established in 1892; although recognized as a field of study before 1900, psychology was almost entirely nonclinical and confined exclusively to the universities. The introduction of intelligence tests was the first push for psychology as a profession followed by the mental test applications during World War I.

## National Mental Health Association (NMHA)
(See Carter, 1961; Ridenour, 1961; Beers, 1953;
Cross, 1934; "NMHA Annual Reports"; Note 14;
Menninger, Note 15; NMHA, 1957.)

Between 1872 and 1888 a National Association for the Protection of the Insane and the Prevention of Insanity existed, but it faded for some years. In 1894 the brother of Clifford Whittingham Beers was disabled with epilepsy and in 1900 he died of a brain tumor. Shortly thereafter, Beers, a 1897 graduate of Yale University and a New York City insurance company clerk experienced a nervous breakdown and threatened or attempted suicide several times. He was committed to an institution in 1901, transferred to the violent ward in 1902, and later transferred to a state hospital. As Beers recalled, "Few, if any, prisons in this country contain worse holes than this cell proved to be" (Beers, p. 151). In September 1903 he was discharged, and in 1905 he began writing *A Mind That Found Itself*. He wrote the book with two primary purposes; the first was to answer a question: "A narrow escape from death and a miraculous return to health after an apparently fatal illness are enough to make a man ask himself: For what purpose was my life spared?" (quoted in Cross, 1934, p. 2). "Without malice toward those who had me in charge, I yet looked with abhorrence upon the system by which I had been treated," Beers wrote (p. 212), so his book, published in 1908, had as it second purpose the intention "to serve as the opening gun in a permanent campaign for improvement in the care and treatment of mental sufferers, and the prevention, whenever possible, of mental illness itself" (p. 225).

On May 6, 1908, Beers, age 32, his father, his brother, four physicians, a judge, a minister, a lawyer, a hospital administrator, a university official, and a social worker organized the Connecticut Society for Mental Hygiene. On February 19, 1909, Beers led "physicians and laymen" (Cross, p. 470) in founding the National Committee for Mental Hygiene, its chief concern being "to humanize the care of the insane" (Cross, p. 471). Beers attracted the leading physicians of his time to the committee. William H. Welch, Johns Hopkins physician and "dean of American medicine" (Ridenour, 1961) served over the years as vice president, president, and honorary president. Adolf Meyer, the "first full-time professor of psychiatry in the U.S. and among the greatest contributors to American psychiatric literature" (Ridenour) served as president or honorary president for years. Headquartered in New York City, in 1912 the committee appointed as its medical director Dr. Thomas W. Salmon, on loan from the New York State Board of Alienists (psychiatrists qualified as expert witnesses in a court of law). The Committee launched numerous initiatives, research, education, training, rehabilitation, community clinics, and world affairs. In 1943 Beers, who had served as the committee's secretary from 1909 until overcome by illness in 1939, died. He was replaced as secretary by Mary Lasker. The committee continued to maintain Beers' contention that it "would be equally the friend of the physician and the patient" (NMHA Annual Report, 1946).

In 1944 conscientious objectors who worked in the Civilian Public Service began describing the poor conditions found in mental hospitals through their bulletin, *The Attendant*. In 1946 with the support of the American Friends Service Committee, these persons organized the National Mental Health Foundation and published a journal, *The Psychiatric Aide*. From 1946 into the 1950s the press published a series of exposés of state mental hospitals.

In 1950 the National Committee for Mental Hygiene, the National Mental Health Foundation (NMHF), and the Psychiatric Foundation merged into the National Association for Mental Health (NASH). The foundation had earlier been organized by the American Psychiatric Association and American Neurological Association as a fundraising entity to finance hospital surveys. The committee's medical director, Dr. George Stevenson, remained the medical director and prominent committee members, such as Mary Lasker, remained on the new board. According to Hunter (Note 16) the NMHF "was a major catalyst in converting the mental health movement from a professionally led elitist organization to a broad membership consumer advocate operator."

However, in his 1961 book, Carter declared: "The problems of mental illness demand social, political, and scientific activity under leadership as vigorous as that of the reform movements of the early century. In none of its several incarnations has the NAMH displayed stomach for such activity, let alone any agreement that the activity might even be necessary . . . [it has been characterized by its] inability to agree on a focus for program" (pp. 195 and 198). Also in 1961 Ridenour stated that NAMH had "taken on a structure entirely different from that of its predecessors, although there is not yet agreement as to exactly what the structure ought to be."

(The NMHA governmental relations program will be discussed subsequently.) The annual reports of the late 1950s and early 1960s are enthusiastic statements of hope, idealism, and energy because of the federal government's actions in this area. The 1962 report, "A national awakening" is indicative of the NMHA approach during this period.

### National Association of State Mental Health Program Directors (NASMHPD)
(See Ridenour, 1961; Schnibbe, Note 11.)

During the 1950s state mental health directors met once a year at the annual meeting of the American Psychiatric Association. In 1954, New York passed the first Community Mental Health Systems Act, whereby the state reimbursed local communities for half of the service costs. By 1959 between sixteen and eighteen states had followed New York's lead in authorizing community care programs. In order to launch a national lobbying effort to establish a federal community mental health care program, a Washington, D.C., secretariat was established in 1959. The directors' concern was that programs in the states were changing so rapidly that they must have an ongoing communication network. Information and lobbying needs resulted in the hiring of a former journalist and Senate employee, Harry Schnibbe, as the NASMHPD executive director.

### National Council of Community Mental Health Centers (NCCMHC)
(See Wolf and Koyanagi, Note 17.)

In 1971 with renewal of the Community Mental Health Centers Act approaching, the community mental health center directors organized their council and retained Jonas Morris, a governmental consultant, to represent them. In 1975 the Council opened its own Washington, D.C., office and retained Morris Associates for their governmental liaison work; in 1978 they terminated the contractual relationship and took on all organizational functions directly.

The NCCMHC has four purposes: to promote the concept, funding, and delivery of CMHC services; to provide technical guidance and support for its members; to serve as a means of cooperation and communication between individuals working in CMHCs; and to work in liaison efforts with other human service agencies as a protagonist for mental health centers.

### THE INDEPENDENT LIVING/SELF HELP GROUPS
(See De Jong, Note 18.)

The Public Law 95-602 "Comprehensive Services for Independent Living" program is seen by some as the federal government's response to a new social movement, the movement for independent living. In describing the movement, Gerben De Jong focuses on the Center for Independent Living (CIL) at Berkeley, organized in 1972, and the American Coalition of Citizens with Disabilities (ACCD), organized in 1974, as the "real beginnings" of the movement. De Jong views independent living as a consumer movement and a social phenomenon characterized by the following philosophies:

- *Consumerism*: "Basic to consumerism is a distrust of seller or service provider. . . . With the rise of consumer sovereignty, professional dominance in disability policy and rehabilitation is being challenged."

- *Self-Help*: The objective of the "self-help movement" is to "give people the opportunity to exercise control over their own lives and the services they use." This movement is fueled by the same "distrust of professionally dominated services" as consumerism. These proponents view themselves as "an alternative service provider" emphasizing peer counseling and advocacy services, which, according to De Jong, are "not provided by mainline human service organizations."

- *Demedicalization*: This concept supplements self-help and consumerism by challenging the dominance of medical professionals and furthering self-care. It maintains that individuals can and should take greater responsibility for their own health and medical care. To De Jong, once medical stability of disability has been obtained, "medical presence is both unnecessary and counterproductive. . . . Disabled persons are insisting that the management of their disabilities is primarily a personal matter and only secondarily a medical matter."

De Jong maintains that the independent living movement has concentrated its energies on a relatively few major disability groups: those with spinal cord injury, muscular dystrophy, cerebral palsy, multiple sclerosis, and post-polio disablement, and on the older adolescent and younger working age adult. This age focus is a function of the disability conditions emphasized to date and the communities (large academic settings) where independent living has taken root.

The CILs or ACCD will not be further described here. Their legislative efforts to date have generally focused on civil rights and affirmative action compliance, transportation, rehabilitation, and independent living as well as crisis issues like congressional reductions in the Social Security Disability Insurance program. UCPA and ARC are associate members of ACCD. They are an alternative service/advocacy system and they have the potential to become more active in the future. They are a factor in planning advocacy approaches in the 1980s.

Tables 3-1 through 3-3 provide comparative data on various constituency organizations.

In his 1980 book, *Conscience and Convenience: The Asylum and Its Alternatives in Progressive America*, David J. Rothman discusses the conflict between conscience and convenience in the development of mental health programs. To Rothman, conscience is "the inven-

**Table 3-1.** Constituency Organizations: A Perspective Using a Common Data Base for Annual Budgets and Government Funding.

| Organization | Founded | Estimated National Budget[a] | Government Grants and Contracts[b] |
|---|---|---|---|
| AAMD | 1876 | $ 1,000,000 | $ 0 |
| EFA | 1898 (1968) | 4,000,000 | 900,000 |
| NESS | 1921 | 3,263,000 | 120,000 |
| UCPA | 1949 | 4,024,000 | 43,000 |
| ARC | 1950 | 2,000,000 | 1,500,000 |
| NSAC | 1965 | 305,900 | 91,200 |
| NASMRPD | 1970 | 285,000 | 45,000 |
| NAPRFMR | 1970 | 62,800 | 0 |
| APA (psychiatric) | 1844 | 10,150,000 | 1,450,000 |
| APA (psychological) | 1892 | 14,000,000 | 0 |
| NMHA | 1909 (1872) | 1,800,000 | 0 |
| NASMHPD | 1959 | 330,000 | 0 |
| NCCMHC | 1971 | 520,000 | 40,000 |

a. Latest available data.

b. Zero in this column indicates that agency is funded entirely through membership dues or private fundraising.

tion of benevolent and philanthropic-minded men and women and their ideological formulations (which) were essential to promoting change." Convenience is the modifications and compromise by "administrators, wardens and superintendents" and others who would have the responsibility for carrying out the reforms advocated by those of conscience.

In *The Organizational Revolution* (1953) Kenneth E. Boulding advanced the thesis that the growth of large-scale organizations in recent decades is a direct reflection of changes in the technical ability to organize. As David Walker (1980) has argued, prior to 1960 only those interests that were large, organized, and relatively well financed were able to pay the price of participating in national politics. Today there has been a

> drastic reduction in the cost of using the political process . . . The new arrivals may not occupy the spacious quarters that house the traditionals, but they can usully muster enough support to rent a modest suite or perhaps only a single office, which frequently is all that is needed physically to manage an effective campaign. (p. 38)

Table 3-2.  Estimated Combined National and Affiliate Budget.[a]

| Organization | Total Budget | Government Grants and Contracts |
|---|---|---|
| AAMD | n.a. | |
| EFA | $   8,000,000 | $   3,100,000 |
| NESS | 113,500,000 | 31,000,000 |
| UCPA | 90,900,000 | 60,160,000 |
| ARC | 187,000,000 | 112,200,000 |
| NSAC | 1,695,000 | 420,000 |
| NASMRPD[b] | | |
| NAPRFMR | n.a. | |
| APA (psychiatric) | n.a. | |
| APA (psychological) | n.a. | |
| NMHA | 20,000,000 | n.a. |
| NASMHPD[c] | | |
| NCCMHC[d] | | |

a.  Latest available data.

b.  State mental retardation budgets are estimated to be $4.5 – $5.0 billion; of this, $3.5 billion is institutional budgets.

c.  State mental health budgets are estimated to be $3.5 billion, not including mental retardation, alcoholism, or drug abuse programs.

d.  Federal appropriations for community mental health centers in fiscal 1980 were $270 million. This does not include nonfederal sources.

## AAMD Governmental Activities
(See Sloan, 1976; Berkowitz, Note 16.)

In 1948 AAMD President Lloyd N. Yepsen, Ph.D., advocated a new theme in presidential addresses, the need for "an organized and consistent attack on the problem of mental deficiency" emphasizing AAMD's main concern, "to safeguard the rights and privileges of the mentally retarded" (p. 199). This theme did not reappear until 1955 when President Gale H. Walker, M.D., criticized AAMD for its low profile in influencing the federal government. In 1964 an ad hoc committee to study legislation was established. In 1969 President Richard Koch, M.D., declared that "AAMD must involve itself in the significant social issues of the day. A formal plan of action for involving AAMD in federal and state legislation was developed that empha-

Table 3-3. National Organizations' Resources for Federal Lobbying and Public Policy Analysis.

| | |
|---|---|
| AAMD | No separate office, half time of a professional lobbyist |
| EFA | No separate office, two professionals |
| NESS | $102,500 Washington, D.C., office budget, two professionals |
| UCPA | $163,205 Washington office budget, two professionals |
| ARC | $168,000 Washington office budget, two professionals |
| NSAC | No separate office, half time of a professional |
| NASMRPD | No separate office, two part-time professionals |
| NAPRFMR | No separate office, half time of a professional |
| APA (psychiatric) | No separate office, six full-time professionals |
| APA (psychological) | APA: one research analyst, AAP: four full-time professionals |
| NMHA | No separate office, two full-time professionals, one half-time professional |
| NASMHPD | No separate office, four full-time professionals (working part time on government activities) |
| NCCMHC | No separate office, two full-time professionals, one half-time professional |

sized cooperative relationships with other organizations. The ad hoc committee on legislation and social issues was continued for two years.

In 1970 President Wesley D. White, Ed.D., declared that "we have the central office that President Chris DeProspo requested twelve years ago and yet we have not really decided as to what its role should be" (p. 272). In 1972 funds were allocated to secure personnel to function in the areas of social and legislative issues and projects and in 1973 the social and legislative issues committee was made a standing committee.

AAMD was established and continues to emphasize itself as a place where all professionals in the mental retardation field can meet to discuss and debate issues of importance. The nature of the organization has resulted in three characteristics: a very cautious organizational approach to governmental advocacy, a severe difficulty in developing organizational consensus on public policy issues, and its members are also members of other mental retardation organizations involved in the same activities.

### EFA Governmental Activities
(See Epilepsy Foundation of America, 1974; McLin, Note 20.)

Many physicians associated with national epilepsy organizations were active in establishing the National Institute of Neurological Diseases and Blindness in 1950. Prominent in these efforts was Dr. William Lennox, who, as early as 1945, had proposed a special Public Health Service Act program for epilepsy.

In 1970 EFA established a legislative committee of the board of directors and hired staff specifically to work in the area of governmental activities. This coincided with the enactment of the Developmental Disabilities Act on October 30, 1970. Implementation of the Developmental Disabilities Act became an EFA priority. EFA has maintained a governmental relations staff ever since. In 1975, by Public Law 94–63, Congress established the Commission for the Control of Epilepsy and Its Consequences, which issued its report in August 1977.

### NESS Governmental Activities
(See Romer, Note 3.)

In 1935, the NESS executive director became personally involved with federal legislation which led to the Title V, of the Social Security Act, the Crippled Childrens Services Program. In 1946 the program services staff and committee was given responsibility for federal legislation. In 1955 the organization established its external affairs committee to work on public relations, organizational liaison, litigation, and governmental activities. In 1973 NESS opened its Washington, D.C., office. Today the organization emphasizes rehabilitation, removing architectural barriers, health financing and planning, and organizational issues such as postage regulation, lobbying regulation, and charitable giving.

### UCPA Governmental Activities
(See United Cerebral Palsy Associations
"Annual Reports; Nielson, Note 21.)

The 1950 UCPA annual report declared a primary purpose of the organization to be "cooperation with government and private agencies concerned with the welfare of the physically handicapped." This coincided with the establishment of the National Institute of Neurological Diseases and Blindness and the appointment of the association's president, Leonard Goldenson, as a member of the institute's advisory council. The 1951 annual report described the establishment of a legislative committee to study existing laws and legislation affecting cerebral palsy in the country; "It cannot be emphasized too strongly that the potential from legislative grants is beyond anything we have been able to raise." In 1953 Harry Lyons, an attorney, was hired as director of the legislative department in the New York national office, which was renamed the legal and legislative committee and department in 1956. Between 1960 and 1969 UCPA purchased the services of a Washington consultant, Colonel Luke C. Quinn, whose services were continued by Mike Gorman from 1969 to 1973. While UCPA's legal and then Washington office focused on program services and rights issues, these consultants were involved in the research and technology areas, a reflection of Leonard Goldenson and Mary Lasker's UCP research foundation interests.

Following Mr. Lyons' retirement in 1968, UCPA opened its Washington office in September and established a governmental activities committee independent from the legal department. The initial staffing of this office was interesting; UCPA's Washington representative, Dr. Elsie D. Helsel, commuted from Athens, Ohio, with secretarial services purchased from NASMHPD, which housed both UCPA and ARC. Dr. Helsel's first Washington-based staff was hired in June 1970. UCPA, ARC, and NASMHPD officials conceived and advocated enactment of the Developmental Disabilities Act. In 1976, UCPA offered to share its copyrighted *Word from Washington* newsletter with ARC, EFA, and NSAC to demonstrate its commitment to the developmental disabilities concept; in September 1976 a joint editorial committee of EFA, NSAC, and UCPA began publishing a revised cooperative Word from Washington.

## ARC Governmental Activities
(See Romanofsky, 1978; ARC, 1979; Note 5; Boggs, Note 6; Marchand, Note 22.)

During its first year in existence (1950), ARC established a legislative committee. In 1954, ARC hired its first executive director, Dr. Salvator George DiMichael, who came from the federal Vocational Rehabilitation Administration. In 1956 ARC published its "Federal Program of Action for America's Retarded Children and Adults" and submitted it to Congressional Representative John E. Fogarty of Rhode Island. This led to the 1958 program to train teachers of the mentally retarded. Under Elizabeth Boggs, Ph.D., first as vice president for program services in 1956 and then president in 1958, federal governmental activities became a primary thrust of the association. With the coming to office of the Kennedy administration and the funding of the president's committee on mental retardation, federal attention to the needs of the mentally retarded greatly expanded.

In 1964 Luther Stringham, a public administrator with a federal government career, became executive director; he hired ARC's first legislative liaison Harry Blank. In 1965 Elizabeth Boggs became chairperson of the legislative committee, which issued its first annual statement of legislative goals, and in 1966 Blank was replaced by Robert Gettings. With the departure of both Gettings and Stringham in 1968, there was no senior staff responsibility for governmental activities between February 1968 and April 1969, when ARC opened its Washington office housed with NASMHPD. It was up to Dr. Boggs and others on the committee to provide continuity and direction to the new staff; she stepped down as chairman of the committee in 1971 and continues as a committee member to this day.

Between April 1969 and January 1975 ARC had four Washington office directors. Since 1975 Paul Marchand has directed the office. In 1971 ARC moved out of the NASMHPD office; in order to keep the working relationship live, ARC launched an ad hoc coalition and in 1973 ARC, UCPA, EFA, NASMHPD, and NASMRPD organized the Consortium Concerned with the Developmentally Disabled (CCDD). The collaborative efforts of the CCDD have characterized most legislative efforts of the developmental disability groups ever since.

In 1978 Peter Romanofsky summarized the ARC success:

> The NARC has been so effective in its legislative and public education programs because of the nature of its grsss-roots structure, the socioeconomic characteristics of its members, the kinds of social action strategies that were utilized, and the able professional leadership of its executive directors and staff. Local affiliates are strong and have always had a vote in the policy making of national and state organizations. (p. 441)

### NSAC Governmental Activities
(See Akerley, Note 8; Benson, Note 9)

NSACs National Affairs Committee was established in 1967 but was not really active until after the Developmental Disability Act passed in 1970. With Mary Akerley as chairperson of the committee from 1972 to 1974 and as president from 1974 to 1976, NSAC's legislative priority was to have autism accepted into the federal definition of developmental disability; this occurred in 1975. Between August 1978 and December 1979, funds were available for Ms. Akerley to be hired as staff member, but these funds have since been exhausted and were not replaced.

### NASMRPD Governmental Activities
(See Gettings, Note 10.)

NASMRPD is much more cautious than ARC and UCPA but much more assertive than AAMD in its lobbying activities on Capitol Hill. First, it is difficult for state mental retardation administrators to speak with much flexibility; they are frequently constrained by their states and governors. Second, many administrators see themselves as implementors rather than policymakers. Third, increasingly state mental retardation programs are using entitlement programs that do not require the level of appropriations and legislative renewals of other programs. Fourth, the priority of these administrators is on obtaining information about federal programs rather than on influencing legislation. When NASMRPD does agree to act it is very effective; a small association of state program administrators seems to be more able to reach consensus on policy approaches than AAMD, ARC, and the other developmental disabilities organizations.

### NAPRFMR Governmental Activities
(See Fritz, Note 12.)

Limited resources (an executive director and a part-time secretary) are the reasons for NAPRFMR lack of lobbying activity. Because of the association's involvement in the CCDD, its resources can be targeted to specific legislative objectives.

### American Psychiatric Association Governmental
Activities (See Fine, Note 20; Cutler, Note 13.)

The American Psychiatric Association has maintained a long involvement in governmental activities and achieved prominence and an excellent reputation under its former medical director, Dr. Walter Barton. As explained by APA staff,

> In 1975, the APA established the Joint Commission on Government Relations (JCGR) which is responsible to both the Board of Trustees and the Assembly of the Association. The Commission includes elected representatives of each of the seven APA geographic areas and has the responsibility for

coordinating the work of the APA's legislative network, comprised of a representative in each of the 75 District Branches. Such network is concerned with legislation affecting mental health predominantly at the Federal level. The JCGR serves as the APA's coordinating body for all legislative and regulatory activities, and acts as a conduit for efforts by other APA components to interact with the Federal legislative and regulatory process. The JCGR meets regularly with the Division of Government Relations (staff level APA personnel) to evaluate, propose and monitor federal and selected state legislative initiatives and regulatory activities to determine the most effective and appropriate means of achieving APA goals through the legislative and regulatory process.

The Division of Government Relations, the staff arm of the APA for all federal legislative and regulatory activities, provides the interface for APA policy with the legislative and executive branches of the federal government. At the same time, the Division seeks to provide the APA insight into and analysis of the health policy developmental process of the Congress and executive branch of government and of legislative and executive activities resulting therefrom, to assist the APA in the development of APA policy respecting such forthcoming activities. To the maximum extent possible, the Division's efforts regarding legislative and executive branch activities are proactive—providing broad-ranging APA input into the legislative and regulatory processes before such legislation is proposed or regulations are promulgated.

In addition to providing APA testimony before the legislative and executive branches and acting as a resource to legislators and their staff with respect to the interests and concerns of psychiatry, the Division's efforts include regular personal contact with government officials, legislators and key staff of both branches of the federal government. (Cutler, pp. 1–2)

Though the American Psychiatric Association may not fully subscribe to the following characterization, it appears to some in the field that the APA government relations program is essentially benefit oriented, its primary objective is to equalize reimbursement for mental illness coverage with physical illness coverage. Among its 1980 concerns are physician reimbursement under Medicare and Medicaid, equal mental health coverage under national health insurance proposals, extension of the Mental Health Systems Act, confidentiality of medical records, health manpower programs, and mental health research issues.

### American Psychological Association Governmental Activities (See Vandervoss, Note 24.)

The American Psychological Association is one of the largest educational corporations and publishers of professional material in the world. Fearing that their public policy work could jeopardize their IRS tax status, in 1974 APA initiated the establishment of the Association for the Advancement of Psychology (AAP). The AAP is solely concerned with public policy issues; their charter mandates that all public policy issues be analyzed from three perceptions: the scientific/academic, the professional, and the social dimension. The two associations are separate legal corporations but the memberships of the two are closely parallel.

The APA currently has a single research analyst who disseminates information on public policy to the APA office of state affairs. The independent AAP has four professionals currently concerned with forty issues that may be classified into three categories: fee-for-service and availability of mental health services concerns; federal funding of research and training programs; and social issues such as the Equal Rights Amendment, Justice Department standing, and nondiscrimination. The AAP claims to be actively involved in such generic issues as housing, education, Title XX of the Social Security Act, income maintenance, and similar concerns.

### NMHA Governmental Activities (See Romanofsky, 1978; National Mental Health Association, 1946ff; McAllister, Note 25; Finley, Note 26.)

In 1955 Congress appropriated $1.2 million for the Joint Commission on Mental Illness; eighteen national organizations participated in its work, which resulted in 1961 in a federal report, *Action for Mental Health*. This was the period of expansion. Between 1955 and 1958, the National Institute of Mental Health (NIMH) budget increased from $14.1 million to $39.2 million. In 1962 the NIMH budget was $143.6 million, a $34.7 million (32 percent increase over 1961. And in 1963 the community mental health centers (CMHC) were authorized. During this period the NMHA relied primarily upon volunteers for its legislative liaison work.

In 1969 Brian O'Connell became executive director and Robert Smucker became NMHA legislative director. NMHA moved its national headquarters from New York City to Rosslyn, Virginia, in 1971 so the agency could have greater access to the federal government. During the late 1960s and early 1970s, NMHA organized its legislative network to campaign strongly against the Nixon administration's efforts to replace CMHCs with prepaid group plans, to include mental illness coverage in national health insurance proposals, and to help with the 1975 override of the veto of the Community Mental Health Centers Act. With the arrival of Mrs. Carter at the White Houe, focus was directed to the president's commission on mental health. In 1978 O'Connell and Smucker left NMHA for independent sector.

Under Jack McAllister NMHA has launched efforts toward several new public policy objectives. Because of his previous experience in the developmental disabilities field, McAllister strongly believes in the advantages of coalition activity, and NMHA has consequently begun working with the CCDD on generic funding issues. The NMHA plans to fight against stigma and discrimination against the mentally disabled. In terms of public policy this means improving federal government employment and benefits and third-party payment practices, as well as working to prevent mental illness and promote mental health.

### NASMHPD Governmental Activities
(See Schnibbe, Note 11.)

By necessity NASMHPD has focused a great deal of attention on the mental health issues, such as CMHCs. Of all the mental health groups NASMHPD has been involved the most in the nonhealth generic programs. Lately legal problems have overwhelmed the association. Three state mental health commissioners are attorneys. Vermont Department of Mental Health and Mental Retardation, as an example, has nine attorneys on its staff. The staggering array of lawsuits in which it is engaged has reduced the association's other public policy concerns.

## NCCMHC Governmental Activities
(See Wolfe, Note 17.)

The NCCMHC focus has been on the renewal and federal funding on CMHCs. These centers are federal clients, created and nurtured by federal mandates, and are dependent on the federal dollar. Only in the last year or so have CMHCs begun considering other public means to support centers financially.

## KEY FACTORS IN CONSTITUENCY ORGANIZATIONS' GOVERNMENTAL ACTIVITIES

### Overview: Tying in with the Conceptual Framework

The theoretical ideas offered earlier provide partial explanations of the mental health/developmental disability (MH/DD) agencies' performance and effectiveness in governmental activities.

*Origins of MH/DD Organizations.* Stephen Strickland (1972), Jeffrey Berry (1977), Robert Salisbury (1969), and David Sills (1957) discuss the importance of the entrepreneur or political organizer to organization development. This explanation is appropriate as demonstrated by the examples of William Lennox and EFA, Edgar Allen and NESS, Clifford Beers and NMHA, the Goldensons and UCPA, Mary Lasker and NMHA and UCPA, and Bernard Rimland and NSAC. David Sills has stressed the importance of specific disabilities to organization development. Entrepreneurs, parents, concerned lay persons, and physicians who founded the organizations treated here focused on specific disabilities and devoted substantial time and resources to correcting the disadvantages of neglect, psychosocial stress, financial hardship, and discrimination suffered by persons bearing the disability.

Earl Latham (1965) described the objective of professionals to control their physical and social environment in order to survive and prosper. They attempt to standardize and maintain their unique specialization in order to enhance their control and influence. This explanation partially explains the establishment and operation of AAMD, American Psychiatric Association, and American Psychological Association. This theoretical argument is much more appropriate for the two APAs than AAMD since AAMD represents several professions.

David Truman (1971) discusses specific catalytic factors, so-called disturbances, that alter the equilibrium of a group and promote change or new groups. A major change in government activity is such a disturbance. The debate over the renewal of the Community Mental Health Centers Act led to the establishment of NCCMHC. The trend in developing state-financed community care programs and the desire for federal assistance resulted in NASMHPD. And the growing importance of federal monies to state mental retardation programs prompted creation of NASMRPD.

Burton Weisbrod (1977) maintains that the failure of government to provide collective goods and the consumer demand for such goods results in the establishment of nonprofit organizations. The demands of all consumers do not generally develop simultaneously; so rather than a single agency promoting services to the disabled, various parents and consumers have come together when dissatisfaction reaches a certain level. Clifford Beers was personally so dissatisfied that he started NMHA. Better examples of Weisbrod's explanation are the parents in New York City who between 1945 and 1949 established UCPA and the parents in Minneapolis in 1950 who established the ARC. Consumer dissatisfaction with education and mental health care for the mentally disabled was so great in 1965 that physicians and parents joined together to found NSAC.

*Kinds of MH/DD Organizations.*   Robert Alford (1975) describes the major structural interests and their continuing struggle for control. The "dominant structural interests" are the professional monopolies who control the production and distribution of health services. These groups are largely satisfied with the fee-for-service approach. The problem is how to find a viable method for dividing up the resources among themselves. The two APAs are examples of these interests.

Alford's "challenging structural interests" are the "corporate rationalizers"—the hospital administrators, health planners, and public health agencies—that desire control of the organization and delivery of services. NASMHPD and NASMRPD are examples of "corporate rationalizers."

Last Alford describes the "repressed structural interests" as the groups that will remain unserved unless extraordinary political energies are mobilized. The voluntary disability specific organizations believe their consumers remain underserved despite their political efforts.

Paul Feldstein (1980) reviews "concentrated interests" as those groups whose members' jobs and income are seriously affected by government programs. These groups are willing to pay more and be more active for lobbying. In contrast "diffuse interests" are those whose members' jobs and income are not dependent on government. At first glance it might seem that only NASMRPD, NASMHPD, NAPRFMR, and NCCMHC are concentrated interests whereas the other organizations are diffuse interests. As professionals become more and more dependent on third-party reimbursement, which is either derived or regulated by government, their organization's become concentrated interests too. Every one of the MH/DD voluntary organizations is receiving substantial government grants and contracts, which makes them concentrated interests as well. Each of these groups should have a primary motivation to protect and expand its governmental role. But they will continue to compete for control according to Alford's conceptualization.

*MH/DD Organization Characteristics and Performance.* Norman Ornstein and Shirley Elder (1978) argue that single-focus consumer organizations are usually more politically successful than public interest consumer groups. Because their concerns do not involve a broad range of citizens, their proposals do not gain wide media coverage, which means opposition is less likely. This explanation could be partially responsible for the success in having specific disabilities listed in federal programs while a broader national health insurance proposal has repeatedly failed.

Burton Weisbrod argues that the larger the number of consumer demands, the greater the amount output by the voluntary sector. This is true of the large output of the ARC and the small output of NSAC. But it does not explain the modest output of EFA and NMHA (compared to their numbers) and the strength of UCPA (in terms of its numbers). Stigma, nature of the disability, organizational capacity, and individual initiative are important dimensions.

Paul Feldstein discusses the problem of voluntary and other organizations whereby there is little incentive for individuals to contribute because they will benefit anyway if the group is successful; this is the so-called free-rider problem. The unaffiliated ARC, UCPA, NESS organizations are group examples of this. A significant sector of nonprofit organizations is composed of former affiliates of MH/ DD national organizations that did not like the price of contributing. The best example is the New York ARC, a large, wealthy, influential organization that has operated independently for years. Independent groups diminish the effectiveness of the national organizations but benefit if their former national agency is successful.

Mancur Olson (1971) maintains that groups with larger numbers of members generally perform less efficiently than groups with smaller numbers. Large groups tend to be exploited by smaller groups. The larger the group, the smaller fraction of benefits received by each group member and the greater the organizational costs. Olson's "privileged group" is one where at least one member has an incentive to see that the collective good is provided and their effort is noticeable. This probably explains the success of the NASMHPD and NASMRPD in attaining public policy goals. Olson's "intermediate group" is one where no single member gets a share of the benefit sufficient to give him an incentive to provide the good but his effort is noticeable. This is probably true of all these MH/DD groups that have chapters or members in the hundreds (EFA, NESS, UCPA, NSAC, NAPRFMR, NCCMHC). The "latent group" is one where a member acts or does not act with no impact one way or another. ARC with 1,900 state and local chapters and NMHA with over 800 chapters are probably latent groups. AAMD and the two APAs, with thousands of individual members, are latent groups. Only a selective incentive will stimulate a rational individual in a latent group. AAMD, composed of many different types of professions, has no incentive; however, opposing fee-for-service payment and maintaining control are the selective incentives for the APAs' members to act.

As Jeffrey Berry (1977) maintains, organizational size is a key factor in determining the scope of a lobbyist's work. It determines the amount of lobbyist specialization permitted, the type of backup available, the scope and variety of issues to be addressed, and the ease of compliance with the 1976 Internal Revenue Service limitations on the lobbying activities of nonprofit organizations. Organizational size has previously been compared; more important to total size is the amount of unrestricted private income available to the organization. The professional organization (AAMD and the two APAs) have the greatest available private income; however, the AAMD budget is too small for this to be important. EFA has almost one-quarter of its national office budget from government, NSAC has almost one-third, and ARC has three-quarters of its income from government.

## PARTICULAR STRENGTHS AND WEAKNESSES

From the theoretical perspective, a number of MH/DD organizations have specific strengths and weaknesses. The two APAs have many strengths: they are dominant structural interests, they have the greatest available private income, and they have incentives to overcome their latent group tendencies. NASMRPD and NASMHPD have two strengths; they are challenging structural interests and operate as privileged groups. EFA, ARC, UCPA, and NSAC have the strength of a single disability focus, which seems to increase the intensity of its members. Last, in terms of strength, EFA, NESS, UCPA, NSAC, NAPRFMR, and NCCMHC are intermediate groups.

ARC, NESS, and UCPA suffer because of a number of free riders, unaffiliated groups. NMHA and AAMD appear to be latent groups. NAPRFMR and NSAC are too small to have the desired national impact. EFA, NSAC, and ARC are probably too dependent on the federal government for their national office income. Every MH/DD organization has a concentrated interest in expanding and protecting the role of the federal government in delivering services.

### Role of the Developmental Disabilities Program

The first developmental disability act was passed in October 1970 and aimed to benefit those with mental retardation, cerebral palsy, and epilepsy. The 1975 amendments added autism to the definition, and the 1978 amendments terminated categorical references, emphasizing severity and functional dimensions instead.

Justification for the 1970 definition is important. All three of the conditions are major causes of substantial handicaps to adults disabled in childhood, as documented by recipients of Social Security Disability Insurance (SSDI). These three disabilities accounted for 80 percent of all adults disabled in childhood receiving SSDI. All three of the conditions imply multiple handicaps requiring both special and similar services. It is frequently estimated that between one-half and two-thirds of persons with cerebral palsy are mentally retarded and that 20 percent to 30 percent of persons with epilepsy are mentally retarded; thus, the primary diagnosis of any of the three is likely to be accompanied by a wide spectrum of other disabilities. These are long-term, substantial, and frequently multiple handicaps that do not fit into neat categories. *Commonality of service needs* is a concept frequently discussed. Mental illness does not have such specific yet overlapping parameters.

The initial developmental disability (DD) legislation in 1970 gave state DD councils much flexibility in designing their programs to improve the quality, scope, and extent of services for persons with developmental disabilities. The 1975 amendments were more directive regarding the role of DD councils. Council responsibilities were to (1) supervise the development of and approve the state plan, (2) monitor and evaluate the implementation of the state plan, (3) review and comment on other federal/state plans that should serve persons with developmental disabilities, and (4) submit periodic reports to the U.S. Department of Health, Education, and Welfare. The council's name was changed from "advisory" to "planning" and it was expected to become a planner, monitor, evaluator, coordinator, and advocate. The DD program was expected to access other funding sources to implement state plans; however, program funds could continue to finance direct services. Because federal funds could support both planning and services, confusion regarding the proper mix of planning and service remained. The 1975 amendments emphasized the importance of the state plan as a tool to improve and expand services for persons with developmental disabilities by monitoring, linking with, and influencing other federal/state plans. Additionally at least 10 percent of fiscal year 1976 DD funding (rising to 30 percent in succeeding years) had to be spent to implement deinstitutionalization.

The *Rehabilitation, Comprehensive Services, and Developmental Disabilities Act* (1978) retained the state planning council, its review and monitoring responsibilities related to other federal/state plans, and its 1970 and 1975 effort to examine the quality, scope and extent of services to persons with developmental disabilities in the state. The plan is to examine four different areas of "priority services" (p. 76) (case management, child development, living arrangements, and nonvocational social development) and "financially support, coordinate and otherwise better address, on a statewide and comprehensive basis, unmet needs in the state for the provision of at least one of the areas of priority services." (p. 87) Not less than $100,000 or 65 percent of the state's federal DD funds shall be expended on "service activities" in the service priority areas. The 1978 law changed the council's role to emphasize "joint" (p. 85) development of the state plan with the administering agency and to focus on "priority" services.

The utilization of generic programs will be discussed later; in this regard, the DD program has been highly successful. But the DD program itself has been quite modest; fiscal year 1980 DD appropriations are shown in Table 3–4. The basis of the DD program is the leverage of other public funds.

## Role of the National Institute on Mental Health

Although the mental health groups have not been actively involved in the utilization of generic benefits, they have been very successful at establishing a large, strong federal base specifically for mental health. Table 3–5 shows fiscal year 1980 appropriations for the Alcohol, Drug Abuse, and Mental Health Administration (ADAMHA). With ADAMHA, NIMH, and the CMHCs, the mental health field has a strong categorical base from which to operate.

## Role of Consumers and Parents in MH/DD Advocacy

The heart of the federal/state DD program is the state DD planning council, which is legally mandated to have parental and consumer membership (50 percent by the 1978 amendments). The DD Council can provide an excellent forum for consumer initiative; it is here that consumers can be key members of groups responsible for planning, developing, and improving the quality of services for developmentally disabled persons. The council can provide support for consumers in securing their rightful place in service delivery activities. The council can be a source of information to consumers and a resource for incorporating local consumer data and perspective at the state level. The DD act is the only major piece of federal legislation currently being implemented at the state and local level that requires consumer involvement in the planning, development, and delivery of services for handicapped individuals (Warren, 1979).

Table 3-4.  1980 Federal Appropriations for Developmental
Disabilities.

|  | Amount, $ Millions |
|---|---|
| State grants | 43.1 |
| Protection and advocacy | 7.5 |
| Projects | 4.7 |
| University-affiliated facilities | 7.0 |

*Source*:  Ross's analysis of the U.S. Government's Fiscal Year 1981 Budget.

Table 3-5.  1980 ADAMHA Appropriations.

| Program | Amount, $ Millions |
|---|---|
| Research | 146 |
| Training | 90 |
| Community | 290 |
| State | 7.6 |

*Source*:  Ross's analysis of the U.S. Government's Fiscal Year 1981 Budget.

The ARC and UCPA were organized by parents of disabled children, and Elizabeth Boggs and Elsie Helsel, both parents and prime movers in ARC and UCPA, were also the prime architects of the 1970 DD act. So it is not surprising that the 1970 act required that one-third of the council membership be consumers. Between 1970 and 1976 most of these consumer members were parents, particularly parents of the mentally retarded. Under the sponsorship and urging of UCPA, Congress amended the 1978 act to emphasize full involvement by primary consumers, the developmentally disabled themselves.

It is a common feeling in Washington that the strength of the DD movement is the consumer agencies. Parents and consumers associated with ARC, UCPA, and NSAC (and in the last few years EFA) are congressional witnesses and governmental advocates. They are willing to personalize their situations. They are willing to explain what it is like to be disabled or have a disabled family member or child.

There is also a common feeling in Washington that the strength of the mental health movement is the professional organizations. The board of NMHA does not appear to be a cross section of America; they appear to be mostly upper and upper middle-class persons. Many are family members but they generally do not identify themselves as such. Because they do not stand up, because they are unwilling to personalize their situations, legislators and others may have a different level of response to NMHA requests. Legislators feel the intensity, urgency, and purity of the parent of a mentally retarded child and the person with cerebral palsy; they probably do not have such a feeling toward a NMHA witness who is standing as advocate for someone else. This difference in consumer advocacy is one factor determining the success of lobbying and other governmental activities.

### Role of Professionals in MH/DD Advocacy

The heavyweights in the MH field are generally perceived to be the professionals, as stated previously. Whether this observation is valid or not, it is the way in which strengths are perceived, and in politics the way one is perceived is probably more significant than one's real situation. The two APAs in particular but also NASMHPD and NCCMHC are composed of professionals. As explained earlier, the primary focus of the APAs is on fee-for-service reimbursement, training, and research issues. Thus, they do not focus on the quality of life of persons with disabilities, income maintenance, social support services, housing, education, and transportation.

In the MH field, there is no equivalent to AAMD (although it can be argued that the American Orthopsychiatric Association attempts this role). AAMD offers a neutral professional forum with academic backup where mental retardation professionals come together to discuss and debate concerns. There appears to be no respected national professional forum in the MH field.

### Voluntary Health Agencies as Providers

During the 1970s a significant change occurred that has tainted the voluntary health agency as consumer advocate while increasing its sophistication about and commitment to government grants and contracts utilization. The ARC nationally advocates a philosophy of obtaining and advocating rather than providing; yet, it is the most dependent of all the groups on government for its income. Likewise NMHA focuses on advocacy rather than service provision, but its affiliates are increasingly utilizing government funds. So all of the groups have a concentrated interest in protecting and expanding the government's involvement in MH and DD.

### Voluntary Health Agencies and Distinct Medical Diagnosis

Each of the DD voluntary agencies are organized around disabilities with clear etiological characteristics whereas NMHA represents a wide variety of conditions. Whereas science understands the causes of cerebral palsy, epilepsy, and mental retardation better than the causes of the types of mental illness, it is easier to recommend methods to ameliorate, reduce, or prevent the disability. So in some ways the disability predetermines the dynamics of an organization and the environment in which it operates.

### The Importance of Federal Generic Programs

A comparison of the DD and ADAMHA categorical programs for handicapped persons (Table 3-6) and generic programs (Table 3-7), which benefit handicapped persons, in terms of fiscal year 1980 appropriations, offers the economic and financial implications of each.

Table 3-6.    DD and ADAMHA Categorical Program Funding.

| Program | Fiscal FY 1980 Appropriation, $ Millions |
|---------|------------------------------------------|
| DD      | 62.3                                     |
| ADAMHA  | 533.6                                    |
| Total   | 595.9                                    |

Source: Ross's analysis of the U.S. Government's Fiscal Year 1981 Budget.

Table 3-7.  Generic Service Funding.[a]

| Program | Amount, $ Billions |
|---|---|
| Supplemental Security Income | 5.590 |
| Social Security Disability Insurance (strictly benefits for the disabled) | 15.263 |
| Medicaid | 11.250 |
| Medicare | 23.238 |
| Title XX social services | 2.700 |
| Title IV B child welfare services | 56.500 |
| HUD Section 8 rent subsidies | 19.600 |
| Total for the seven generic programs with major benefits to the disabled | 77.700 |

a. Except Social Security Disability, not all benefits go to the disabled, but funds for the disabled are substantial. The federal government cannot specify allocations within these programs for the disabled.

It is in utilizing generic programs that the DD organizations have been most successful and that the MH organizations have been least successful. The DD groups have formulated or influenced the initial legislation whereby the MH organizations frequently attempt to utilize these programs several years after their enactment.

A review of the various coalitions for generic services and the membership of MH/DD agencies reflects this involvement.

1. Council for Exceptional Children Interagency Coalition: ARC, UCPA, NESS, NSAC, and NASMRPD.

2. Council of State Administrators of Vocational Rehabilitation Ad Hoc Coalition on Vocational Rehabilitation Appropriations: ARC, UCPA, NESS, NSAC, NASMRPD, EFA, NAPRFMR, and sometimes NASMHPD.

3. Ad Hoc Coalition on Independent Living: ARC, UCPA, NESS, EFA, NAPRFMR, and sometimes NSAC and NMHA.

4. Title XX social services coalition: ARC, UCPA, NASMRPD, and NASMHPD.

5. Consortium Concerned with the Developmentally Disabled Task Force on Housing: ARC, UCPA, NESS, NASMRPD, NAPRFMR, and sometimes EFA, NSAC, NASMHPD, and NMHA.

6.  Save our Security Coalition: ARC, UCPA, NESS, NSAC, NASM-
    RPD, EFA, NAPRFMR, and NMHA.

The MH/DD Child Health Assurance Program (CHAP) Coalition
offers a unique example of collaboration. In the 95th Congress,
CHAP bills for both the mentally ill and the developmentally disabled were singled out and excluded from coverage. The two coalition groups testified separately; during a Senate hearing, Senator
Abraham Ribicoff of Connecticut suggested that the two groups
work together. The Childrens Defense Funds facilitated the establishment of the MH/DD CHAP Coalition. Leadership in the DD field
has evolved from NSAC and UCPA to EFA because of staff changes.
In the MH field, NMHA assumed leadership because of its close ties
to the Carter administration. Members of the MH/DD CHAP Coalition are listed in Table 3-8. The future of this coalition is uncertain.
It is clearly a single-issue coalition. One result has been NMHA
membership in the CCDD Task Force on Health (Hatton, Note 27).

The Mental Health Liaison Group meets as a single coalition
effort. There is no dividing of responsibility and frequently there is
no true sharing of substance, beyond general information, because
of the lack of trust and because of competition over turf. An example of the working relationship is that eight versions of the Mental
Health Systems Act (HR 4156) were drafted in 1979 before the act
was finally passed. A Washington newsletter reported: "Unable to
muster a quorum . . . Chairman Waxman of the House Commerce
Health Subcommittee chided mental health lobbyists last week for
their bickering and lack of effective backing for a bill . . . He admitted the future of the legislation is dim."

In February 1973 eighteen national organizations founded the
Consortium Concerned with the Developmentally Disabled (CCDD).
It soon became obvious that there were the workers and those
who came just to gain information. In November 1974 the CCDD
organized itself into task forces. Only organizations willing to devote
staff time to the task force could join a task force. Division of responsibility is thus a key to any success CCDD might earn. Once a
year the CCDD meets and reexamines the need for and performance
of its task forces. Currently there are six task forces: Developmental
Disabilities Act, appropriations, housing, health, employment, and
Social Security Act. It is not the intention of the CCDD to dupli-
cate functions of the other coalitions to which DD agency members

Table 3-8. CHAP Coalition Organizations.

| Developmental Disabilities | Mental Health |
|---|---|
| American Speech-Language-Hearing Association | American Academy of Child Psychiatry |
| Epilepsy Foundation of America | Association for the Advancement of Psychology |
| National Association for Retarded Citizens | American Association of Children's Residential Centers |
| National Association of State Mental Retardation Program Directors, Inc. | American Psychiatric Association |
| National Easter Seal Society | American Psychological Association |
| National Society for Autistic Children | Mental Health Association |
| United Cerebral Palsy Associations | National Association of Private Psychiatric Hospitals |
| | National Association of State Mental Health Program Directors |
| | National Council of Community Mental Health Centers |
| | National Congress of Parents and Teachers |
| | American Association of Psychiatric Services for Children |

belong. The mental health liaison group has organized subcommittees around such topics as Medicare and housing and urban development.

## Agency Staff Continuity and Washington Lobbying

Jeffrey Berry (1977) has observed that "The individual skills of a lobbyist become even more significant in low-resource organizations that have only one or two staff professionals. . . . In these cases, the value of representatives who have issue expertise, procedural knowledge, and the battle scars of front-line experience becomes magnified." (p. 108) Both the MH and DD organizations have very capable Washington representatives; however, there appears to be a greater continuity in DD representatives. Longevity and a network of personal relationships characterize the DD field.

Elsie D. Helsel was a member of both ARC and UCPA in the 1950s as a parent seeking responses to her needs. She served on ARC's Residential Care Committee during the 1950s and UCPA's Professional Services Program Committee from 1958 to 1968. A member of CEC, she also served as vice president for education of the Ohio AAMD in the early 1960s. From 1966 to 1969 she served as assistant director of the division of special studies and project director of the accreditation project for AAMD. In 1968 she was hired as UCPA's Washington representative; she retired in 1974 to direct the Ohio University UAF. From 1975 to 1981 she has served on UCPA's governmental activities committee, chairing the group from 1978 to 1981.

Elizabeth M. Boggs was a member of ARC from the beginning as a parent seeking responses to her needs. She served as vice president for program services from 1956 to 1958, ARC president from 1958 to 1960, and chairman of the governmental affairs committee from 1965 to 1971. From 1961 to 1963, Boggs served on the President's Panel on Mental Retardation. In the 1970s she has served as chairman of the National Advisory Council on Developmental Disabilities, a member of the AAUAP long range planning committee, and a member of the President's Committee on Mental Retardation (PCMR). From 1964 to 1978 she served on AAMD's legislation and social issues committee, chairing the group for many years.

When Helsel and Boggs established UCPA and ARC Washington offices in 1968–69, they were housed by NASMHPD. Together with Harry Schnibbe, they conceptualized the DD act. In 1971 Clarke Ross was hired as Schnibbe's legislative assistant and in 1972 he was hired by Elsie Helsel and UCPA; in August 1976 he became UCPA's Washington office director.

Robert Gettings was hired in 1966 as ARC's governmental affairs analyst; in 1968 he went to the staff of PCMR; and in 1970 he became the first executive director of NASMRPD. Between 1974 and 1976 he chaired the AAMD legislative committee. While Helsel and Schnibbe provided guidance to Ross, Boggs provided similar ideas to Gettings. These five persons have remained involved in DD federal legislation.

When Elsie Helsel first thought of retirement, Hal Benson, Deputy Commissioner for Mental Health in North Carolina, was looking for an opportunity to come to Washington. He had worked with

Schnibbe and Ross in NASMHPD. In September 1973 he was hired as UCPA's state program consultant and in September 1974 he became UCPA's Washington office director. In 1976 he moved on to EFA and today is NSAC's executive director.

Paul Marchand, an ARC executive director in Rhode Island and then R.I. DD council executive director, came to ARC's Washington office in 1973 and became director in 1975. In 1980 he was appointed to the AAMD legislative committee. Jack McAllister, an ARC executive director in Florida, became mental retardation director for the State of Florida, served briefly as a staff consultant to PCMR, became the EFA executive director in 1976, and moved to NMHA in 1979. Myrl Weinberg, today's ARC Washington office assistant director, worked in the State of Arkansas mental retardation office and then NASMRPD.

The MH/DD fields suffered when Mary Akerley, who led NSAC governmental activities first as a volunteer and then as a staff member from 1972 to 1979, departed because of NSAC funding difficulties. While leading NSAC's efforts, she had also served on NMHA's Children's Committee from 1972 to 1974 and Public Affairs Committee from 1974 to 1978. What involvement NMHA had in DD and education were largely the result of Mary's attention. It will be some time before NSAC regains the experience and insight that Mary had developed. Bill McLin, with fourteen years in various positions with the Cancer Society, became EFA's governmental affairs director in 1976 and its executive director in 1979.

Harry Schnibbe has the greatest experience in MH public policy issues and has trained many entry level staff. But there is great turnover in NASMHPD staff and the association loses experience, continuity, and consistency with every change. Robert Smucker directed NMHA's governmental relations program from 1969 to 1978 but since then the organization has been in transition and experienced turnover in its governmental relations staff. Chris Koyanagi has worked, on a part-time basis, on CMHC legislation since 1972 and in 1980 she moved from NCCMHC to NMHA.

The CCDD is organized by task forces to facilitate the maximum involvement of each member's agency strength. Contributing to the CCDD success is the continuity of personal experience. By working together week in and week out for years, its members have developed sharing and respect. The MH field generally lacks this advantage. For example, the American Psychiatric Association governmental relations director, Jay Cutler, has had a long and distinguished career working in the U.S. Senate, and the MH field is fortunate to have such experience; but it is not the same as continuity of private agency relationships that promote trust, respect, delegation of responsibility, and genuine sharing.

## SUMMARY: THE BALKANIZATION OF INTEREST GROUPS AND ITS IMPACT ON POLICY FORMULATION

Philip Selznick's classic study, *The TVA and the Grass Roots* (1949), documented the close relationship between organizational goals and organizational survival. Dissolution is not the only course of action open to an organization when its purposes are either achieved or become irrelevant; objectives are modified or changed so it can stay in business. Peter Blau in *The Dynamics of Bureaucracy* (1955) called this process the "succession of goals" or "the reverse of the displacement of goals." David Sills' 1957 study of the National Foundation for Infantile Paralysis documents the validity of these observations as applied to voluntary health agencies. So one must assume that each of the organizations described in this chapter will exist for some time.

David Walker (1980) has described the proliferation of programmatic groups paralleling the enactment of more and more specific categorical federal programs. The national politicization of nearly all issues is one reason for this. Another is the reduced cost of participating in Washington. A third is the "ever present lure of federal money." A fourth is the easier access to and greater responsiveness of members of Congress and the relatively easy access to the courts because of class action suits and fee-splitting. The impact of administrative decisions on our lives is a fifth reason. To Walker, "the current interest group scene in Washington is a not-too-cloudy mirror image of the profuse specialized pluralism of the nation as a whole" (p. 42).

In a *Harper's Magazine* article entitled "The balkanization of America" (May 1978) Keven Phillips argues that the increase in groups has resulted in more fragmentation in politics; these groups become narrower and more specialized in their interests and focus on more specific policy areas. This trend has resulted in substantial problems in gaining consensus to implement a comprehensive or national policy. Phillips maintains that this trend could result in

John C. Calhoun's negative veto/concurrent majority system (cited in Ornstein and Elder, 1978).[a]

Walker fears decisionmaking now is "heavily overburdened." The volume of reauthorizations and the demands to add specialized subfunctional programs and new legislative areas, not to mention the pace of legislative activity, is overwhelming national decisionmakers. For example, Paul Marchand (Note 22), ARC's Washington office director, has described the failure of the federal government to address the needs of the person who is both mentally ill and mentally retarded. This was initially part of the special concerns section of the Mental Health Systems Act but was later dropped. No one disagrees with the need to address this problem; without a target, it will not be addressed. But it is an example of Walker's point.

The Madisonian system allows and promotes competing political organizations to vie for governmental action. But the proliferation of groups has overwhelmed the system to the point, as described by Walker (1980), that "the politics of posturing, then, has replaced the politics of fair play and common sense; and, if they persist, the specter of a huge promise–performance gap again arises" (p. 45). The CCDD, as a coalition, seems to be ahead of the Mental Health Liaison Group in overcoming this politics of posturing. Maybe this is why generic programs are targeted more to the developmentally disabled than to the mentally ill. The mental health field must develop a more viable coalition strategy, the CCDD must strengthen its coalition efforts, and the two fields must come together. Several possible steps would help promote this:

1. Rather than accepting the proliferation of narrow specialization and survival of organizations, thought should be given to
   a. Sharing offices;
   b. Single newsletters with joint editorial committees;
   c. Formalized and unified sharing of information;
   d. More unified lobbying campaigns;
   e. Long-term goals and possibly actual merger (NASMRPD and NASMHPD for example).

a. John C. Calhoun's early 1800s "theory of the concurrent majority" advocated each of the various interest groups of the society having a veto over any major policy proposal that affected them. Conversely a concurrent majority of all interest groups would have to support a policy proposal for it to be adopted. To Calhoun, the various factions combined to define the community, or national, interest (Ornstein and Elder, 1978, pp. 10–11).

2. Mental health consumers, their parents, and other family members, must be helped to overcome stigma and to serve as their own advocates, by
   a. Possible NIMH grant activity.
   b. Financial incentives to ARC, UCPA, EFA, and NSAC to share experience and expertise with NMHA and others in this area.

3. Greater attention and promotion should be given to MH/DD coalition efforts, including
   a. Possible NIMH/ADD (Administration on Developmental Disabilities) grant activity;
   b. Studying the experience of CCDD;
   c. Strengthening the Mental Health Liaison Group;
   d. Strengthening CCDD;
   e. Concerted MH/DD joint activities;
   f. Neutral professional forum for MH/DD like AAMD (strengthening the American Orthopsychiatric Association).
   g. In-house intangibles, attitudes.

4. Consumers and parents must be less self-righteous and more understanding of administrative realities.

5. Administrators must be less defensive and more willing to recommend possible solutions, rather than reacting to and complaining about the proposals of others.

6. Professionals must be less protective; less parochial; less concerned with status, control, fee-for-service; and more willing to recommend possible solutions.

7. Salary levels and organizational status of government activities' staff and volunteers, should be enhanced in the hope of promoting greater continuity and longevity.

This chapter ends on the thought of merger. At UCPA's 1980 annual conference, Dr. Clement Bezold (Note 28), director of the Institute for Alternative Futures, described four alternative scenarios facing the United States in the year 2025:

- Continued growth and success. Technology in the service of an energetic, achievement-oriented free society enables a country to continue growing and everything just keeps on getting better.

- Societal collapse or foul-weather. Depletion of resources or social upheaval result in the end of industrial society as we know it. A cooling climate also results in loss of significant productivity in the North Central agricultural regions.

- Conserver or disciplined society. Everything is controlled through government force or voluntary conservation. There is less consumption and a gradual abandonment of the growth ethic.

- Transformational society. This society has given up on material growth of industrial civilization as its key value and seeks inner or personal development.

Six hundred UCPA affiliate representatives met in small groups to discuss how Bezold's alternative futures would relate to UCPA in the year 2025. It is interesting to note that in the final analysis no one believed that UCPA would exist in the year 2025 in its current form. In the continued-growth scenario the work groups saw the association as a member of a larger allied group concerned with the welfare of all developmentally disabled people.

Participants utilizing the collapse scenario had two views. One eliminated the national organization but predicted the emergence of autonomous and less effective local groups. The other view, like that expressed by those who believed in continued growth, foresaw a large allied organization with a cerebral palsy component.

Likewise the conserver society report contained two views. One also used the allied concept, but the second predicted a Big Brother government that prohibited UCPA advocacy efforts. In such a society the national organization would be allowed to exist to help provide services to those in institutions.

The transformational society held three views. The first, resembling that of the collapse scenario, warned that some local groups would replace the national organization. The second foresaw a tremendous increase in the number of affiliates, with every community of any size having an organization focused on family support services. The third view was that UCPA would evolve into an international organization with an emphasis on sharing expertise and resources with third-world nations.

Maybe merger is a strategy we can pursue to alleviate the Balkanization of constituency organizations and its negative effect on MH/DD policy formulation. All these ideas may be impossible; but, do we have a choice?

# REFERENCES

Alford, Robert R. *Health care politics: ideological and interest group barriers to reform.* Chicago: The University of Chicago Press, 1975.

American Psychiatric Association. *Biographical directory of fellows and members of the American Psychiatric Association.* Washington, D.C.: 1963.

Applebaum, Richard. *Theories of social change.* Chicago: Rand McNally, 1970.

Association for Retarded Citizens: *Action together: Information exchange.* Arlington, Texas: Association for Retarded Citizens, September 1979.

Beers, Clifford Whittingham. *A mind that found itself.* Garden City, N.Y.: Doubleday, 1907 (1953 printing).

Berry, Jeffrey M. *Lobbying for the people: The political behavior of public interest groups.* Princeton, N.J.: Princeton University Press, 1977.

Blau, Peter. *The dynamics of Bureaucracy.* Chicago: University of Chicago Press, 1955.

Carter, Richard. *The gentle legions.* Garden City, N.Y.: Doubleday, 1961.

Cross, Wilbur L. *Twenty-five years after: Sidelights on the mental hygiene movement and its founder.* Garden City, N.Y.: Doubleday, Doran, 1934.

Ellis, Susan J., and Noyes, Katherine H. *By the people: A history of Americans as volunteers.* Philadelphia: Michael C. Prestegard, 1978.

Epilepsy Foundation of America. *History of the epilepsy movement in the United States.* Washington, D.C.: 1974.

Feldstein, Paul J. The political environment of regulation. *Regulating health care: The struggle for control.* New York: Academy of Political Science, 1980, pp. 6–20.

Latham, Earl. *The group basis of politics: A study in basing-point legislation.* New York: Octagon Books, 1965, pp. 1–54 and 209–227.

Miller, Jerry W. *Organizational structures of nongovernmental postsecondary accreditation: Relationship to uses of accreditation.* Washington, D.C.: National Commission on Accrediting, 1971.

National Association for Mental Health. *Relationship of NAMH with organizations in allied fields of mental illness and health.* New York: July 27, 1957.

National Mental Health Association. *Annual reports.* 1939–1940, 1940, 1943, 1944, 1946, 1949, 1950–51, 1951–52, 1955, 1956, 1957, 1960, 1961, 1962, 1963, 1970, and 1978.

National Society for Autistic Children. *New directions for the 1980's: Goals and priorities.* Washington, D.C.: October 1, 1979.

Ogburn, William F., and Nimkoff, Meyer F. *Sociology.* Boston: Houghton Mifflin, 1964, pp. 37–40 and 407–421.

Olson, Mancur. *The logic of collective action: Public goods and the theory of groups.* Cambridge, Mass.: Harvard University Press, 1971.

Ornstein, Norman J., and Elder, Shirley. *Interest Groups, lobbying, and policymaking.* Washington, D.C.: Congressional Quarterly Press, 1978.

Pryor, David. How America takes care of her own. Bookworld. *The Washington Post*, June 29, 1980, p. 3 and 6.

*Rehabilitation, comprehensive services, and developmental disabilities act* (PL 95-902). Washington, D.C.: Government Printing Office, November 6, 1978.

Ridenour, Nina. *Mental health in the United States: A fifty-year history*. Cambridge, Mass.: Harvard University Press, 1961.

Romanofsky, Peter (ed.). *Social service organizations*. Westport, Conn.: Greenwood Press, 1978, pp. 436-443.

Salisbury, Robert. An exchange theory of interest groups. *Midwest Journal of Political Science*, 1969.

Selden, William K. *Accreditation: A struggle over standards in higher education*. New York: Harper & Brothers, 1960.

Selznick, Philip. *The TVA and the grass roots*. Berkeley: University of California Press, 1949.

Sills, David L. *The volunteers: Means and ends in a national organization*. Glencoe, Ill.: The Free Press, 1957.

Sloan, William, and Stevens, Harvey A. *A century of concern: A history of the American Association on Mental Deficiency, 1876-1976*. Washington, D.C.: American Association on Mental Deficiency, 1976.

Strickland, Stephen P. *Politics, science and dread disease: A short history of United States medical research policy*. Cambridge, Mass.: Harvard University Press, 1972.

Truman, David. *The governmental process*. New York: Knopf, 1971.

United Cerebral Palsy Associations, Inc. *Annual reports*. New York, 1950, 1951, 1952, 1953, 1955, 1968, and 1974.

United Cerebral Palsy Associations, Inc. *Annals of UCPA 1949-1974*. New York, 1974.

United Cerebral Palsy Associations, Inc. *UC People, Etc*. New York, May/June, 1980.

Walker, David B. Constitutional revision, incremental retrenchment, or real reform: An analysis of current efforts to curb federal growth. *The Bureaucrat*. Washington, D.C.: American Society for Public Administration, National Capital Area Chapter, Spring 1980, pp. 35-47.

Warren, Frank. Role of the consumer in planning and delivering services. In Wiegerink, Ronald, and Pelosi, John (eds.), *Developmental disabilities: The DD movement*. Chapel Hill, N.C.: Developmental Disabilities Technical Assistant System, 1979.

Wiegerink, Ronald, Parrish, Vince, and Buhl, Iris. Consumer involvement in human services. In Wiegerink, Ronald, and Pelosi, John (eds.), *Developmental disabilities: The DD movement*. Chapel Hill, N.C.: Developmental Disabilities Technical Assistant System, 1979.

Weisbrod, Burton A. *The voluntary nonprofit sector: An economic analysis*. Lexington, Mass.: D.C. Heath, 1977.

# REFERENCE NOTES

1. Manchester, Robert A., president-elect of Rotary International. Speech to the National Easter Seal Society Convention, Louisville, Ky.: November 1975.

2. The National Easter Seal Society. *Profile.* Updated.

3. Romer, Joseph, director of governmental affairs, National Easter Seal Society. Conversation, July 9, 1980; correspondence, August 15, 1980.

4. Eaton, Nina, vice president, United Cerebral Palsy Association. The relationship between local, state and national: Historical perspective. Remarks to the 34th Annual Conference of United Cerebral Palsy Association of New York State, Monticello, N.Y., June 9, 1980.

5. National Association for Retarded Citizens. *NARC highlights.* Arlington, Texas: National Association for Retarded Citizens, undated.

6. Boggs, Elizabeth, Ph.D., Former President, Association for Retarded Citizens. Conversation, July 7, 1980; revisions, August 21, 1980.

7. National Society for Autistic Children. *A brief history of the National Society for Autistic Children.* Washington, D.C.: NSAC, undated.

8. Akerley, Mary, past president and past director of National Affairs, National Society for Autistic Children. Conversation, July 9, 1980.

9. Benson, Harold, executive director, National Society for Autistic Children. Conversation, July 10, 1980.

10. Gettings, Robert, executive director, National Association of State Mental Retardation Program Directors. Conversation, July 7, 1980.

11. Schnibbe, Harry, executive director, National Association of State Mental Health Program Directors. Conversation, July 8, 1980.

12. Fritz, Joni, executive director, National Association of Private Residential Facilities for the Mentally Retarded. Conversation, July 9, 1980.

13. Cutler, Jay B., J.D., Special counsel and director of government relations, American Psychiatric Association. Letters of August 26 and October 6, 1980.

14. National Committee for Mental Hygiene and American Foundation for Mental Hygiene. *The next crusade in public health.* 1930.

15. Menninger, William C. *Suggestions for immediate consideration by the board of directors.* November 9, 1951 report to the National Association for Mental Health.

16. Hunter, Richard, former executive director of the National Mental Health Foundation and current assistant executive director of the National Mental Health Association. Conversation, May 15, 1980.

17. Wolfe, John, executive director; and Koyanagi, Chris, legislative assistant, National Council of Community Mental Health Centers. Conversations, July 8, 1980, and September 2, 1980.

18. De Jong, Gerben. *The movement for independent living: Origins, ideology and implications for disability research.* Paper presented to the American Congress of Rehabilitation Medicine Annual Conference. New Orleans, La.: November 17, 1978.

19. Berkowitz, Albert J., Ed.D., executive director, American Association on Mental Deficiency. Conversation, July 10, 1980.

20. McLin, William, executive director, Epilepsy Foundation of America. Conversation, July 8, 1980.

21. Nielsen, Charles, assistant to the executive director, United Cerebral Palsy Associations, Inc. Conversation, July 8, 1980.

22. Marchand, Paul, director, Governmental Affairs Office, Association for Retarded Citizens. Conversation, July 7, 1980.

23. Fine, Theodora, assistant director, Governmental Relations Office, American Psychiatric Association. Conversation, July 11, 1980.

24. Vandervoss, Gary, Ph.D., executive director, American Psychological Association; and Martin, Clarence, executive director, Association for the Advancement of Psychology. Conversations, July 10, 1980, and July 29, 1980, respectively.

25. McAllister, Jack, executive director, National Mental Health Association. Conversations, May 21, 1980 and July 11, 1980.

26. Finley, Jim, legislative assistant, National Mental Health Association. Conversation, July 8, 1980.

27, Hatton, Melinda, assistant director for governmental relations, Epilepsy Foundation of America. Conversation, July 11, 1980.

28. Bezold, Clement, Ph.D., Director, Institute for Alternative Futures. *Four scenarios of the future of health.* Address to the annual conference of the United Cerebral Palsy Association, Inc., Kansas City, Mo. April 4, 1980.

# 4 NOT JUST THE AGED, NOT JUST HEALTH CARE, AND NOT JUST NURSING HOMES
## Some Proposals for Policy and Legislative Changes in Long-Term Care

*William C. Copeland and
Iver A. Iversen*

Long-term care has been a concern in human services policy for generations, but only since the early 1960s has it elicited a consistent response at the national level. The view prevailing earlier held that long-term care was primarily a matter of state or local concern. There was federally subsidized foster care for children, but no other manifestation of a national interest in long-term care. The response of the state governments to the need for long-term care, although varying in scope and quality, has been remarkably consistent: state hospitals for the mentally ill, state schools for the retarded, state schools for the deaf and blind, but nothing for the aged except inappropriate institutionalization and state (or locally) subsidized care in a poorly regulated network of nursing homes.

The turning point appears to have been Medicare and Medicaid (Title XVIII and Title XIX of the Social Security Act), the key legislative item affecting long-term care being the federal subsidization of nursing home care. Both are primarily health care measures, and both are tailored to specific eligibility groups. Medicare, originally intended for the aged retiree, has since been expanded to cover the

This work was supported, in part, by Grant no. 54–P–71407/5–03 for a Developmental Disabilities Project of National Significance from the Administration on Developmental Disabilities, Office of Human Development Services, U.S. Department of Health and Human Services.

159

disabled former wage earner. Medicaid was, and still is, intended for indigent aged, blind, or disabled persons in need of medical care or indigent families with dependent children, with some latitude given the states in defining medical indigency.

The basic response to long-term care reflected in Medicare and Medicaid has changed little over the years. The focus was and continues to be the nursing home. Coverage for long-term care in state institutions, except for certain groups such as the mentally ill who are neither aged persons nor dependent children, was mainly effected by redefining such institutions to be skilled nursing facilities (SNF) or intermediate care facilities (ICF). More recently, for the mentally retarded, a special class of nursing home was created—the intermediate care facility for the mentally retarded (ICF/MR)—and state institutions caring for this group are now required to meet special regulations governing this type of facility.

Senate and House documents, Department of Health and Human Services (DHHS) publications, and reports of DHHS–sponsored research and demonstration meetings leave the unmistakeable impression that long-term care relates primarily to the aged, and except for health-related day and in-home services, the vehicle for providing long-term care is the nursing home. It is true that the aged are the primary group of interest because of their number, and it is also true that nursing home care is a crucial (or, perhaps again because of their number, *the* crucial) element in a set of long-term care opportunities. But it is by no means true that the aged are the only group of interest, that a long-term care concept applicable to the aged can be readily extended to the other groups, or that the nursing home, to the exclusion of all others, is the preferred level of care for all aged persons in need of long-term care.

## Other Target Groups

More than 300,000 mentally retarded and developmentally disabled persons, as well as more than 500,000 chronically mentally ill, receive some form of long-term care. (About one-third of these persons are also aged.) These numbers do not include the physically handicapped (those not classified as mentally ill, mentally retarded, or developmentally disabled) or the hundreds of thousands of children in some form of out-of-home care at any point in time.

## Other Forms of Long-Term Care

Besides nursing homes, long-term care is provided through state institutions, specialized care residences (such as ICF/MRs), supervised (nonmedical) residences, specialized foster care, family subsidies, independent living, and a host of community-based and home-based support and emergency care programs. The development of these residential and generic service programs has been haphazard. Their linkage with one another has been fragmented, and their relative position in attracting funds has been a function of their length of time in existence and the degree to which they were perceived as meeting medical rather than other, more appropriate, criteria. A preferred approach would be to find some rational way of developing current and potential program and financing linkages between related types of care opportunities.

## Health Care is Not the Only Support Needed

Chronically ill or disabled populations need health care, but the episodic medical care that tends to be the concern of many of those who write regulations for government health programs falls far short of addressing the long-term care needs of these populations. The key needs for many of the aged, the mentally ill, and the mentally retarded or developmentally disabled tend to be multidimensional and multidisciplinary. Their needs span a broad range, including medical services, nursing services (but not necessarily in a nursing home), psychological services, developmental programming services, income maintenance, transportation, day services, work activity services, and social rehabilitation services.

They have the further characteristic that whatever their profile of needs, if one or more of these needs is not met, then the effect of any investment in meeting the other needs tends to be attenuated. If there is not a flexible package of services covering the whole spectrum of living supports, the people in long-term care tend to miss out on services that are needed and tend to receive services that are not needed. Under current financing programs the services that are provided but not needed tend to be medical services, inefficient, ineffective, expensive substitutes provided in expensive care contexts for the group of services usually called *psychosocial* services, which can usually be provided in less expensive care contexts. The problem in planning for long-term care, therefore, is to provide financing for all needed services and not just a few.

Planning for long-term care policy and legislation should take account of all affected target groups, all needed care opportunities, and all necessary services. The result would be a more reasonable concept of long-term care, one that would permit addressing the legislative, administrative, programmatic, and fiscal issues in a more rational, cohesive, and manageable manner. R.J. Samuelson's 1978 *National Journal* articles on the demography of aging, its effects on service needs and income maintenance, and the associated cost projections for the next thirty years, provide convincing testimony that such changes are needed.

## THE GENERAL CONTINUUM OF CARE

The following approach would make the long-term care problem more manageable: Organize legislation, management, financing (and financing incentives), and program development into continua of care around homogeneous target groups such as the aging, the physically handicapped, the mentally ill, the mentally retarded and developmentally disabled, and the child welfare populations. Each of these target groups becomes a constituent part of the long-term care initiative. This approach has a number of advantages.

1. Instead of requiring legislation and administration covering all of long-term care at once, it calls for separate legislation for the separate target groups of interest. Massive legislative changes tend to be almost impossible in the Congress as it is now constituted.)

2. It permits the federal government to deal simultaneously with a number of interest groups having relatively harmonious concerns. (Dealing with all mental retardation groups alone, for example, is possible. Dealing with all aging, all mental health, and all mental retardation groups at once is almost impossible.)

3. It forces federal, state, and local governments into total program budgeting. This is important because no level of government knows its own costs or the total costs of any one system. News that came out of our deinstitutionalization technical assistance

project in 1979 that mental retardation and related problems cost about $10.8 billion per year in public funds came as a surprise to DHHS Secretary Patricia Harris, who believed she had only one small ($65 million per year) mental retardation/developmental disability program. In California, for example, the "official" state budget lists mental retardation services as costing about $500 million per year in federal and state funds. However, this sum represents only about one-third of the approximately $1.5 billion of the federal, state, and local mental retardation funding. Most of the remainder is concealed under other account rubrics, such Supplemental Security Income (SSI), Social Security Disability Income (SSDI), state SSI supplement, Medicaid, Medicare, U.S. Department of Housing and Urban Development (HUD) and local housing authority budgets, Title XX of the Social Security Act and its associated state budget, Vocational Rehabilitation, state mental health, Education for All Handicapped Children Act (PL 94-142), and state and local education costs.

4. It forces states to engage in integrated placement, case management, financing, and evaluation for each identified target group.

5. It helps to align federal and state policy and program with the currently accepted principles of preference—that is, least restrictive environment, most normalized appropriate placement, and least costly appropriate behavior on the part of state and local governments in program development and client placement. (Since current federal financing policy tends to encourage law-breaking by states by financing institutions and nursing homes that are providing inappropriate care and refusing to provide financing for appropriate community services because they are "social" and not "medical" in nature, the continuum-of-care approach also clarifies where the problems are and how to fix them.)

6. In the medium to long term, a continuum-of-care policy will save all actors money. In the short term, it saves only states money, and this is precisely the stimulus needed to ensure the massive program changes required at the state and local levels. (About fifteen states are responding to these stimuli now, and more will soon.) In the long term, because of the higher cost of institutional and nursing care (which will become increasingly more expensive than community care because of regulation-

induced costs), continuum-of-care programs having a set of built-in deinstitutionalization incentives will cost less for all actors.

To develop an explicit continuum of care, there are some minimum requirements:

1. Financing that provides incentives in the preferred direction of the flow of persons;

2. A placement, or placement monitoring, organization;

3. A technology of appropriate placement, such as an activities-of-daily living scale, the scores of which correspond to different level-of-care needs;

4. Defined levels of care, each of which serves distinctly different level-of-care needs;

5. Data on the current placement of persons in the target group, the flow of persons into the placement system, the flow of persons among parts of the system, and the flow of persons out of the system;

6. Data on the costs of care for each level of care, with projections of future cost and expected revenues by source, for each defined subpopulation within the system.

Given the continuum-of-care concept, with its minimum requirements, we are now in a position to specify what is required for policy changes with no change in regulation or law; regulation changes with no change in law; and changes in the law. As one example of planning for a continuum of care we shall discuss the case of a continuum for the mentally retarded/developmentally disabled (MR/DD) together with recommendations for changes in policy needed to make it easier to design such continua.

## THE CONTINUUM OF CARE FOR MR/DD PERSONS: DEFINITION AND POLICY IMPLICATIONS

A continuum of care is a set of care opportunities (for a group of persons characterized by similar or identical problems) that are ordered according to their intensity, their cost, their restrictiveness of environment, or some other dimension. A continuum can be implicit, simply having emerged as a set of fragmented care opportunities that can be described according to various levels or it can be explicit, organized for programmatic purposes, say for least restrictive or most appropriate program placement, or organized for fiscal purposes, say for least cost to one or more of the major fiscal actors.

In most areas the continuum of care is implicit. It "just grew." In the MR/DD area, the continuum's growth was influenced by fiscal history (especially Section 1121 and Title XIX ICF/MR legislation, and Title XVI of the Social Security Act), program theory (the rise of habilitation approaches and normalization goals), and court decisions (right to treatment in the least restrictive environment).

The current continuum of care for MR/DD includes the following care opportunities, running roughly from most to least restrictive: state institutions, SNF/ICFs, ICF/MRs (community-based—both large and small), supervised group and apartment living, foster care, home care, and independent living (including family subsidies).

It seems established that the great majority of those housed at the more restrictive end of the continuum can be housed (and served) at the less restrictive end of the continuum; and, once having moved into that end of the continuum, there is noticeable improvement in function. It is less well established, but nevertheless strongly asserted, with fragmentary evidence, that the more restrictive the program (holding the amount of service constant) the more expensive it tends to be.

If these assertions are true (and we believe them to be true), one would wonder why MR/DD persons continue to be housed in state institutions and nursing homes in such great numbers (more than 250,000 in 1979). We can identify some of the reasons:

1. The historic position of the institutions. Until recently the burden of proof was on community placement, not on the institutions (an MR/DD person was considered eminently institutionalizable, and the burden of proof was on those who claimed that the person would be more appropriately placed in the community). Beyond this, the institution was well organized, had an appropriations history, and had an agreed-upon model of "treatment," none of which was available in the community until recently.

2. The funding of institutions was administratively easy and clean, requiring only one major federal account—Title XIX—and one state account; the funding of community services required many accounts and was messy.

3. Federal funding tended to provide perverse incentives. That is, federal funding, and especially Medicaid, tended to encourage (and still does) institutional, nonnormalized forms of care and to discourage the more normalized forms of care in the community.

4. Even when the fiscal incentives might be reorganized to provide incentives for normalized community care, standard federal and state budget and management practices tend to make that more difficult.

The first of the foregoing reasons is weakening under the power of new approaches in habilitation and attacks through the courts. The others continue.

If there is to be a well-managed, explicit continuum, where all incentives tend toward the most appropriate level of care for each MR/DD person in the system, the other three factors must be changed. The last factor can be modified, but the task is not related to Medicaid. Because the other two factors are so related we will discuss what must be done with Medicaid and the probable fiscal effects of those actions, in order to move into an adequate continuum funding approach for MR/DD persons.

### Funding along the Continuum of Care: Neatness and Messiness

In general, the more institutional the care, the cleaner its funding. State institutional care is funded under a single account: Title XIX of the Social Security Act. Less restrictive forms of care invariably require multiple accounts, one or more for the residential component and one or more for day programming and other generic services. As a result, multifunded services, even when the money available in the separate accounts is adequate, are difficult to develop and organize. The general rule of civil service behavior, therefore, is: When possible, organize services only around clean funding (see Table 4-1).

Table 4-1. Sources of Funding.

| Level of Continuum | Residential Room and Board and Service Cost | Service Cost Outside Residence |
|---|---|---|
| Institution | Title XIX | |
| Community ICF/MR | Title XIX | Title XX, Title XIX (for regular medical costs), state grants, county levy, Office of Special Education or local school levy, vocational rehabilitation |
| Supervised living | SSI, HUD Section 8, food stamps, Title XX | Same as above |
| Home care | SSI or Social Security Administration, state subsidy, Title XIX | Title XIX or XX |
| Family subsidy | State subsidy | |

The further we move into the community end of the continuum of care, the more diverse the funding. The need for normalized, separated, community-based services may require a large number of different funding sources. One or more changes can be made to make community services administratively neater. First, put all generic services outside the residence (respite care, transport, social development, work preparation, infant stimulation, work activity) under Title XIX. Then put supervised living care, in toto, under Title XIX. The activities of a supervised living approach are very close to those in an ICF/MR (for persons of higher functional capabilities). Alternatively fund only the habilitation/supervision activities of the staff (about half the budget), while allowing the room and board function to be funded under SSI, HUD Section 8, and food stamps. (The second alternative provides a higher federal matching rate in most states, thus making the increased administrative complexity "worth it" to the state.)

## Funding along the Continuum of Care:
## Correcting Perverse Incentives

For a continuum of care where the incentives are toward normalized, community-oriented kinds of care and services, the following two rules hold: The more normalized the level of care, the less it should cost in total. The more normalized the level of care, the less it should cost each relevant fiscal actor.

Under current funding, the first rule nearly always holds, but the second is violated constantly by the design of the system. A truncated continuum is exemplified in Table 4-2, where the levels of care are laid out from least to most normalized.

The continuum in Table 4-2 is in a state with 50 percent Medicaid matching, with active treatment in all levels but ICF/SNF, and with separated active treatment in the community ICF/MR and the supervised living levels. In many states, counties share certain costs with the state government (say 50 percent of nonfederal Medicaid costs).

For such states, the incentives for the federal government are ordered almost as one would want; however, the incentives of the state governments are toward community ICF/MRs or toward SNF or ICF programs. The incentives of the counties are the worst. Their fiscal preferences would be the institution first and the SNF or ICF second, both undesirable choices. In states where there are no local shares, the state's incentive is toward care in SNF or ICF programs (and in most cases, those programs do not include active treatment programming). From that sort of state's point of view, community ICF/MRs cost them as much as institutions.

Even if the SNFs and ICFs offered active treatment programming, but on an internal basis only, as the state institutions do, this less-

Table 4-2.  Cost per Client per Year in a Perverse-Incentive Continuum.

| Level of Care | Federal | State | Local | Total |
| --- | --- | --- | --- | --- |
| Institutions | $12,000 | $12,000 | $    0 | $24,000 |
| SNF/ICF[a] | 7,000 | 3,500 | 3,500 | 14,000 |
| Community ICF/MR | 7,500 | 3,750 | 8,750 | 20,000 |
| Supervised living | 2,500 | 4,750 | 4,750 | 12,000 |

a. For this level of care no active treatment program is required by law and regulation.

normalized level of care would still be fiscally preferable from the state's point of view. Community ICF/MR and supervised living programs would cost the state more.

How can the incentives be made less perverse? A series of actions could be taken by the Health Care Financing Administration (HCFA) vis-à-vis Medicaid:

1. An "intergovernmental" provision for state–local matching. In those states where there is state–local Medicaid sharing for other than state institutions, there should be the same matching formula for state institutions.

2. An enforced requirement for active treatment in a place physically and administratively separate from the SNF or ICF but funded by Medicaid.

3. The required funding of day activities, workshop activities, and related activities as physically and administratively separate from ICF/MRs in the community (as is now permitted in New York, Massachusetts, and Michigan, but on very narrow grounds).

4. The optional funding of personal care staff (now allowed) and rehabilitation staff for Individual Habilitation Plan-related activities, in supervised living programs; and the funding of related day programs, as needed, as in (3).

With that series of policy actions, the fiscal incentives of the continuum displayed in Table 4–2 would more nearly fit the preferences of the normalization approach. That is, the fiscal results would be as in Table 4–3.

At this point, the total cost criterion is more nearly met, and the second (the more normalized the environment, the lower the cost to each actor) is also almost met. This approach also meets the "admin-

Table 4-3.  Cost per Client per Year in the Reformed-Incentive Continuum.

| Level of Care | Federal | State | Local | Total |
|---|---|---|---|---|
| Institutions | $12,000 | $6,000 | $6,000 | $24,000 |
| SNF/ICF | 9,500 | 4,750 | 4,750 | 19,000 |
| Community ICF/MR | 10,000 | 5,000 | 5,000 | 20,000 |
| Supervised living | 8,000 | 2,000 | 2,000 | 12,000 |

istrative neatness" criterion of the previous section. Thus, the fiscal incentives for a normalized care-oriented continuum of care would be more nearly met.

## Fiscal Consequences: A Raid on the Federal Treasury

Changes of the sort we have recommended in Medicaid funding would result in an increased level of federal participation at almost every level of the somewhat truncated continuum of care used for the example. The answer to the question of whether such changes would require raiding the federal treasury appears to be no. In a study of funding for institutions and community care, our simulation of various policy options and state reactions found that deinstitutionalization policy approaches (which included heavy emphasis on gradually phasing out institutions, coupled with increases in community funding, especially in Medicaid) would cost less for both federal and nonfederal governments over the next six years than would alternatives in which current (status quo) trends are extrapolated over the same period.

*Current Public Funding of MR/DD Services.*    Public funding from all sources of MR/DD activities was approximately $10.8 billion in fiscal year 1979. About $4.3 billion was federally funded; the rest, by state and local governments. A majority of the total spending was for some form of institutional care rather than for normalized care. The overwhelming proportion of Medicaid funding was for institutional care, although there are clear precedents in law, regulation, policy, and current practice for the reversal of federal funding practices—especially Title XIX Medicaid.

*Examining Federal Funding Policies and State Reactions.*    A National Policy Simulation Model for the Developmental Disabilities is being developed by the staff of the Hubert H. Humphrey Institute of Public Affairs DD Technical Assistance Program. The model estimates federal and nonfederal costs of different types of deinstitutionalization policies for MR/DD populations. The first runs of that model concentrated on the institutional and community costs of serving such populations. The major federal focus was on Medicaid costs in the institutions and on Medicaid, Title XX, SSI, and other costs in the communities, as well as state and local costs for each type of care. For the first phase of this model, SNF/ICF costs, PL 94-142 special educational costs, most SSI payments, and non-ICF/MR Medicaid costs (as for occupational therapy (OT), physical therapy (PT), speech therapy, physicians, hospital, and other costs) are not included. These latter will be included in the next phases of the model.

As phase I of the model stands, $5.45 billion of the $10.8 billion in total costs are currently included. Given current data, the federal government is now paying about $1.14 billion for care in public institutions for the mentally retarded (almost totally through Medicaid), and about $430 million for community care (with Title XX paying the largest amount of a number of accounts, including Medicaid, vocational rehabilitation, DD, and other federal sources), for a total of $1.57 billion. The remaining $3.88 billion consists of state and local funds. The distribution of current funding is shown in Table 4-4.

*What Happens under Different State and Federal Policies?*  The National Developmental Disability Policy Model is a computerized model of the MR/DD system that accommodates analysis of a large variety of "what if" questions. A current report on that model examines eight major options or strategies in caring for MR/DD populations in state institutions and in the community and explores a number of suboptions for each of the major options. The major options include, for example, the national status quo option, which examines what will happen if the recent historic trends in the states continue with respect to the transfer of persons out of the state institutions into the community-based service system and the movement of per-

Table 4-4.  1979 Public Funding for MR/DD Activities as Defined by Phase I of the National DD Policy Simulation Model, $ Billions.

| Payment Source | State Institution Costs | Community-Based Costs | Total Costs |
|---|---|---|---|
| Federal | 1.14 | .43 | 1.57 |
| State/local | 2.15 | 1.73 | 3.88 |
| Total | 3.29 | 2.16 | 5.45 |

sons out of the population at risk in the community into the community system (the out-of-the-woodwork phenomenon). The model thus facilitates examination of the fiscal effects of providing services that draw more persons out of the community together with the fiscal effects of differing deinstitutionalization policies.

The national status quo option, which assumes that the federal government will not change its behavior can be examined from two points of view for state reactions. In one suboption we can assume that the states continue historic trends in seeking federal reimbursements. In another we can assume that the states operate as intelligent maximizers, getting the most reimbursement they can out of the current rules.

For other options we can make some assumptions about aggressive federal deinstitutionalization policies. We can examine a "mild" deinstitutionalization policy and its effects, for example, moving from the current sixty-eight persons per 100,000 population to a California status quo option, with forty state institutional residents per 100,000 population in 1985, as a goal for the nation in 1985, or a "Pennhurst" option, which assumes no state institutional beds at all by 1985, as a goal for the nation. The results in 1985 from four of these models are instructive. They are tabulated in Table 4–5, in comparison with current (1979) funding. Examining the projections is revealing.

Table 4-5. 1985 Public Funding for MR/DD Activities for Four Different Policy Options, as Defined by Phase I of the National DD Policy Simulation Model, $ Billions.

| Options | Federal Costs | State Costs | Total Costs |
|---|---|---|---|
| Current (1979) funding | 1.57 | 3.88 | 5.45 |
| Pennhurst strategy | 3.55 | 7.95 | 11.50 |
| California status quo | 4.20 | 9.44 | 13.64 |
| National status quo (historic trends) | 5.41 | 9.52 | 14.93 |
| National status quo (historic trends with state maximization of federal funds) | 7.03 | 7.90 | 14.93 |

Costs for the part of the national MR/DD system encompassed in the current version of the model (state institutions and community services but not including nursing homes) increase 111 percent by 1985, even in the option with the smallest cost increase, the Pennhurst, which is the radical deinstitutionalization option. The increase in gross costs for the most expensive options, those based on historic trends, is 174 percent over the same period. A key determinant of this large increase is the expected 130 percent increase in institutional per diem costs from a 1959 national average of $59.00 to $136.00 over the next six years, which is caused by general inflation plus the regulatory inflation driven by current ICF/MR regulations and their interpretations.

Under the assumptions of the current version of the model, it is clear that the greater the deinstitutionalization initiative, the lower the gross costs of the total system. From the point of view of the federal government, the status quo option continuing current historic trends is the most expensive. If federal policy continues as it has in the past five years, and the states continue as they have, then the federal cost increase will be 250 percent over the next six years. If the states become more aggressive in collecting federal reimbursement, however, as it appears they already have, then federal costs will increase about 350 percent by 1985.

The states can be fiscally indifferent to the two most extreme options. A radical deinstitutionalization strategy (the Pennhurst strategy, resulting in no institutional beds in 1985) would cost the states about as much as a status quo strategy in which the states maximize federal revenues (by investing in the certification of all institutional beds occupied by 1985 and by "Medicaiding" every community service that can be included under Title XIX of the Social Security Act). The practical result, in terms of state policy, would seem to be that the states have the choice of two courses of action.

1. *The states can concentrate on federal funds maximization.* The states' major efforts can be spent in upgrading and redesigning their Medicaid reimbursement systems in order to secure maximum yield from the federal government, while at the same time appropriating the funds needed to bring institutional beds and personnel to the level needed for compliance with the ICF/MR regulations, providing a capital program for community ICF/MR

beds and supervised living beds, and redesigning nonresidential services to meet Medicaid standards (even if a "hard line" HCFA policy demanded the nonnormalized unification of all services under each community ICF/MRs roof).

2. *States can concentrate on deinstitutionalization and community services development.* The states' major efforts can be spent in planning a six-year phasedown of state institutions, with a design of a complete community system, heavily subsidized by a normalization-oriented Medicaid funding system, which would pay for small ICF/MRs, care and rehabilitation staffing for supervised living facilities, nonresidential habilitation (day activities, workshops) and respite care programs, and case management systems.

Either of these approaches would cost the states about the same amount; but the first alternative would cost the federal government about twice as much. The practical result, in terms of federal policy, would seem to be that one of two courses of action could be pursued (with no recourse to legislation).

DHHS (and especially HCFA) can take an "easy line" toward state institutional programming and investment (essentially the current policy) and a hard line toward community programming (essentially the current policy). This will result in a continuation of the status quo, with the expected results.

DHHS can take a hard line toward institutional investment. For example, it can provide deficiency waivers for institutions only where there is a specific, performance-oriented plan for phaseout of institutional beds. In the absence of a deficiency plan, it could require detailed commitment and monitoring (under the utilization review provisions) for institutions. It could require tightly administered rate-setting policies, in which state uses of cost allocation to put overhead for child development (CD) and mental illness (MI) into mental retardation (MR) costs were forbidden, in which any capital allowances in the per diem other than use allowances would be forbidden, and in which detailed justification of support costs (as opposed to care costs) would be required, under specific criteria defining the costs that would be allowed in the support area. It can cooperate closely, on an ongoing task force basis, with the Justice Department's Civil Rights Division on institution-related cases. At the same time, it can take an easy line toward the funding of community care through Title XIX. That is, although virtually all forms of community care and habilitation for MR/DD persons can now be designed to be funded by Medicaid, there is considerable ambiguity, ambivalence, and designed waste in the process of qualifying these services under HCFA's current interpretation of the regulations. What needs to be done by DHHS (and especially HCFA) is to publicly support the specific regulatory policies that set forth the possibilities for Medicaid-funded programming in the community in line with the best practices in the field today.

The advantages of the second of the two courses of action are clear. From fiscal, programmatic, and legal points of view, it would seem to make sense to move to normalized community funding approaches under Title XIX.

### Funding along the MR/DD Continuum: A Summary of Policy Recommendations

A number of changes are needed in current HCFA policy to achieve a reformed continuum. Some are changes in the regulations, but most are changes in how the regulations are interpreted.

Much of what is recommended below is already clearly permitted under current regulations. Where not clearly permitted, precedents exist in a number of states, in the form of HCFA approvals that indicate a permitted departure from or reinterpretation of the regulations. The recommended changes actually are changes in emphasis in subpolicies that could be made as part of the issuance of a more general policy. Institution policy changes needed are as follows:

1.  Use the current deficiency correction policy, which allows for optional phasedown of state institutions, as an incentive to developing performance-oriented phasedown plans over the next five or six years. This would require a regulation change, which was written for issuance in the spring of 1981.

2.  In the absence of a phasedown-oriented plan for correcting the deficiencies of state institutions, require tightly monitored utilization review, with a reduction of matching funds for any person who could be receiving care in a less restrictive environment and for any person who is not receiving active treatment in accord with the level of care provided.

3. Require tightly administered rate-setting policies, with restrictions on cost allocation, capital allowances, and payment for unneeded support costs in state institutions.

4. Require active treatment programs in SNFs and ICFs, on a separated basis, for all MR/DD residents.

5. Develop an intergovernmental provision for state–local matching, requiring the same intrastate (state–local) matching for justifications as for community ICF/MR facilities. This would require a change in the regulations.

Community policy changes that are needed are as follows:

1. Publicly commit to ICF/MRs with fifteen or fewer beds and with separate Medicaid-funded day activities and respite care. A requirement for the separation of the residential and generic service functions should also be written into the regulations. The Minnesota model, which operates under the HCFA regulations on a more normalized basis than we have seen in the mini-institutions of other states, should be adopted.

2. Define day activity and other day programming costs as fundable from residential costs under Medicaid. Develop a concept that is less medical and less expensive than that funded, for example, under New York State Statute, Section 365(a), Subsection (2)(c) of the Social Services Law.

3. Develop technical assistance concepts on how the personal care attendant or a higher level employee, funded under Medicaid, may be used to staff the Individual Habilitation Plan activities in supervised living facilities.

4. Develop a technical assistance concept on how case management activities can be funded as an administrative cost under Medicaid.

Other changes that should be made include:

1. Use the Institute of Medicaid Management to hold a series of regional meetings in which all relevant regional office personnel and members of the state departments of health, welfare, mental retardation, and housing authorities—all in one room at one time—can be given the word on the new policy.

Table 4-6.  Sources of Medicaid Funding for the MR/DD Continuum of Care, by Type of Service According to the Code of Federal Regulations (*CFR*).

| | *Residential* | *Nonresidential* |
|---|---|---|
| State institutions ICF/MRs | 42 CFR 440.150 and related provisions | . . . |
| SNF/ICF[a] | 42 CFR 440.40(a), 440.150 and related provisions | 42 CFR 440.90 or 440.70(e) or 440.130(d) (day activity workshop services); 42 CFR 432.50(b)(1) or (b)(6) (case management services) |
| Community-based ICF/MRs, more than sixteen beds[b] | 42 CFR 440.150, and related provisions | Same as above |
| Community-based ICF/MRs, fewer than sixteen beds[c] | 42 CFR 440.150, and related provisions | Same as above |
| Supervised community living (group homes with fewer than sixteen beds; apartment living)[d] | 42 CFR 440.170(f) (for staff only) | Same as above |
| Home care | . . . | Same as above |

a. MR/DD persons should be placed in SNFs and ICFs only if the person's physical condition is such that nursing care is required round the clock and there is a program of active treatment, preferably separate from the SNF or ICF.

b. These are allowed, under current regulations, but do not appear to meet the demands of current "best practice."

c. Includes multiple residence/centralized services, where there are one or two persons per site.

d. Can include Independent Group Living Concept, as defined in HUD Regulations, 24 CFR 882.

2.  Provide a technical assistance concept on how full continuum management for ensuring fiscal control and appropriateness of placement may be paid for out of Medicaid administrative funds.

A summary of what provisions of current regulations fit what level of the continuum, by type of service, is presented in Table 4-6.

## INCREMENTAL LEGISLATIVE STEPS
## TOWARD CONTINUA OF CARE FOR
## VARIOUS LONG-TERM CARE
## POPULATIONS

If it is accepted that a desirable policy would be movement toward explicit continua of care designed for specific target groups (the aging, mentally ill, mentally retarded and other developmentally disabled, physically handicapped, and child welfare populations) and organized by levels of care, ranging from most restrictive to least restrictive, and linked by case management/placement services, then a number of "small" legislative initiatives are needed, most of which would be in the legislative area of the U.S. Senate finance committee and the U.S. House of Representatives ways and means and commerce committees.

The initiatives call for minor changes, mostly in Title XIX, which support the following major objectives:

1. Reorganize currently available information to make it more relevant to policy.

2. Change federal and state fiscal incentives from support of institutional care to support of community care, so that the DHHS incentives support the preferences of program theory and law.

3. Increase program flexibility in the planning and delivering services in long-term care.

4. Provide new information for policy purposes.

5. Increase local innovation and control.

6. Increase consumer choice.

7. Provide incentives to retrain institutional personnel and new personnel for management and service delivery in the community.

Recommended changes, listed separately for the major objective they serve (they may serve more than one major objective), are as follows:

### Making Available Information More
### Relevant to Policy

*Separate (by Statute) the Medicaid Reporting for Each of the Long-Term Care Populations.* There has been much talk in DHHS about the need to deal with long-term care as a separate issue in discussion of National Health Insurance. The information to make the discussion far more insightful is potentially available, especially in the more than twenty states with operating Medicaid Management Information Systems (MMIS).

Unfortunately the information is now reported by category of vendor, rather than by category of person. As a result, we know the cost of SNFs by state, but we do not know the cost of Medicaid to the different types of persons in SNFs. Thus the cost of care for any given person in a SNF is reported for the SNF, but the person's cost for physician care, lab tests, trips to an acute general hospital, PT and OT costs (unless such costs are included in the SNF per diem) cannot now be ascertained. A further example: the cost of the mentally ill in nursing homes, who go to a short-term acute hospital for treatment, is included under short-term hospitals, but not under a "mentally ill" classification. Yet, as much as one-eighth of the total cost for short-term general hospitals may be for the mentally ill, with about two-thirds of the mentally ill being persons who were in nursing homes, or who would enter them after hospitalization (a heavily chronic brain syndrome population).

In states with Medical Management Information Systems (MMIS), however, those costs could be ascertained by type of patient or client, since a medical cost history can be assembled within the MMIS for a given person, then "spread" for acute general hospital costs, physician costs, and other costs incurred by that type of person.

We propose that person-type by vendor-type by location-type expenditure reporting be required for all states, with an almost immediate phase-in for the MMIS states, after a two-year research and demonstration project in three states to provide "debugged" models, to report on costs incurred by the following groups:

• Aged (divided into young and old aged and, if possible, into those with a mental illness and mental retardation diagnosis versus "all other")

In state institutions
  ICF/MR
  Mentally ill and geriatric
In SNFs
In ICFs
All other

- Mentally retarded and developmentally disabled (under 65)

  In state institutions
    ICF/MR
    Mentally ill and geriatric
  In SNFs
  In ICFs
  In ICFs/MR in the community
    In ICFs/MR of sixteen beds or more
    In ICFs/MR of fifteen beds or less
  All other
  (Should be divided into ages 22–64 and ages 0–21, if possible, for those in custody of state or local MR/DD systems.)

- Chronically mentally ill (under 65)

  In state institutions
  In SNFs
  In ICFs
  All other
  (Should be divided ages 22–64 and ages 0–21, if possible, for those in custody of state or local mental health systems.)

Medicaid costs for children in custody of state and local child welfare systems (or receiving medical assistance under the foster care or adoptive subsidy provisions). These should be broken into three groups:

- Mentally retarded/developmentally disabled
- Mentally ill
- All other

  In state institutions
  In county institutions
  In SNFs

In ICFs
In residential treatment institutions
In other out-of-home group care
In subsidized adoption
In family foster care
   In minimum-pay-level care
   In some form of extra-subsidy care
In independent living
Living with own family

Despite the apparent complexity of the reporting taxonomies, nearly all of the coding already exists within Medicaid systems (age, primary diagnosis, location of residences, number of beds). Only for some child welfare categories, and only in part, since some are already done, would new codes need to be developed. For the child welfare categories, such new codes will be under development in the coming year, since they must be available under the new child-tracking requirements of PL 96–272 (IV B and IV E reform amendments of 1980, for the Social Security Act). Once the additional codes are added, and the states are required to use the basic Medicaid history for reporting in the modes recommended, a new standard reporting system should be available for most of the states (and more than 85 percent of all clients) by 1985 or 1986.

*Amend Title XI of the Social Security Act.* This amendment would require DHHS to present total budgets to Congress for each major long-term care target group. At present Congress, the administration, and the state and local governments are flying blind on the effects of their spending and saving decisions on the long-term care. Not only do they not know how much medical assistance spending is involved for any one target group (and thus make incorrect decisions), they also do not know what total spending is. Most decisionmakers in legislatures and administrations have ignored the chronically mentally ill in the community on the ground that they are for the public fisc a relatively low-cost group; recent evidence in Minnesota shows, however, that they may be costing the federal and state governments as much as persons in nursing homes. Support for the mentally retarded and developmentally disabled by the federal and state governments amounted to about $10.8 billion in 1979, from Title II (Disability) of the Social Security Act, as well as Titles XVI, XVIII,

XIX, and XX; from CHAMPUS in the Department of Defense, vocational rehabilitation and PL 94-142 in the Department of Education, food stamps and Section 8 in HUD (a total of about $5.0 billion in federal support), with the rest coming from state budgets, schools, institutions, nursing homes, child welfare and social service budgets; and from local budgets for county welfare or for special education.

A further example is the "official" public budget of California, which puts support for MR/DD persons at $500 million per year; the actual public cost from all sources is about $1.5 billion. The National Institute of Mental Health, the Administration on Aging, the Administration for Developmental Disabilities, and the Administration for Children, Youth, and Families should be required by Congress to assemble budget data by state, for "their" target groups, by account (with the goal of being able to allocate by location and account, in a way analogous to the Medicaid taxonomy), so that full continuum budgets, by level of the continuum, are available to Congress on a state-by-state basis. At that point Congress (and the administration and the individual states) will begin to understand the total public costs and the changes in types of costs as well as total costs year by year for long-term care. At the same time it is only at that point that the informational basis for negotiated state block grants like those for health maintenance organizations will be possible for individual target groups.

## Change Federal and State Fiscal Incentives
## to Support Normalized Communities

Institutional funds matching would first have to be reduced, and the difference between the original match and the reduced match transferred to community services for the mental illness and mental retardation groups. Similarly nursing home matching funds could be reduced for all mentally ill and mentally retarded without physical conditions requiring round-the-clock nursing care or (in the case of the mentally ill) without conditions of senility or chronic brain syndrome and the difference between original match and reduced match transferred to community care account. Active treatment could be required for all those mentally ill and MR/DD remaining in SNFs and ICFs, with active treatment to be included in per diems as a specific item.

Rehabilitative and developmentally oriented (rather than medical) Medicaid benefits could be expanded and clarified for case management, day activities, respite care, transport between residence and day activity site, allowance for staff services in nonmedical residence and family care (own family or other) services in the community. Eligibility for nursing home versus home care should be examined with a view toward changing the mix.

Given the driving force of inflation and regulatory requirements for the institutional and nursing home care, it will become increasingly possible to provide enriched programs in the community, at savings to the public fisc, if federal fiscal and other regulatory incentives are used to encourage the states to move persons in need of long-term care into less restrictive environments.

### Increase Flexibility in Planning and Delivering Long-Term Care Services

*Allow the States to Provide Medicaid-Financed Services by Target Group.* At the present time, except for specific kinds of named services (psychiatric services for persons over age 65 and under age 21, intermediate care facility services for the mentally retarded, and others), most Medicaid-financed services must be provided to all. This includes virtually all community services for special long-term groups. Thus, if day activity services are to be provided for the mentally retarded, they must also be provided for the aged, the mentally ill, the physically handicapped, children, and all others.

Given the exigencies of planning and implementing new kinds of services in the states, this introduces fiscal uncertainties and administrative difficulties the states find insurmountable. As a result, nothing is developed.

The introduction of HR 6194, the Pepper–Waxman bill, which provides 90 percent federal matching for such long-term-care-oriented community services under Title XIX, is one response to this problem. If the states were able to plan total service ladders by individual target-group continuum, however, such a large financial incentive to the states would not be needed. Thus, a state could begin with the community services for the chronically mentally ill or the mentally retarded, without the need to bring them up for all groups. Planning and implementing such services without such an authority is especially difficult because of the problems of planning for the aging. In general, less expensive services in the community can be installed for most of the other groups, at no increase in cost for the population currently being served and at only relatively small increase for the population not being served now. That is, the numbers of persons not now in the public sector who would be attracted into the public sector by the presence of new, attractive community services (if the services were well designed) would be small and relatively controllable. For the aging, matters are perceived by a number of research people and budget people to be different. They believe that the potential response of the aging to increases in the supply of community services is not understood; therefore, developing large new supplies of community "institutionalization-preventive" services may inadvertently loose another 5 percent or so of the aging (on top of the current 15 percent) upon the public fisc. Thus, it is believed, much more research and testing of the waters for continuum-of-care design is needed for the aging than for the other long-term-care groups. Waiting to solve the design problems for the aging, under current Medicaid law, however, will hold up progress for the other groups. This will mean one or two strategic approaches for the states.

The states could do nothing more than currently in the community (such community services as have been built are mainly built on Title XX; and, therefore, given the closed end, they have already reached their zenith and will be under an inflationary squeeze—as they have been since 1972. This will result in another buildup of institutional and nursing home services. In the mental retardation area, this has apparently been happening in two ways: (1) A number of states that aggressively deinstitutionalized through the early and midseventies stopped doing so, and now seem to be aiming at upgrading all or nearly all remaining institutional beds, with no large reductions for the future (because of the combination of inflation and regulation-related cost increases, this will result in a large increase in costs to the federal government as well as the state). (2) A number of states have been using nursing homes (illegally) for reinstitutionalization of persons transferred out of state mental retardation institutions or coming out of the community during a time of closed admissions in the institutions; there are now between 100,000 and 175,000 such persons in nursing homes, most not receiving active treatment, in the MR/DD category alone. This flow into nursing homes can be expected to increase, so long as states cannot provide the program that MR/DD persons are supposed to have, such as day services, case management, and the like, under Medicaid. And, at the same time, HCFA continues not to enforce its policies on active treatment in ICF/MRs. (HCFA, it should be noted, has recently decided to enforce these policies but has not yet moved forcefully on the problem.)

On the other hand, the states could move into a "massive Medicaiding" of community services, using ICF/MRs and Medicaid-supported day services that are provided on the grounds of the community ICF/MRs (against all program theory of "best practice"), providing services more expensive than they need be, in order to satisfy current doctrine in some offices in HCFA about the "medical" nature of all Medicaid services. This will lead to a lack of the less expensive and more appropriate services that can be provided through supervised living, personal care, independent living, and developmental-program-oriented, independently administered day services. Although this is not as costly as the first strategy, it will be far more costly than need be. If it is possible to provide services by target group, together with the expanded and "rehabilitation-oriented" community services, then we can avoid state recourse to either of the possible strategies just detailed.

*Allow Six-Year Waivers of Social Security Act, Section 1115.*  Waivers could be provided for states wishing to develop complex continuum-of-care systems (three years, given time needed to gear up and interact with state budget cycles, is simply too short; the 1980 disability amendments of the SSA recognized this in their time-unlimited authority for demonstration projects).

### Provide New Information for Policy Purposes

Measures that could be taken include funding total-budget information systems for the following:

- MR/DD, through the Administration for Developmental Disabilities/OHD/DHHS;
- Chronically mentally ill, through NIMH/the Public Health Service/DHHS;

- Aging, through Administration on Aging/the Office of Human Development/DHHS;
- Child Welfare Services, through ACYF/OHD/HHS. (Cost: $1 million, each group, each of three years, to develop debugged models; $10 million thereafter, with 50 percent state share, for all four groups, with moderate scaling for population size.)

Funding for small research and demonstration studies related to specific long-term care policy question could also be increased.

Current long-term care research and demonstration funding tends to be concentrated on one set of questions: "channeling" for "aging" patients. There is a whole set of questions not addressed here that should be and whole target groups not addressed that should be: the mentally ill, the mentally retarded, the physically handicapped, and children in need of welfare protection.

### Increase Local Innovation and Control

The law should require that, in the case of law and regulation interpretation by federal officials, the interpretation that most clearly facilitates local innovation and control shall prevail. In addition, a percentage of each Social Security agency's salary and expense funding should be designated for use specifically for unification of formal grant requirements among programs and for specific program integration projects in the states. If not used specifically for these purposes, the money should lapse, and one-half of the lapsed amount should not be reappropriated.

Finally, study should be undertaken of DHHS individual agency finance management practices and audit agency promotion incentives, their effects upon audit practice and deferral and disallowance practices, and their effects on state and local agency operation. This is probably the least understood, but most effective area in squelching state and local innovation and control. What is clear is that the audit threat is the major weapon used by status-quo-guarding bureaucrats in discussions of change and innovation in programs. Because there are so few published rules of behavior in these areas, virtually anything can be alleged to be "liable to audit exception" and thus throttle further discussion. The audit threat has made Title XX, which should be a "program-oriented" program, an almost totally paper-compliance-oriented one (and this is directly traceable to the way the legislation was written). In other programs, the problems are different; one of them is that the audit program itself appears to give "brownie points" for amounts of money defined as exceptions. Yet these amounts are often clearly inflated beyond application of any reasonable rule; the final payback is negotiated and always much smaller. At the same time final paybacks are subject to much political haggling. Congressional oversight responsibilities would seem to dictate a series of Government Accounting Office studies in this area, to see how the system works for both audit and financial management people, and what changes should be made in law, in agency incentives and operations, so that the goal of improved state and local management becomes the clear operational goal of these agencies. Without clear days on this horizon, the other changes in law and regulation may only be tinkering, with respect to improving local innovation and control.

### Increase Consumer Choice

For the long-term care, the key issue of consumer choice would seem to be housing. Without adequate housing for the 600,000 persons needing to be deinstitutionalized or who will be coming out of the private sector into the public sector over the next six to eight years, there will be very few real choices for these people. Without such choices, the pressures will be on keeping state institution beds, increasing nursing home beds, and getting extra lengths of stay and extra admissions in short-term general hospitals. (About 12 percent of all patient days in New York State short-term hospital Medicaid payments are for patients diagnosed as mentally ill, about two-thirds of them are shuttling between hospitals and nursing homes as chronic brain syndrome and senile patients or shuttling between the two, with the other third being "true psychiatric" patients, according to some rough new statistics from the New York Department of Mental Health.) Programs providing integration of income maintenance, jobs and training, housing, supportive services, and medical services appear to cut these costs; the evaluation results of the Hennepin County Community Support Program support this conclusion. Most elements other than housing are being handled already by social agencies. In housing the need is for programs relatively free of red tape. The HUD Section 8 program provides this in markets where rental housing still exists. The HUD Section 202 program for new housing, however, does not help very much where it does not. A better approach would be revenue bond and general obligation bond programs through state housing agencies. A revenue bond exemption in tax law restrictions on these bonds for housing for the aging, mentally retarded and other developmentally disabled persons, the mentally ill, and the physically handicapped should be provided, with an interest subsidy on top of the exemption.

### Provide Incentives to Retrain Institution and New Management Personnel

Earmark the portion of authorized Title XX training funds not now appropriated ($63 million per year) for retraining of institutional personnel losing their jobs through deinstitutionalization and for training of developmental-programming/administrative managers of the network of small community facilities that must be developed on the model suggested by Travis Thompson, of the University of Minnesota (Thompson and Grabowksi, 1978), one of the most successful trainers of successful program personnel in the United States. This would assure that the money is used in a cost-effective way, for pursuing an important public policy goal.

## THE EFFECT OF NEW FEDERAL POLICIES

The ideas in this chapter were formulated before the budget proposals of the Reagan administration. Its specific legislative and policy recommendations were minimalist, suited more to the spirit of the Carter administration. The important question has become: Are the suggested principles usable in what is now a completely different political and fiscal environment?

The environment has changed in a number of ways. Where we had assumed that there would be a continuing open-ended Medicaid account, we now must assume some form of "floating cap," possibly related to inflation and to growth in the underlying population at risk. Where we had assumed a continued federal legislative and executive devotion to the use of fiscal and regulatory incentives as a way of influencing the behavior of state governments, providers, and consumers, we must now recognize that doctrine to be no longer valid. It has been sacrificed to a doctrine of "flexibility."

What this means practically is that the social services-oriented accounts (Title XX, Developmental Disabilities, Maternal and Child Health, NIMH programs) will be cut drastically. For example, the proposed 33 percent cut from federal fiscal year (FFY) 1981–82 will, with the addition of 12 percent inflation, result in a nearly 50 percent cut, in real terms, in funding for the social services in one year. Because the social services accounts have been the key federal supports of community-oriented services for the developmentally disabled and the mentally ill, with Title XX, for example, contributing about $500 million per year for community services for the developmentally disabled and $350 million per year for community services for the mentally ill, this will mean roughly a $375 million cutback in federal support in these areas in FFY 1982.

Major portions of these cutbacks could be repaired, using Medicaid funding, if Title XIX (Medicaid) were to remain open-ended. However, the administration, which has shown formidable strength so far in both House and Senate, has proposed a floating cap for Medicaid. The cap itself would work as follows: FFY 1982 Medicaid funding from the federal government would equal 105 percent of FFY 1981 funding (or an official early estimate of that funding); FFY 1983 funding would equal FFY 1982 funding, plus an amount equal to the "Gross National Product Deflator" (probably for the previous four quarters); and funding in future years would work the same way as in 1983. If the proposed cap is voted through by Congress, then the loss to the states from both social services and Medicaid cutbacks (in current dollars) would be about $28 billion over the 1982 through 1985 budget years (assuming 10 percent general inflation per year for those years). What the states would get in exchange would be enhanced "flexibility" in spending the money.

The increased flexibility in social services would not be worth much, since such funds are already programmatically quite flexible and since some of the major program restrictions in Title XX have also been written into the social service block grant. Some, but not all, of the accountability rules under Title XX would also be deleted, but their deletion would not mean much in cost savings, since most states already have adjusted to them (the "50 percent rule" under Title XX) for some years.

It is not yet clear what the approach to increased flexibility will be under Medicaid. There apparently are two positions being discussed within the administration. The first approach is essentially to leave the entire Medicaid program as it is for the moment, with structural reform coming later, and to provide a broad waiver authority somewhat like the Social Security Act's Section 1115 waiver authority (but without the research and demonstration components) to the secretary of DHHS. States could then come in with their own plans for running a Medicaid program. The second approach is to leave the "basic seven" services (hospital, physician, and so on) as they are now, but only for the categorically eligible populations, and to allow the states an almost total flexibility for the remainder of their programs—whether basic services for the medically needy or other services for any Medicaid-eligible group.

The flexibility in Medicaid, in whatever form it came, would be worth something to the states. This is especially true in continuum-of-care financing for the long-term care of the mentally ill and the developmentally disabled. It is probably true in continuum-of-care financing for the long-term care of the aged as well, but research is needed to clear up points about whether creating new kinds of supply (such as more normalized residential, home-care, and support programs) will create an additional demand for services beyond merely substituting for current higher cost services.

Accelerated deinstitutionalization of the mentally retarded and developmentally disabled, and the simultaneous development of community programs according to a continuum-of-care plan can be shown to be *strongly* desirable fiscally for a state whether the proposed cuts come or not.

That is,

- If there are no social services and Medicaid cuts, there is potential for large initial net savings to states, and later savings to the federal government, from a fast-track deinstitutionalization plan (when compared to historic trends in deinstitutionalization in the states).

- Large savings are still available if there are cuts in social services but not in Medicaid, so long as the state carries out a fast-track deinstitutionalization plan.

- Savings are no longer available at all in most states, or they are quite small in the early years, if they commit to a fast-track deinstitutionalization plan in the face of cuts in both social services and Medicaid.

Even if both accounts are cut, there are still strong fiscal incentives for the states. The major fiscal incentive is a gloomier one to be sure, since we would move from *an incentive to maximize federal funding* to *an incentive to minimize state net losses.* For example, one large northeastern state spent $504 million in state funds (expressed in 1985 dollars and not counting federal dollars) on its publicly supported MR/DD system (over the whole continuum of care) in 1980. If it succeeded in moving about 55 percent of its 1980 institutional population into community programs by 1985, its 1985 net state costs for the whole system would drop to $450 million—even with the proposed social services and Medicaid cuts. If, however, it "froze" the 1980 distribution of patients (the same numbers of patients in state institutions, nursing homes, community residences, and soon in 1985 as in 1980), the net state cost for 1985 for running the system would be about $580 million. This would not only be a large (15 percent) increase from the current level of state-dollar spending, it would be a very large increase (about $130 million per year by 1985) over the net state cost that would result from fast-track deinstitutionalization with continuum-of-care planning. We have similar results for four more of the six states where we have examined the question. In the sixth, there is now virtually no institutional system in the state at the present time (and, of course, far fewer savings accruing to a deinstitutionalization strategy).

Using continuum-of-care financing principles is thus extremely important for the states. For if they fall into the traditional fragmented funding approaches of the past, then any "designed in" strategic approach for cost control and cost containment falls victim to the "clash of interests" strategy, where hospital associations, nursing home associations, residential home operators, physicians, nurses, psychologists, social workers, therapists of all kinds, and advocacy groups press their individual claims on governors, legislatures, and bureaucracies. The results are eventually fiscally and programmatically disastrous since, as we observed in an earlier paper:

> the changes tend to be marginal, their wider effects unexamined, and their relationship to any general plan nil. Yet, such changes, as more and more of them come along, tend to define a new . . . policy for the state—one which grows as if guided by an invisible hand. Unfortunately, such invisible hands do not have the rationality that is vested in the historic invisible hand of clas-

sical economics, which (in theory) guides everything for the maximization of the economic welfare. Rather, the strategy of independent, incremental change provides each contradictory interest, in turn, an opportunity to get its piece of the program quietly installed. The contradictions of the public political scene are thus installed in the relatively non-public fiscal and bureaucratic operations of the human services system. The strategy, if pursued extensively, (without periodic purging) tends to produce a system that becomes immobilized in its own contradictions. (Copeland and Iversen, Note 1)

What we argue here is not for or against the proposed cuts. Rather, we argue that, if there are not cuts, fast-track deinstitutionalization with continuum-of-care planning and financing is fiscally extremely pleasant for states. If there are such cuts, then we would argue that the same strategy is necessary to avoid intense fiscal pain.

The proposed cuts provide more of an "open universe" for the states for dealing with their long-term-care systems. However, they do not provide any indication of strategic direction, program structure, fiscal incentives, information requirements for planning and operation, or, most important, a set of principles for allocation of the reduced, but more flexible, funding.

What they do is to put the onus on each individual state to plan its long-term-care systems rationally. What we have done in this chapter, we hope, in enumerating the legislative and policy changes proposed under the old order, is to provide a set of design principles that can give a state a coherent rhetoric of long-term care planning and financing under the new order.

## REFERENCES

Samuelson, R.J. *The economics of aging: A National Journal issues book*. Washington, D.C.: Government Research Corporation, October 28, 1978.
Thomas, T., and Grabowski, J. *Behavior modification of the mentally retarded*, vol. 2. New York: Oxford University Press, 1978.

## REFERENCE NOTES

1.   Copeland, W.C., and Iversen, I.A. *The deinstitutionalization problem*, part of DD Project of National Significance funding proposal, 1978.

# 5 MENTAL DISABILITIES SERVICE
## Maintenance of Public Accountability in a Privately Operated System

*Valerie J. Bradley*

During the 1960s Americans' notions of how and where publicly supported services for mentally disabled individuals should be provided changed dramatically. Shifts in ideology, a growing body of literature on the weaknesses of public institutions, and the advent of major federal funding programs available to private sector agencies helped change people's perceptions of the appropriate locus of responsibility for mental disabilities services. These factors combined to create a reaction against continued expansion of publicly provided services and the creation of purchase-of-service mechanisms aimed at maximizing the utilization of private sector resources.

Stimulating the shift in emphasis to the private sector was an increasing recognition among policymakers and professionals that large state institutions were by and large not fulfilling the multiple needs of their residents for active treatment, resocialization, and preparation for reentry into the community. Research regarding the capabilities of institutional residents increasingly showed that instead of getting better, long-stay residents in particular lost functioning as they became more "institutionalized" (Goffman, 1961). Moreover, institutions became the target of media exposés that highlighted the lack of adequate staffing and the substandard conditions in many state hospitals around the country. Among reformers in the sixties institutions became known as warehouses remote from local communities and housing individuals whom society wished to forget.

In devising alternatives to large public institutions, reformers turned to the private sector. At the time it seemed incongruous to build a new community-based system with the same personnel and administrative structure that had contributed to the inadequate conditions in institutions. Comparisons between private sector services, both proprietary and nonprofit, and publicly managed institutions inevitably led analysts to affirm the virtues of the former. Such virtues included efficient and economical management, flexibility of programming, capacity for innovation, variety and richness of service offerings, and the healthy dynamic of competition. The intensity of the contrasts between the public and private sector, as viewed by some observers, can be seen in the following quote from Whittington (1975):

> The greatest hidden cost [in the public sector] is the frequent inefficient use of manpower. . . . Public mental health agencies consider themselves fortunate if staff members spend 50% of their time in contact with or on behalf of patients. By contrast, a private program expects at least 70% of staff time in patient contact. In the public agency, much staff time is wasted in meetings of little value to patients, though often billed as inservice training. Most sessions are devoted to satisfying needs for stroking and reassurance. . . . The reason . . . lies in the basic professional and personal insecurity of staff members; they are deprived of adequate feedback as to whether they are doing a good job with their patients. (p. 24)

In addition to the desire to set a different tone for alternative community-based services, reformers also had strategic reasons for relying on private agencies. Given the need for community resources to divert individuals from institutions, it was much more expedient at the time to build on resources that already existed in the community than to initiate publicly operated programs from scratch. There was also a sense that many mentally disabled persons had for too long been shunted off to segregated public institutions and that any reform of the system should include access for such individuals to services previously available only to those who could afford them. California, in its reform of both the mental retardation and mental health systems, relied heavily on existing private sector agencies to begin the transition to the community. The rationale for the development of the state's private, nonprofit regional centers for mentally retarded persons, which contract with other private agencies to meet the specific needs of retarded individuals and their families, was in part based on survey findings that showed a significant unused capacity among private mental retardation programs (California State Assembly (CSA), 1965). All that was lacking to secure service expansion was the development of a purchase-of-service mechanism through which public funds could be channeled to existing caregivers.

The foundation selected for the expansion of community services for mentally ill persons in California was likewise community-based services—the bulk of which were in the private sector. The legislative report (CSA, 1967) that stimulated the mental health reform in the state made this emphasis explicit:

> The State will contract with local Mental Health Departments; local public and private clinics, hospitals, universities, and colleges, or other agencies to provide specific . . . services as set forth in legislation. Wherever possible, the State will contract with existing agencies now performing similar services. (p. 91)

The major, or at least the most direct, influence on the expansion of public funding of private sector agencies was perhaps the advent, in the sixties, of new federal financial incentives. Incentives took two forms: appropriation of funds under the Community Mental Health Centers Act for the development of specialized facilities for the mentally disabled and the development of reimbursement mechanisms for generic health services under Medicare and Medicaid. In the former instance, a conscious choice was made at the federal level to bypass state government and to offer funds directly to nonprofit private corporations. Though states were eligible as sponsors of community mental health centers (CMHCs), only a few states actually took advantage of the new funding (Oklahoma, Massachusetts, and Connecticut). The lack of a more direct connection between the community mental health centers and the administration of state and local mental health systems has, in many states, posed problems for those centers whose funds are now declining or terminating.

Medicare, enacted in the midsixties, made it possible for many states to transfer old and infirm residents of state hospitals into private nursing care in the community. Medicaid made it possible for many indigent individuals to secure mental health services in the community rather than in state institutions. Though Medicaid reimbursement was made available to residents of public mental retardation facilities (in skilled nursing and intermediate care units), reimbursement for individuals in mental hospitals was limited to those under 21 and over 65 years of age. Since the federal reimbursement under Medicaid was at least 50 percent—and higher in most states—the incentive to serve mentally ill persons in alternative private facilities in the community was significant.

The sixties was a period of changing expectations and attitudes regarding the care and treatment of mentally disabled persons. Many state and federal policies were set in motion that would, over the next several years, significantly change the form and content of services to mentally disabled individuals. The purpose of this chapter is to make these trends explicit, to show the ways in which these initial policies have driven the system of care, and to point out the ramifications of these trends. The discussion is not meant as a general critique of private sector services. In fact the argument presumes that without private sector participation, the goals of deinstitutionalization, normalization, and the least restrictive means of care would not be possible. The purpose of this chapter then is to explore the ramifications of continuation of current policies and to begin a dialogue regarding what the appropriate role of the public sector should be in the management and/or the direct provision of services to mentally disabled individuals.

## IMPLEMENTATION DURING THE 1970s

During the 1970s states began to carry out the policies of the 1960s through increased deinstitutionalization and explicit moves to divest themselves of some of the responsibility for the direct provision of services for mentally disabled persons. Several states passed community mental health statutes that established county, multicounty, or regional administrative units for the management of the burgeoning community-based system. Almost all of these designated units were given the capacity to contract with a range of private agencies for the provision of residential and support services.

As the investment in the community system expanded, the population in state institutions continued to decline. In some states, such as California, the community investment grew beyond the allocation to state institutions (Bradley, 1972). In that state, the decline in the investment in public facilities was accomplished in part by the closure of several institutions. Although the movement of funds out of public facilities into the community did not happen as dramatically in other states as it did in California, significant strides were made in the expansion of community resources. Former and potential institutional residents were diverted to a broad array of private sector programs including halfway houses, group homes, family care homes, and nursing homes.

Not all mentally disabled persons found their way into the community through the organized mental health system. Many who left institutions went into private board and care homes and for all intents and purposes were no longer visible to public or private mental health agencies. Whereas many of these individuals chose to disassociate themselves from the mental health system, others had little choice given their lack of resources and the inadequacy of case management mechanisms in local communities. Many of the board and care residences were not adequately governed by state certification and/or licensing provisions and reports increased regarding resident abuse and inadequate conditions. Several states have developed at least minimal certification standards for board and care residences, but the capacity of states and localities to monitor such facilities is still significantly limited.

During the seventies, additional federal incentives were developed that made it possible to expand the use of private sector facilities for mentally disabled individuals. The creation of the Supplemental Security Income (SSI) program raised income maintenance benefits and expanded eligibility among disabled persons in many states. SSI payments became the basic funding source for the support of many mentally disabled individuals in a variety of nonmedical residential arrangements. Since mentally disabled individuals are not eligible for full SSI benefits while residing in public institutions,[a] maintaining individuals in the community in private nonmedical facilities relieved pressure on limited state resources.

The advent of the Intermediate Care Facility for the Mentally Retarded (ICF/MR) provisions under the Medicaid program in 1974 made it possible for many states to use federal funds to develop specialized facilities for mentally retarded persons in the private sector. Although Medicaid funds had been generally available for nursing and medical services for mentally retarded persons, the more pro-

---

a. Under the original provisions of the SSI program, no publicly operated residential arrangements could receive SSI maintenance payments from their clients. These provisions changed as a result of the Keyes amendment, enacted in 1976, which exempts facilities with no more than sixteen beds.

grammatic and habilitative thrust of the new regulations made it possible for states to use ICF/MR funds to support more specialized and normalized living arrangements.

As more funds became available for the support of mentally disabled persons in private facilities, interest groups made up of various private providers began to develop at the state and federal level. During the seventies, multiple groups were initiated and expanded including associations of nursing homes, providers of children's services, board and care operators, private residential facilities, private psychiatric hospitals, group home operators, community mental health centers, and vocational rehabilitation providers. Such groups became a counterbalance in the state legislature and before Congress to the pressures generated by public employee unions and others interested in the perpetuation of publicly operated services. In fact the growth of private sector interest groups worked to the advantage of those who sought continued deinstitutionalization because of the coincidental interests of private constituencies and reformers in the expansion of alternative community-based services.

During the middle and late seventies, large corporate chains began to enter the field of services for mentally disabled persons. Initially such chains preferred to provide nursing care, but increasingly the large organizations have taken on the provision of small group care at multiple sites. Although the individual entrepreneur still makes up a significant portion of the provider community, the overall character of the private sector in many states has subtly begun to shift from single to multiple providers. It can be argued that the provision of services to mentally disabled persons may be more efficiently carried out by larger and better managed enterprises, it is worth noting this phenomenon and attempting to understand its ramifications for public policy and public accountability to mentally disabled individuals.

A review of the seventies shows the flowering of policies begun in the sixties. Contracting out for services became the norm in the community, the system of services for mentally disabled persons was significantly diversified, and the political power of private mental disabilities agencies increased. Further, the provision of care to mentally disabled persons became, in some quarters, a business, as reflected by the growth of large proprietary care providers. Though the trend toward deinstitutionalization was somewhat slowed by the end of the decade and many professionals began to reassess the importance of public institutions in the continuum of services for mentally disabled persons, the pressures to shift resources from public institutions to community alternatives are still strong.

It is important to pause, therefore, and reflect on the influences that have shaped the system to date and to investigate what role, if any, publicly operated services have in the system of community care for mentally disabled individuals—especially assuming the reduced presence of public institutions. It is also important to understand in what ways public managers can ensure the stability of private sector programs while maintaining flexibility in policymaking and general program design.

## RESIDUAL ISSUES

Continuation of the policies of the 1960s and 1970s—deinstitutionalization coupled with increased reliance on the private sector—will eventually result in a significant reduction of public involvement in the provision of services to mentally disabled individuals. Before this happens, it is important to review past policies and to explore potential modifications and readjustments that may be necessary to ensure a responsive system. In order to sort out the fundamental issues that should be addressed in any future policymaking, it is important to note some of the realities of the community-based system for mentally disabled individuals. In the absence of such an analysis, weaknesses in current planning, management, and capacity may overtake the important gains made in the past.

An important reality mentioned earlier is the change in the character of some of what is regarded as the private sector. Until lately the private sector in most states was comprised of voluntary agencies, including organizations spawned by entities such as associations for retarded citizens and long-standing charitable organizations. With the exception of nursing home enterprises, proprietary and nonprofit agencies were by and large small and limited to one or two facilities. With the growth of both state and federal allocations to community services larger organizations have been attracted to the marketplace. In the state of Pennsylvania, for instance, one large proprietary chain owns and operates 150 small group homes for mentally retarded individuals. In other states, large nursing home chains have developed multiple ICF/MRs housing a significant portion of the more disabled mentally retarded population.

The emergence of large chains into the provision of services for the mentally disabled individuals may also signal a similar consolidation of private sector services currently taking place in the health sector. Traditionally, nonprofit organizations have been a major provider of hospital services in this country. With the rapid escalation of health costs and the increasing administrative burdens placed on hospitals, many nonprofit hospitals have begun to flounder. In recent years, several such hospitals have been taken over by larger, seemingly more sophisticated and heavily capitalized, proprietary chains. Though such changes in auspices may not reflect any changes in patient services, they do reflect a distinct change in the character of hospital administration and the potential disappearance of the voluntary agency in the hospital business.

One of the factors that may contribute to a "consolidation" of private sector services in the area of mental disabilities is the precarious state of existing voluntary agencies and the difficulties encountered by small entrepreneurs entering the current marketplace. Voluntary agencies around the country have been increasingly squeezed financially by inflation and state reimbursement policies. Inflation has significantly increased the cost of credit (the lifeblood of many agencies) at the same time that state payment schedules have fallen further and further behind. The situation is complicated by the fact that some state and federal reimbursement policies disallow interest expense as a legitimate overhead item. In order to stay afloat, many voluntary agencies have gone to foundations in order to secure funding to cover severe cash flow problems (Baird, note 1). The problem became so acute in Massachusetts that a consortium of voluntary agencies and foundations pressured the state legislature into creating a revolving fund to speed state reimbursements.

A recent series of papers commissioned by the federal Office of Management and Budget entitled *Managing Federal Assistance in the 1980s* highlights many of the problems faced by voluntary and nonprofit agencies providing publicly reimbursed services. The problem areas identified include the inability of agencies to claim interest, complex overhead requirements, late state and federal payments, and the impact of confusing and conflicting legal requirements (U.S. Office of Management and Budget, 1979).

The problems for a new entrepreneur are even more onerous than those faced by a small provider who is already in business. Many state and federal programs do not provide prospective financing to offset the costs of initiating a service. With respect to residential programs, this would include such expenses as securing the site, making necessary rennovations, seeking waivers and zoning variances, and recruiting and training staff. Many small providers do not have the capital to make such initial investments even though the state may allow for the amortization of such expenditures through the reimbursement rate. Complex eligibility criteria also dissuade many small entrepreneurs from entering the market. Interviews with potential providers, conducted in preparation of a case study of the Connecticut mental retardation system, for instance, clearly indicated the difficulty such providers have in meeting the complex state and federal requirements and their frustration with the process (Lewin et al., 1977).

If it is true that many voluntary agencies may not be capable of weathering inflationary and cash flow pressures, that fewer and fewer small providers are capable of entering the system, and that larger chains with investment capital have a distinct advantage in the market, then power in the private sector will be increasingly centralized among fewer and fewer providers. As control among a small group of large corporate entities increases, the power of the state and federal government to influence service directions and priorities decreases. This lack of diversity among private providers may be especially problematic in smaller states where one or two providers can essentially control a significant sector of the service system. For example, during the late seventies, a large nursing home chain made a proposal to a small western state to develop nursing care and ICF/MR beds for deinstitutionalized residents of the state's institution for mentally retarded persons. Had the state accepted the proposal, the corporation would have virtually controlled almost all of the nursing care beds for mentally retarded persons in the state. Although there is every reason to believe that the nursing home chain would have provided adequate care to their clients, the state's ability to redirect resources and to alter program directions would have been substantially hampered. Instead, the state chose to limit the size of ICF/MR facilities and to encourage a more pluralistic provider community.

The decentralization of services for mentally disabled persons has also placed significant burdens on state mental disabilities agencies—many of which are not fully equipped to do adequate monitoring and quality assurance. Though many state legislatures have provided funding for the support of community-based services, they have not been as generous in their support of expanded state resources to guarantee public oversight of contract services. The growth of case management in many communities has expanded the ability of mental disabilities agencies to ensure adequate services, but many case managers are burdened by enormous caseloads that limit their ability to make frequent checks on the circumstances of their clients.

The ability of the state mental disabilities agency to ensure the quality of services provided in the community is further complicated by the fact that, in many states, the program agency has little or no authority over licensing and certification of private mental disabilities agencies. This is true with respect to both nonmedical residential programs and Medicaid-funded agencies serving mentally disabled persons. In some states, licensing and Medicaid certification are vested in the state department of health, which is administratively separate from the mental health and/or mental retardation agency. Though some mental disabilities administrators may be able to influence licensing and certification standards, they have little responsibility for on-site surveys and the program qualifications of licensing and survey staff.

The rapidly increasing use of the ICF/MR provisions of Medicaid to expand community residential services for mentally retarded persons also raises questions regarding the future ability of states to conduct effective monitoring of private sector resources. The problem is exemplified by Pennsylvania's current plan to build on Medicaid funding for the future expansion of community living arrangements in that state. Currently Pennsylvania's mental disabilities system is managed at the local level by county administrators who in turn contract with a range of private agencies to meet the needs of their mentally disabled citizens. By virtue of the contract, county administrators are able to monitor the provision of services and to influence the types of clients who are served by local agencies.

New or current agencies wishing to take advantage of Pennsylvania's plan to use Title XIX for residential programs will be certified by the state's department of health and licensed by the Pennsylvania Department of Public Welfare. As a result, newly certified ICF/MR facilities will be technically outside the purview of the county mental health and mental retardation agency. Thus the county administrator loses the previous quality assurance and placement powers he had under the contractual arrangement (Human Services Research Institute, 1980). Though the Pennsylvania Office of Mental Retardation in Pennsylvania is currently addressing this problem, it does point out the potential problems involved in ICF/MR conversions in other states where the groundwork has not been laid ahead of time.

As deinstitutionalization continues, states are contemplating the move of more disabled individuals into the community. Because of the complexity of the problems of such individuals, the inadequate payment levels available for their support and the lack of adequate backup resources in many states, private agencies have been reluctant to serve the most disabled segments of the mentally disabled population. Given that these are the individuals most in need of services, it would seem important, if continued deinstitutionalization is a feasible goal, for state and federal policymakers to determine the appropriate level of payment and locus of responsibility for the provision of services to this clientele.

As deinstitutionalization continues, there is evidence of increasing concern among parents in particular regarding the stability of community-based agencies. While mentally disabled persons were in institutions families were assured that the state had a permanent and tangible commitment to provide services. Once institutional residents are moved to the community, the commitment of the state is perceived by some parents to be less concrete. Further, there is increasing concern regarding the longevity of community residential arrangements, especially among parents of more severely disabled individuals. They question whether or not providers will still be in business in ten or twenty years when parents may no longer be around to protect the interests of their disabled grown child.

All of these issues have major ramifications for the future development of public mental disabilities policy. The key is to develop a series of strategies that maximize accountability while at the same time maintaining the stability and programmatic viability of the community-based system. It is not an easy task but surely one that is worth the investment. Unless these issues are addressed, the current diversity and richness of the provider community may be jeopardized and the well-being and security of more disabled individuals may be in question.

## PROPOSALS FOR THE FUTURE

The final portion of this chapter delineates some of the steps to be taken to meet the challenges of a decentralized service system and to ensure the provision of responsive services to mentally disabled individuals.

## Reexamination of Public Provision of Services

Reviewing policy on mental disabilities of the past two decades shows a clear intention on the part of policymakers to shift the locus of responsibility for services to the private sector and away from the public provision of services. This policy has served the system well and has made it possible to develop a range of community-based services in an expeditious fashion. However, given the more disabled nature of the residual population in public institutions and the plans for continued deinstitutionalization, it may be important to reinspect conventional wisdom regarding the public provision of services—in this instance, in the community. Several pros and cons should be considered:

### Pros

- Public operation of community living arrangements would enhance the stability and accountability of such residential programs.
- The availability of publicly operated residences might serve to allay the fears of many families regarding deinstitutionalization.
- The development of publicly operated residences would provide resources for more severely disabled individuals who currently are being only minimally served in the private sector.
- The creation of publicly operated facilities would to some extent counter the opposition of public employee unions to the expansion of community-based services.

### Cons

- In some states, the development of publicly operated residences in the community would create differential pay scales between staff of state-operated facilities and personnel employed by private facilities currently under contract with the state.

- The development of publicly operated residences in the community would require retraining of some more traditionally oriented state institutional employees.

- Public operation of small residential facilities would involve numerous management problems, including the necessity for central purchasing, the development of new job descriptions, the refinement of current shift requirements, and so forth.

- The development of publicly operated residences at the local level might, in some states, interfere with the power and authority of local mental disabilities administrators to manage the local system.

Obviously, the ultimate resolution of the issue of public provision of services will depend on individual states' circumstances and political and administrative traditions. The issue should, however, be assessed carefully before the next phase of deinstitutionalization takes place.

### Profit vs. Nonprofit

Although some states have developed distinct policies with respect to purchase of services from profit versus not-for-profit agencies, other states have merely allowed the system to grow without establishing any basic principles. No value judgment is implied in this recommendation, but it does seem important that policymakers come to grips with some fundamental issues:

- Is the profit incentive necessary to ensure resource development and capital investment?

- Is there any fundamental difference between the outcomes of for-profit and not-for-profit services?

- Do current state policies discriminate against a particular organizational arrangement? Is this appropriate?

- Is there a viable way of controlling profit taking in the field of mental disabilities? Is it desirable?

Again, each state will make policy decisions based on its own individual needs, but the airing of these issues is important to any systematic analysis of purchase of service policies.

## Options for Ensuring Diversity and Accountability

States should consider how much of the market can or should be controlled by one provider and what the ramifications are over time of allowing one corporate entity to develop a monopoly. (The State of Michigan currently limits the number of beds that any single corporate entity can operate within the mental retardation system.)

States should consider a variety of means for ensuring the stability of private sector residential programs both by maintaining adequate levels of reimbursement and developing contingency plans for the discontinuation of private sector residential services. Michigan handles this problem by maintaining ownership of the physical facility in which the residential program is housed and contracts with nonprofit agencies for program and staff support. In this way, if a program goes out of business, state staff can manage the program on a temporary basis thus eliminating the need to dislocate the clients.

## Multiple Monitoring Mechanisms

Given the scarce resources available to states to monitor the multiplicity of decentralized services for mentally disabled persons, policy planners should explore the creation of a hierarchy of monitoring and quality assurance mechanisms. Less costly forms of monitoring at the local level such as citizen or lay evaluations and case management should be included in any analysis. States should assess the information needed for quality assurance at all levels of the system and should pay special attention to the ways in which individual client circumstances can be monitored.

## Protections for the Small Entrepreneur

In order to maximize the participation of small providers and to ensure the stability of those currently providing services to the mentally disabled, states should analyze a variety of aspects in their current contracting and purchase of service policies:

- Do current reimbursement schedules jeopardize the cash flow status of small agencies?

- Are current rate structures adequate to meet the actual costs of small agencies?

- Do overhead policies exclude interest and other legitimate costs of doing business?

- Is "seed money" or "up-front" financing available to the small provider wishing to provide a new service in the mental disabilities market?

- Are provider eligibility requirements so complex that small providers are incapable of completing the paperwork?

- Is technical assistance available at the state and local level to help potential providers through the maze of requirements, sign-offs, waivers, and so forth?

In designing ways of attracting small entrepreneurs and stabilizing those currently providing services, policymakers must also be concerned with the administrative viability of specific programs. It may be the case that some small agencies do not have the requisite management ability to ensure the efficient provision of services. This recommendation does not, therefore, imply that small providers should be supported at all costs, but rather that obvious and unreasonable constraints to their operation be removed.

### Involvement in Licensure and Certification

In order to maximize programmatic input into existing licensing and certification standards applicable to mental disabilities agencies, states should explore ways of involving state mental disabilities staff in the preparation and/or refinement of such regulations.

### ICF/MR Conversions

As part of any plans for the development of ICF/MR facilities in the community, states should include provisions that link such facilities to the ongoing mental disabilities system. Such mechanisms might include case management for residents of such facilities, participation of mental disabilities staff in certification and surveys required under Medicaid, inclusion of mental disabilities staff on utilization review groups, and formal linkages between ICF/MR facilities and local mental disabilities units.

## Conclusion

There are many ways of ensuring public accountability in the provision of services to mentally disabled persons. The danger is that continued pursuit of the policies of the 1960s and 1970s without a closer look at the current realities and future ramifications may result in a shift in the locus of control over mental disabilities services. Without some more comprehensive plan and analysis, states may become nothing more than funding conduits with very little leverage to alter priorities and shape the system.

## REFERENCES

Bradley, Valerie J. California moves rapidly to community-centered mental health programs under 1967–68 legislation. *California Journal*, June–July 1972, 185.

California State Assembly, Subcommittee on Mental Health Services. *A redefinition of state responsibility for the mentally retarded*, Sacramento, 1965.

California State Assembly, Subcommittee on Mental Health Services. *The dilemma of mental commitments.* Sacramento, 1967, p. 91.

Goffman, Erving. *Asylums.* Garden City, N.Y.: Anchor Books, 1961.

Human Services Research Institute. *Historical overview II.* Washington, D.C.: U.S. Department of Health and Human Services, December 1980. (Part of the U.S. Department of Health and Human Services five-year longitudinal study of the *Halderman v. Pennhurst State School and Hospital* case.)

Lewin and Associates and Human Services Research Institute, *Deinstitutionalization of mentally retarded and other developmentally disabled persons: The experience in five states.* Washington, D.C., 1977.

U.S. Office of Management and Budget. *Managing federal assistance in the 1980s*, Volume G: *Recipient Related Issues*, Washington, D.C., August, 1979.

Whittington, H.G. A case for private enterprise in mental health. *Administration in Mental Health*, Spring 1975, p. 24.

## REFERENCE NOTE

1. Baird, Douglas. *Institutionalizing deinstitutionalization.* Unpublished paper presented at the National Council on Foundations Conference. Dallas, Texas: 1980.

# 6 MENTAL DISABILITY
## The Role of the Family

*Robert M. Moroney*

Advocates for the mentally disabled have important stories to share, and how the story is told, the story teller's ability to make the tale interesting, even compelling, is often as important as the message itself. As advocates, we often find ourselves competing with one another to tell the best story, not for personal satisfaction, but to gain support for our respective positions.

Advocates for the chronically mentally disabled in general are also advocates for specific policies, services, and target populations. Practitioners, analysts, and planners are much more effective in their jobs when they take an advocacy position, identifying with and sensitive to the needs of specific population groups. Unlike the professional who appears detached and objective, the professional who is committed can argue convincingly for more sensitive and meaningful policies and services. Unfortunately this entails the danger that the efforts of advocates will become fragmented and divisive and in the long run, all mentally disabled persons will lose. I witnessed this phenomenon in 1977 when I was a member of a task force connected with the President's Commission on Mental Health. During a three-

This chapter draws heavily on R. Moroney, *Families, social services and social policy: The issue of shared responsibility*, ADM-80-846, Washington, D.C.: U.S. Government Printing Office, 1980, and R. Moroney, *The family and the state: Considerations for social policy*, New York: Longman, 1976.

209

day meeting, a number of professionals discussed the needs of American families and eventually produced a series of recommendations to the commission. Each had been asked to present for discussion a paper on a particular subgroup of families. Unintentionally each of us became advocates for "our" families and attempted to demonstrate that their needs were, in fact, the most important. But whose needs are the greatest? Is it the single-parent family, families with teenagers who become pregnant, families caring for the handicapped, American Indian families, black families? All of these and other categories of families are at risk, but is it inevitable that, in assisting one group we do so at the expense of others?

We would like to believe that priorities and other resource allocation decisions are made rationally and fairly. We would like to believe that the criteria used by those responsible for making these decisions are reasonable, clearly thought through, and likely to be agreed upon by most people, consumers as well as providers. In practice, however, neither the policymakers nor the professionals concerned with services for the disabled are this rational. For example, families with severely handicapped children find themselves competing for these resources with families caring for the frail elderly. Even among families caring for handicapped children we find parents and professionals who are advocates for specific groups of children—the mentally retarded child, the autistic child, the child with a physical disability. This competition is compounded by the fact that those interested in developing support services for parents are forced to compete with those attempting to upgrade the quality of care in institutions. Each of these concerns is valid and all have a legitimate claim on society's resources, yet decisions as to where resources should go seem to be grounded more in a belief in social Darwinism—survival of the strongest—than on rationality.

If agencies find themselves competing for these resources today, what might we expect for the future? In periods of retrenchment agencies dealing with some groups of handicapped persons may find themselves at a distinct disadvantage, perhaps because their numbers are small relative to other groups or because certain disabilities attract less attention than others or because some groups of the disabled and their families are less well organized for lobbying than others. One can imagine an extreme scenario with advocates for different groups vying with each other to prove that some disabilities are more important than others, that some handicapped persons are more worthy than others. It may be argued, for example, that children should be given priority over the elderly since their lives are just beginning; that the blind or mentally retarded should be favored over the alcoholic since they themselves were not responsible for their disability; that adults should receive disproportional amounts of resources since they contribute to overall economic growth by working while children and the elderly are basically consumers. Although each group is sincere and rational in what they do, the enemy becomes "other disabled" and survival is achieved only at the expense of others.

However disturbing and perhaps debatable, this overview, historically two kinds of criteria have been introduced in establishing priorities for the allocation of resources. The first is the notion of "worthy pool," a notion deeply embedded in long-standing Poor Law tradition. The influence of criterion should not be underestimated, for it has had a significant effect on decisionmaking, especially in the more enlightened period of the modern Welfare State. The worthy poor— usually the elderly, the handicapped, and children—historically were assisted because they were considered dependent through no fault of their own. All others were held responsible for their condition, and it was considered that there was something deficient in their moral makeup.

However, since the 1950s another criterion has become the basis for setting priorities: the human investment or human capital perspective. Using cost/benefit and cost-effectiveness approaches, decisions are made on the basis of expected return for the investment. Programs are compared in terms of the return (economic) for each dollar spent. The rationale is simple and in keeping with certain basic American values and the bottom line is easy to measure: Did people as a result of the program become independent, enter or return to the labor force, pay taxes and contribute to overall economic growth? This criterion is not totally congruent with the first criterion (worthiness versus nonworthiness), and some of the people with whom we are concerned, such as severely mentally retarded persons, receive a lower priority under the second criterion. Furthermore, in times of economic retrenchment the human investment criterion becomes most important.

Most of this book deals with institutional services for the chronically mentally disabled, services for people who often have no immediate family or whose family is unable or unwilling to provide care. Many recommendations on financing, professional roles, management of institutional and community-based care are offered. But an agenda that concerns cost containment, efficiency, and a more effective mental health system would be incomplete without a discussion of the role of families of the mentally disabled, an issue that is usually almost ignored. It is an unhappy truth that social problems increase during fiscally troubled times, and more rather than fewer programs are needed. There is a need for vision and new initiatives in periods of retrenchment. For the mentally disabled, their families can be and often are capable caregivers, and national policy should help alleviate the stress and strain they are bound to experience in that capacity rather than substituting services provided outside the home.

## SOCIAL POLICIES AND FAMILY CARE

Since the 1930s the State has assumed that it has the responsibility to meet, either directly or indirectly, the income, employment, housing, and medical care needs of its citizens. In a sense it guarantees their physical and social well-being. This principle has been upheld through the years, but there has been little consensus as to which specific types of policies best serve the goal of promoting welfare or which interventions are most appropriate in achieving this goal. In fact, there has been continuous and often bitter debate on these issues. The disagreement can be reduced to a number of fundamental questions: Should services be provided as a right or only made available to individuals and families when they demonstrate their inability, usually financial, to meet their basic needs? Should benefits be provided to the total population or restricted to specific target groups, usually defined as "at risk"? Should the State develop mechanisms to continuously improve and promote the quality of life, or should it restrict its activity to guaranteeing some agreed upon minimum level of welfare, a floor below which no one is allowed to fall? Should it actively seek to prevent or minimize stressful situations both environmental and personal, or should it react to problems and crises as they arise? On one level these questions are shaped by financial considerations, on another by disagreements on basic values. Arguments are offered that support the thesis that the country can afford only so much social welfare. Resources are limited and need to be given to those with the greatest need. Selective provision rather than universal coverage is viewed as more effective and less costly. In fact, selective provision is more likely to result in more services and higher levels of benefits for those truly in need and are not "wasted" on those individuals and families who can manage on their own. Finally, by introducing means testing or other criteria for eligibility determination, potentially excessive demand or utilization is minimized and the state will indirectly encourage individual initiative and responsibility. This position is countered with the argument that a residual approach, one that basically reacts to crises or problems after they have occurred, is shortsighted and that present economies might result in tremendous future demands. Furthermore, policies and services developed from this stance tend to stigmatize recipients, segregate them from the mainstream of life, and strengthen an already fragmented service delivery system.

The underlying issue is the relationship between families and the State—more specifically, the appropriateness of governmental intervention in family life. Under what conditions is intervention appropriate? For what purposes? In which areas of family life? What functions of care are appropriate for the family to carry out? What should they be required to do? What should be shared by both?

These questions are raised within a framework of a number of key assumptions. The most basic is that the structure of the Welfare State has been shaped by a number of beliefs concerning the responsibilities families are expected to carry for the care of the socially dependent and a set of conditions under which this responsibility is to be shared or taken over by society. Admittedly this framework assumes that both the family and the State have responsibility for the provision of care to dependent members. The legitimacy of this general proposition is rarely contested. Serious problems and disagreements emerge, however, when attempts are made to translate the idea of shared responsibility into specific social policies and programs, for then it becomes necessary to define which functions are appropriate to each. What does sharing mean in real terms, and what is to be shared? What do families want the state to provide, and conversely, how does the State view the family?

There seems to have been agreement that society, through the State, had the right and responsibility to step in when individuals could no longer meet their own needs and did not have resources to fall back on. As early as the seventeenth century, the poor law made provision for widows with children through its outdoor relief policy. Children could be and were removed from their families and apprenticed if the State felt the family environment was not suitable. Today this principle has been interpreted to cover the State's right to intervene in a family situation where a child has been or is in danger of being abused or neglected. The child is accepted by society as an individual with certain rights and that one of these is protection from physical harm. Furthermore, few today would feel the State interferes with individual privacy when it removes an isolated elderly person to a nursing home when he or she is unable to meet basic survival needs. To the contrary, people are shocked and angry when they hear of an elderly person starving or freezing to death unattended. The emphasis in these situations is on the need to protect the individual who might harm himself or others or be harmed. In such clearcut cases the State provides a substitute family by providing for some basic survival needs.

Over time the State has also assumed a degree of responsibility in less extreme situations where it is thought that families or individuals are unable to cope adequately. In practice, each generation appears to define what form of intervention is appropriate and under what conditions. This does not mean that each generation discards past policies and develops their own. The process has been incremental, characterized more by marginal adjustments than by radical change. Examples of these are the numerous income maintenance, food stamp, manpower, and educational programs. Intervention usually took place after a crisis or breakdown, whether individual or structural. Whereas in the earlier period of the poor law, services were made available only as a last resort, forcing families to admit to pathology or "family bankruptcy," the current role of the State is still seen as marginal though not as repressive or personally demeaning. Legislation by and large still sees social welfare as a system concerned with a relatively small proportion of the population, a residual group unable or unwilling to meet their own needs. In general, then, the State has been reluctant to intervene if that intervention in any way was perceived to interfere with the family's rights and responsibilities for self-determination.

This residual approach, consistent with earlier social philosophies of laissez-faire and social Darwinism, is gradually becoming balanced with the belief that society, especially as represented by government, should assume more direct responsibility for assuring that basic social and economic needs be met. Incorporating many of the earlier poor law policies, this evolution has produced a number of uncertainties, however, and the borderline between society assuming increased responsibilities through its social welfare institutions and the family retaining appropriate functions has become less clear.

## ARE FAMILIES CAPABLE OF GIVING CARE?

Large numbers of Americans are convinced that significant changes in the family have occurred. The family is viewed as a social institution under attack, one that has been weakened over the preceding decades, one that is in danger of annihilation. This deterioration is in turn the reason why modern families are unable or unwilling to carry out functions that have historically been their responsibility. It is further charged that those functions, which include child care and the care of the handicapped and ill, are being transferred to extrafamilial institutions—the social welfare system. We hear complaints that parents are being shunted off to nursing homes or retirement homes by their adult children and handicapped children to institutions by their parents. More and more people, including elected officials, are arguing that government must find ways to restore the family to its earlier position of strength, to reverse the trend. To do so, it is suggested, would be in the best interest of society and the American family. Implicit in this position is the belief that families should care for their dependent members, especially the handicapped, and that families in the past were more caring and responsible.

This concern is not new. For example, the issue of family responsibility for the care of dependent persons, including children, the handicapped, and the elderly, has been the subject of continuous debate over the past 350 years. Most social welfare programs have been developed on the premise that the family constituted the first line of responsibility when individuals had their self-maintaining capacities impaired or threatened. It was further expected that families would support these persons until the situation became overwhelming and then, and only then would society, either through the public or private sector, intervene.

This approach has been based on the principle that family life is and should be a private matter, an area upon which the state should not encroach. The family was and is viewed as the last sanctuary to which individuals could retreat and as a fragile institution in need of protection. The appropriate role of the state, then, was to develop policies that would protect and strengthen families. More often than not this has resulted in intervention only when absolutely necessary. What was "necessary" was never clear and was subject to various interpretations.

If this shift of responsibility is taking place, if families today are increasingly giving up the caring function, and if the state is being looked upon as the primary source of social care for handicapped persons, such a trend has serious economic and social implications. How much social care can the state afford to provide? To what form of society would we be moving?

For many people there is little question about this shifting of responsibility. It exists. Policymakers, planners, and administrators point to the increased demand for social services and the mushrooming of public and private expenditures for social welfare programs. Human services professionals who have direct contact with families—such as physicians, nurses, social workers, and therapists—conclude the same from their growing caseloads, especially the numbers of families who are seeking institutional care for their aged parents or handicapped children.

Some argue that this shift is related to a larger evolutionary process in which the nature of the family itself is changing. In its emerging form, characterized as more isolated than the extended family of the nineteenth and eighteenth centuries, the family as structured cannot function effectively as caregivers. Society, then, must respond by changing its perception of the caring function, and in doing so will of necessity expand the role of the Welfare State. This position begins with the notion of a weakened family system.

Others would argue that families may be less able or willing to provide care but see different causes. Family structure may be changing, but the major reason for families giving up their responsibility is related to how the Welfare State has been organized. Few services are available to support families. In fact, it is argued that services are designed to substitute for families.

A third position argues that in its evolution and expansion, the Welfare State itself has adversely affected the family's willingness to provide social care. Intentionally or not a growing Welfare State has weakened the family. By providing increased amounts of social welfare services, it has changed people's expectations. Families are merely responding to policies that they interpret as encouragement or even pressure to transfer the caring function. In this sense, the State presents itself as a more effective institution.

From the foregoing discussion a number of "facts" emerge. First, Americans are concerned about the health of the family. They are convinced that it has been weakened and that this weakness has resulted in families divesting themselves of the care for their handicapped members. Second, people not only believe that this is happening, they are equally certain they know why it has happened and what should be done about it. Solutions range from expansion of the Welfare State, to restructuring the social welfare system, to dismantling the Welfare State through gradual retrenchment. Third, and most important, most of these beliefs, rationales, and recommendations are not based on a systematic analysis of relevant data. They are often based on values or ideology and all too easily drift into an abstract debate about social ideals. Each group "knows" what is good, what should be done.

The remainder of this chapter will examine the evidence with a view to clarifying this issue of family and state responsibility in the care of the handicapped. It is organized around three major topics. First, what do we know about the handicapped and families caring for handicapped persons. Are families giving up this function, as charged? If not, are they capable caregivers? Second, how does the state respond to the needs of the handicapped and their families? What are our current policies? Under what conditions are services provided? In the final section I will attempt to identify policies that might be more responsive to families caring for the handicapped with special attention given to those with severely mentally retarded children.

## FAMILY CARE OF SEVERELY RETARDED PERSONS

The prevalence of severe mental retardation (IQ 0–50) shown in Table 6–1 is drawn from the studies of Tizard (1974) and Kushlick (1964). The peak prevalence rate is estimated at 3.6 per thousand persons aged 15 to 19. This prevalence rate is probably close to the true prevalence rate for all age groups up to 15 in so far as severe

Table 6-1.  Estimated Prevalence of Severe Mental Retardation (000).[a]

| Year | Under 15 | 15 and Over | Total |
|------|----------|-------------|-------|
| 1950 | 146 | 243 | 389 |
| 1960 | 200 | 271 | 471 |
| 1970 | 208 | 320 | 528 |
| 1980 | 184 | 377 | 561 |
| 1990 | 209 | 411 | 620 |
| 2000 | 211 | 449 | 660 |

a. The rates used were: for the population under 15 years of age, 3.6 per 1,000; for the population over 14, 2.2 per 1,000 giving a total prevalence rate of 2.5 per 1,000.

Sources: Population figures for 1950–2000 were derived from U.S. Department of Commerce, Washington, D.C.: Social Indicators 1976, U.S. Government Printing Office, December 1977, p. 22.

retardation is almost always present from birth or early infancy (Tizard, 1972). Given these rates, it can be estimated that there will be 561,000 severely retarded persons in the United States by 1980. Over 180,000 will be severely retarded children.

The projections for the next twenty years are based on extremely conservative assumptions. They begin with the position that the prevalence among children is not increasing substantially and that the possibilities of preventing severe retardation are limited, given current knowledge. The projections further assume that the ratio of children to adults will remain the same, 1:2, although, as many more severely retarded children now are surviving to adult life, the number of adult retardates is increasing. Therefore the rate of 2.2 per 1,000 for the population over 14 years of age will possibly be higher. Regardless, the figures are useful, especially for the younger age group and offer reasonable estimates for planning future services.

Severe retardation usually brings with it a range of physical disorders such as epilepsy and visual, hearing, and speech defects. Abramowicz and Richardson (1975) found that approximately one-half of all severely retarded persons have at least one additional handicap and that one in four have multiple associated handicaps. Their findings are supported by other studies (Conroy and Derr, 1971; Tizard and Grad, 1961). Table 6-2 gives estimates of type and degree of physical and behavior difficulties associated with severe retardation.

One in five of all severely retarded persons needs assistance in personal care functions such as feeding, washing, dressing; one in eight

**Table 6-2.** Incapacity Associated with Severe Mental Retardation, Percentages.

| Incapacity | Under 15 | 15 and Over | Total |
|---|---|---|---|
| Nonambulant | 24.06 | 6.23 | 11.45 |
| Behavior difficulties requiring constant supervision | 14.06 | 11.23 | 12.06 |
| Severely incontinent | 12.55 | 5.20 | 7.34 |
| Needing assistance to feed, wash, and dress | 28.33 | 15.49 | 19.25 |
| No physical handicap or severe behavior difficulties | 21.00 | 61.85 | 49.90 |
| Total | 100.00 | 100.00 | 100.00 |

*Source*: Adapted from *Better Services for the Mentally Handicapped*, Cmnd 4683, HMSO, 1971, p. 6, Table 1.

had severe behavioral problems, and one in fourteen was severely incontinent. With the exception of behavior problems, those under 15 years of age are more likely to have associated handicaps. Children were twice as likely to be incontinent and need assistance in personal care functions and four times more likely to be nonambulant. Eighty percent of the severely mentally retarded children were likely to have a physical or behavior problem compared to 40 percent of the severely retarded adults.

Based on the prevalence rate of 3.6 per 1,000 for this age group, over 44,000 severely mentally retarded children are not ambulant, 52,000 need assistance in feeding, washing, and dressing, 23,000 are severely incontinent, and almost 26,000 have severe behavioral problems.

Severe mental retardation is not, then, just a measurement of the intelligence level of an individual. For children it means that someone will have to provide care and supervision over and above what "normal" children require. This decision to maintain the child in the family setting seriously affects the family life of the other members. The trends regarding institutionalization of severely mentally retarded persons over two decades are shown in Table 6-3.

Table 6–3. Institutionalized and Noninstitutionalized Severely Mentally Retarded.

| | Estimated Number of Severely Mentally Retarded | Resident Population in Mental Retardation Institutions | Estimated Number of Severely Mentally Retarded in Institutions | Percentage Not in Mental Retardation Institutions |
|---|---|---|---|---|
| 1950 | | | | |
| Under 15 | 146,000 | 25,845 | 23,260 | 84.07 |
| 15 and over | 243,000 | 108,408 | 97,567 | 59.85 |
| | | | | (68.94) |
| 1960 | | | | |
| Under 15 | 200,000 | 46,269 | 41,642 | 79.18 |
| 15 and over | 271,000 | 128,458 | 115,612 | 57.34 |
| | | | | (66.61) |
| 1970 | | | | |
| Under 15 | 208,000 | 48,141 | 43,327 | 79.17 |
| 15 and over | 320,000 | 153,851 | 138,466 | 56.73 |
| | | | | (65.57) |

Eight of every ten severely retarded children and slightly more than two of every three of all ages are not in institutions, percentages that have remained fairly constant since 1950. Not all of these are being cared for by their families. A number may be in foster care, nursing homes, boarding homes, hostels, or other facilities. Although it is impossible to determine the numbers involved, it is fair to estimate that, at least for children, most live with their families if they are not institutional residents. This suggests that more than 165,000 severely retarded children will be living with their parents or other relatives in 1980.

Recent surveys of values and beliefs associated with family life, marriage, expectations, and roles of adults would argue against "family care." It is demanding, disruptive, and requires family members, especially the mother, to make major adjustments to family life. Although there are alternatives, such as nursing homes and institutions for the mentally retarded, most families apparently choose to provide care, often for long periods.

However, there have been slight shifts in institutional trends. The data are inconclusive at this time and the long-term pattern still unknown, yet it is clear that once a placement is made, it usually means long-term care. There is also some evidence to suggest that families who are not provided support are less willing to take handicapped members back into their homes after an admission to an acute care facility (Morris et al., 1976; Beggs and Blekner, 1970; Lowther and Williamson, 1966).

The literature documents the pressures and strains caring for the disabled families experience. Not all families are experiencing all of these stresses, but all of these families are "at risk" in that statistically they are more likely than families without handicapped members to have problems. There are significant commonalities in the types of strains among these families. In fact, they are probably common to families providing care to all of the physically handicapped. In turn, these pressures can be translated into the services that families could benefit from. They include:

- Additional financial costs (Sultz et al., 1972; Aldrich et al., 1971; Holt, 1958; Dunlap, 1976)
- Stigma (Schonell and Watts, 1956; Kershaw, 1965; Gottleib, 1975)

- Time consumed in personal care, such as feeding, washing, dressing (Aldrich et al., 1971; Bayley, 1973)

- Difficulty with physical management, e.g., lifting, ambulation (Sainsbury and Grad, 1971)

- Interruptions of family sleep (Bayley, 1973; Hewett, 1972)

- Social isolation, attitudes of neighbors and kin (Holt, 1958; Tizard and Grad, 1961)

- Limitations in recreational activities (Holt, 1958; Aldrich et al., 1971)

- Handling behavioral problems (Bayley, 1973; Justice et al., 1971; Younghusband et al., 1971)

- Difficulty in shopping and other normal household routines (Bayley, 1973; Younghusband et al., 1971)

- Limited prospects for the future (Bayley, 1973; Younghusband et al., 1971)

The family, then, is clearly not giving up the caring function. Large numbers of handicapped persons are living with and being cared for by their relatives—far more than are in institutions. The family has been instrumental in preventing or delaying long-term admissions to institutions, thus reducing a potentially heavy demand on social welfare services. Many families have provided what can only be described as a staggering amount of care, and yet the evidence is that they want to do so. In this sense, the family has been a significant resource for handicapped persons and a resource for the social welfare system.

## The Social Welfare Response

How has the State responded? Is there evidence of commitment? Are services such that they clearly emphasize supporting families or are they organized to take over the caring function when families are unable or unwilling to continue as caregivers? Who is the object of the policy or service—the individual or the family?

Expenditure levels show in relative terms the value a society places on social objectives. In this sense it can be interpreted as an indicator of the social welfare effort (Wilensky, 1975). Within this framework, the nation has made a commitment to the social well-being of its citizens. Expenditures have increased significantly over the past three decades whether measured by per capita expenditures (up 314 percent since 1950) or expenditures as a percentage of the gross national product (up 1,000 percent during this same period).

Within the U.S. Department of Health, Education, and Welfare a number of programs have been developed that in principle could be supportive to families with handicapped members. (See Table 6-4.) Thirteen of these are administered by the Office of Human Development and Social and Rehabilitative Services, nine by the Office of Education, seven by the Social Security Administration, and two by the Public Health Service. These thirty-one programs were obligated at $102.7 billion in fiscal year 1976. Seventy-one percent of this total was accounted for by various income maintenance programs, 25 percent by programs paying for medical care services and 4 percent for the provision of services. Although this investment is significant, the distribution itself raises some questions. A fundamental issue in developing an improved support system for families caring for handicapped members lies in the dominance of the income approach. Federal policy has been primarily an income policy, and although income supports are needed, their value may be lessened by the absence of a network of support services.

This general pattern raises a number of troublesome questions. The emphases on income maintenance (71.4 percent) and the financing of medical care (24.5 percent) are based on the assumption that services are either less important or that individuals and families can obtain these services if they have the means to pay for them. This assumption, however, has not been borne out. In some instances there has been market failure; in others, the income support has not been adequate.

The income maintenance programs clearly support handicapped persons but are implicitly neutral toward the family. Their purpose is to offer protection against the loss of earnings resulting from retirement or disability so that the individual will not become indigent. The major exception is the Public Assistance Program, which does have an emphasis on the family, but the existence of a handicapping condition is neither a part of eligibility determination nor will it substantially affect the level of the benefit.

The second largest area of federal expenditures is for medical care. Medicare, accounting for 67 percent of these funds, is used primar-

**Table 6-4.** Federal (HEW) Programs Potentially Benefiting Families with Handicapped Members.

| Catalogue Number | Agency | Title | Obligations FY 1976 |
|---|---|---|---|
| *Specific Services, $ Millions* | | | |
| 13.427 | OE | Educationally Deprived Children/Handicapped | 96 |
| 13.433 | OE | Follow Through | 59 |
| 13.443 | OE | Handicapped, Research and Demonstration | 11 |
| 13.444 | OE | Handicapped, Early Childhood Assistance | 22 |
| 13.446 | OE | Handicapped, Media Services and Films | 16 |
| 13.449 | OE | Handicapped, Pre-School and School Programs | 100 |
| 13.450 | OE | Handicapped, Regional Resource Centers | 10 |
| 13.520 | OE | Special Programs for Children with Learning Disabilities | 4 |
| 13.568 | OE | Handicapped, Innovative Programs, Severely Handicapped | 3 |
| 13.624 | OHD | Rehabilitation Services and Facilities | 720 |
| 13.627 | OHD | Rehabilitation, Research and Demonstration | 24 |
| 13.630 | OHD | Developmental Disabilities, Basic Support | 32 |
| 13.631 | OHD | Developmental Disabilities, Special Projects | 19 |
| 13.635 | OHD | Special Programs, Aging, Nutrition | 125 |
| 13.636 | OHD | Special Programs, Aging, Research and Development | 6 |
| TOTAL | | | 1,247 |
| *Income Maintenance, $ Billions or $ Millions* | | | |
| 13.761 | SRS | Public Assistance–Maintenance | 5.9 B |
| 13.803 | SSA | Retirement Insurance | 45.1 B |
| 13.804 | SSA | Special Benefits for Those Over 71 | 185 M |

| 13.805 | SSA | Survivors Insurance | 16.8 | B |
| 13.806 | SSA | Special Benefits, Disabled Coal Miners | 961 | M |
| 13.807 | SSA | Supplemental Security Income | 4.4 | B |
| TOTAL | | | 73.3 | B |

*Medical Care–Financial, $ Billions*

| 13.800 | SSA | Medicare–Hospital Insurance | 12.2 | |
| 13.801 | SSA | Medicare–Supplementary Insurance | 4.7 | |
| 13.714 | SRS | Medical Assistance Program | 8.3 | |
| TOTAL | | | 25.2 | |

*General Social Services, $ Billions or $ Millions*

| 13.600 | OHD | Headstart | 462 | M |
| 13.608 | OHD | Child Welfare, Research and Development | 15 | M |
| 13.754 | SRS | Public Assistance, Social Services | 16 | M |
| 13.771 | SRS | Social Services, Low Income | 2.2 | B |
| 13.707 | SRS | Child Welfare Services | 53 | M |
| 13.211 | PHS | Crippled Childrens Services | 77 | M |
| 13.232 | PHS | Maternal and Child Health Services | 219 | M |

| Total, $ Billions | | | 3 | B |
| Grand Total, $ Billions | | | 102.7 | B |

*Source:* Adapted from Family Impact Seminar, *Toward An Inventory of Federal Programs with Direct Impact on Families,* George Washington University, February 1978, pp. 37ff.

ily to pay for inpatient hospital care and services provided by physicians. Home health services accounted for only 1.3 percent of the total. Medicaid, on the other hand, can provide for a much broader range of medical care, including services in the home. However, less than 1 percent of the funds is used for this kind of support.

Approximately 4 percent of the total funds obligated were for the provision of social services. Of this $4.2 billion, 71 percent were for services to the general population, with the remainder used specifically for handicapped persons.

Although considerably less is expended on services, even here major problems exist. Most services are income-related so that only individuals or families of low income are eligible. Although many families caring for handicapped members do receive and benefit from these services, more are ineligible. Again, this criterion seems to assume that those whose income is too high to qualify have the means to obtain services. A final problem is that, with few exceptions, these benefits and services are provided to individuals and not to families.

While services and financial support are provided to handicapped persons—the elderly, the sick, and the disabled—their families are not the object of the policy or service. Little emphasis, if any, is given to supporting families caring for mentally retarded children. Although these services and benefits may indirectly support these caregivers, they are not provided with this in mind and it is spurious to argue that if individuals living in families receive support, the entire family is supported. Such a belief may appear logical, but practice has shown otherwise. Overall, these policies have tended to ignore the family with a handicapped member, just as they ignore families in general.

### Policies to Support Families

A basic notion throughout this analysis is that the family can be defined as a social service. Although this concept is ambiguous and for some a term that demeans the family, it is a useful way to describe certain functions of the family. From a social policy perspective, it provides a framework for examining the relationship between families and the State and for identifying effective services. The essence of such policies and services is a commitment to the principle that families and other social institutions need to interact in providing support to handicapped persons.

Social services have come to be defined as those services designed to aid individuals and groups to meet their basic needs, to enhance their social functioning, to develop their potential, and to promote general well-being. The starting point, then, is that families are a social service in that they, as well as the community, society, and the State, carry out these functions for family members. Furthermore, it is clear that families are providing more social care to handicapped members than are the health and welfare agencies. It is not argued that families are "better social services," that de facto they are better equipped to carry out these functions. Any statement such as this tends to bring sharp criticism and examples where families are not capable or where individuals have been harmed by relatives; few people are not aware of the rising numbers of reported child abuse or spouse battering. In general, however, families are functioning well in the care of children and other dependent family members. There is an American tendency to establish dichotomies, to argue that either families or the state should assume primary responsibility. For example, twenty-five years ago, professionals advised families with severely retarded children to place them in institutions. It was better for the child; it was better for the other children in the family; it was better for the parents. Parents who wanted to keep the child often found themselves under considerable pressure and were told that they had neither the skills and knowledge, nor the resources required to assist the child in researching his or her potential. Many ambivalent parents were made to feel guilty if they resisted institutional care. They were led to believe that such a decision would not be in the best interest of the handicapped member in terms of his or her physical and social well-being. A second and equally convincing argument for institutionalization was that in providing care, intense strains are placed on the total family unit, creating problems for the other children or between parents. The pendulum recently seems to have swung back, however. Professionals now seem to feel that community care, including family care, is superior to institutional care. Furthermore, it is extremely difficult given current practices in the various states, to institutionalize a severely retarded child who is very young. The current thinking among professionals is that institutional care is not in the best interests of the child or family as a whole, and much pressure is brought to bear on parents, as was the case in the 1950s. Despite occasional exceptions to these polar positions, solutions tend always to be seen in either/or terms and the value of diversity overlooked. It is likely that in some situations families can provide better care, whereas in others the State would be the more appropriate caregiver. A range of policies is needed, and specific policies may have multiple purposes. Policies might then be located on a continuum whose end points are extreme forms of substitution (the State becoming the family for the individual) and total lack of State involvement in family life. The needs of families and individuals vary and they change over time; ideally the State would respond to those variations with policies that support families when they need support and substitute for families when they are incapable of meeting the needs of their members. Even this postulation is incomplete since it suggests a progression from no services to supportive services to substitute services, the last only when the family breaks down. In many cases a family may need some other social institution to temporarily assume the total caring function of a severely retarded child but would reassume primary responsibility after the crisis has been dealt with. From this point of view, both functions (support and substitution) are necessary and neither can be offered as more important nor desirable than the other.

If these premises are accepted, it becomes critical that current policies be evaluated and future policies developed within a framework where the family is identified as a social service interacting with other social institutions. The overriding question thus becomes "What is the most desirable, effective, and feasible division of responsibility between the family and extrafamilial institutions in meeting the needs of individuals and in what ways can these institutions relate to each other to maximize benefits?" This question emerges from certain biases. It presupposes the value of a relationship based on bilateral exchanges. It argues that neither institution is capable by itself. The data presented in this chapter suggest that such an exchange based on the notion of shared responsibility does not exist. A number of reasons were offered to explain why this has happened. Two are critical and must be dealt with directly. The first is that, whereas families exist, they tend to be deemphasized or ignored when policies are formulated. The focus is primarily on individuals. The second reason is as complex. Whereas the notion that interference in family life is dysfunctional, noninterference has come to be equated with nonintervention. So services exist to take over family functions, but few are available to support families.

The case can be made that a caring society must involve some sense of shared responsibility. The essence of sharing begins with a recognition of the contribution that families are making. It requires also moving from a unilateral relationship to one based on exchange. If anything, families should be supported by a caring society if that society is concerned with its future.

## STRATEGIES TO SUPPORT FAMILIES

Families have always provided the primary environment for rearing and nurturing children. Some specific child-rearing tasks have changed over time; for example, the formal education of most children today is accomplished not in the family setting but in schools. Although some tasks have changed, several factors involved in the successful rearing of children have remained fairly constant. Parents in general have needed and continue to need time, energy, resources, and knowledge in order to fulfill their parenting roles. Usually, their successful performance as parents also involves satisfaction from the continuing development of their children.

And yet certain significant social changes have created varying degrees of stress for most families that affect their care for their children. Stresses tend to have a deleterious effect because they detract from and drain the time, energy, resources, and knowledge that the parents are able to bring to raising their children; they also tend to diminish the satisfaction they may experience in child rearing. If these factors are related to successful child rearing when the children are not handicapped, it should be obvious that they are important to parents with handicapped children. These parents also need time, energy, knowledge, and resources if they are to experience some degree of personal satisfaction and function as effective caregivers.

Strategies to strengthen these parents can be grouped under three general headings: hard services, process skills, and counseling skills. *Hard services* include respite care, income support, assistance in physical adaptations to the home, and homemaker services. *Process skills* are mechanisms to build parental capabilities in management (the executive function), mediation with service providers, and linkage functions. *Counseling* includes educational services, information, and when necessary short-term therapy. Families caring for handicapped children experience financial stress not only because of the costs directly associated with raising such children but because they must forego the second income of one parent, usually the mother. Finding themselves spending a great deal of time caring for these children and having limited opportunity for recreation, they often feel socially isolated. They may also have difficulty carrying out normal household routines.

The need for respite care services is well documented. Although the value of such services to the family is indisputable, their development has been slow and their coverage spotty. Traditionally, the major purpose of respite services has been to respond to a crisis or a need for immediate relief. More often than not the handicapped child was removed from the home and returned after the crisis had passed. Respite care was seen to be appropriate when the caregiver became ill or when the parents were experiencing marital difficulties. The provision of such services was associated with the occurrence of a problem and was not viewed as an ongoing supportive service. Only recently have professionals identified the value of respite services in preventing crises or problems and advocated their provision on a regular basis.

The earlier notions of crisis and pathology as they relate to respite care have been merged with the recent idea of normalization. If parents are to experience any semblance of normal family life, they need time away from the handicapped person, time to be someone other than a caregiver, time to relax. Comprehensive respite care services include the provision of overnight care, babysitting during the day, and longer periods of out-of-home care for vacations. Most families find these services in short supply or too costly, in part because of the apparent lack of commitment to integrate respite care into our service delivery system as other countries have. For example, local authorities in the United Kingdom set aside a percentage of their nursing home beds for short-term admissions. Even if the homes have waiting lists for more permanent admissions, these places are reserved so that families may have one- or two-week vacations. Community hostels for the mentally retarded are used in the same way.

The rationale for this policy is simple: If given regular relief, families are able to function more effectively as caregivers so that long-term admissions or complete transfers to institutions are prevented or at least delayed. In this context the British are using their institutions to achieve social as well as health objectives. In the United States institutional care means long-term care usually financed by Medicaid. This program, with its single emphasis on medical care, is not structured to finance respite care for family members. The institutions themselves are also not organized to provide this service. Respite care does not begin when the handicapped person is admitted to the institution. The severely retarded child is likely to feel frightened when moving to a strange environment and to need contact with institutional personnel before being admitted. In the United Kingdom this contact is feasible since the institutions are community-based, are under local social service departments, and have a great degree of staff interaction. The family is visited before the admission, and, if feasible, the handicapped person can visit the institution. In-home respite care faces the same funding/financing problems as those of out-of-home care. As discussed earlier, most community social services are currently provided through Title XX of the Social Security Act. Respite care relative to other services has low priority and, when available, tends to be restricted to families with low income.

A second area is that of financial assistance. Current policies ignore the financial burden that caring for a handicapped person places on most families. There are programs for the handicapped person and for families with extremely low incomes, such as Social Security Income (SSI) and Aid to Families with Dependent Children (AFDC), but none to offset the costs associated with care. A number of countries have established income-maintenance programs that focus on families providing care for the handicapped, rather than on the handicapped person. In 1971 the British government introduced the Constant Attendance Allowance (CAA). Initially a sum of money was provided to the caregiver in situations where a handicapped person required frequent attention all day and most of the night. Two years later, the program was expanded to include those who needed such care either day or night, and a second benefit was established at a lower rate. The sole determinant of eligibility was the level of handicapping condition. Age of the handicapped person and family income were not material. Although the benefits were not large, the program did achieve two complementary objectives: In many instances, the grant made a real difference in the family's financial status; less measurable but in the view of the program designers as important, families were told in a tangible way that their efforts were recognized, that they were not ignored. The psychological benefit of the grant outweighed the actual amount of the transfer. Also, the financial support was not given to the handicapped person but to the caregiver. Moreover, there were no requirements that the money be spent on predetermined services and goods; the recipients could use the grant in any way they wished.

The Danish social welfare system has a comparable program. Persons who are considered fully unemployable or whose earning capacity is negligible qualify for an income grant equal to the old-age pension. Only one criterion determines eligibility: age of the handicapped person. If the person is between 15 and 67 years of age, he or she is eligible; after 67 he or she automatically transfers to the national old-age pension. Family income is not a factor. If a person is so handicapped as to require constant attendance on the part of others, a non-income-related allowance equal to the full basic rate (pension) is paid. For children payment may be paid to parents or other relatives for their care in their own homes. If the condition and circumstances of the child involve special expense to the home in excess of what a nonhandicapped child would cost, an allowance is paid. As with other programs, family income is not considered in determining eligibility.

Although income support to families is common in most Western countries, it has not become a part of American effort. For many people it would be inconceivable, if not unnatural, to pay families to care for their dependent members. Parents or adult children should provide care because they are expected to do so. The normal response is to want to care, whether from a sense of duty or from love. The basis of this position emerges from a historical belief in acceptable moral principles. The payment of money to carry out "natural" family functions is viewed as harmful in that the moral reasons for caring—duty, love, responsibility to care for one's own—are replaced by less altruistic motives.

Such an attitude has been instrumental in blocking attempts to initiate a family or children's allowance. In the belief that children can place a family in economic risk, most other Western countries have such policies, but the United States views such policies as inherently harmful to family well-being. All societies are concerned with strengthening families. Other countries attempt to reduce as many stresses as possible through constant-attendance allowances and family and children allowances. Allowances are major preventive measures in that, if stress is reduced and risks minimized, the family is more capable of survival as a unit.

The United States' position is that only weakened families need support from the social welfare system. And yet our policies are ambivalent. Money is given to strangers to function as the family of a person in need of care. Foster parents are paid to care for children who have no natural parents or whose parents are incapable of providing a caring environment. Others are paid to care for handicapped persons residing in institutions. The staff, in effect, functions as a substitute family by providing for the physical and social needs of the residents. Policies have been initiated that provide financial incentives to prospective adoptive parents. Previously many low-income families wanting to adopt a child may have found child rearing costs prohibitive.

The reluctance to support natural families but willingness to assist substitute families, needs to be reexamined. The moral issue aside, there is no empirical evidence that providing financial support results in families that are less responsible or less caring. The European experience to date suggests the opposite. When relieved of the financial stress associated with the care of a handicapped person, when given a visible sign that someone is interested in them, most family caregivers are encouraged to continue providing care.

Although there is no national policy, many natural experiments are offering financial support to families. One such program is the MR–Family Subsidy Program administered by the Minnesota Department of Public Welfare. A task force on the family was formed in response to a request by Minnesota's commissioner of public welfare to study the issues and problems of families providing for their handicapped child in the natural or adoptive home. This task force, over 75 percent of whom were parents of handicapped children, was charged with identifying the problems faced by such families, assessing support offered to the family unit by state and local programs, and identifying gaps in the service delivery system.

Based on its analysis, the task force recommended the establishment of a program that would provide financial support for all expenses related to the child's disability needs. Expenses associated with the raising of a normal child would not be covered under the program. Eligibility would be based solely upon the disability needs of the child and not on the income of the family. The program was established in 1975 under the Minnesota Statutes, Section 252.27, Subdivision 4. The program, on an experimental basis, subsidizes fifty families a maximum of $250 per month. Although it is similar in principle to the constant-attendance allowances of the United Kingdom and Denmark, the Family Subsidy Program restricts family expenditures to seven categories: (1) diagnostic assessments, medical expenses, medications; (2) special diets and clothing; (3) special devices, ranging from medical to recreational equipment; (4) parental relief and child care costs; (5) educational and training programs; (6) preschool program costs; and (7) transportation costs.

The typical child in the program was eight years old, with an IQ below 35, suffering from one or two additional handicapping conditions, of which cerebral palsy, seizures, difficulties in mobility, and hyperactivity were most frequent. These children were found to be comparable to children institutionalized in the state hospitals, and yet they did not have a history of placement out of the home. Although a number of families were considering institutionalization, relatively few did once they joined the program.

A constant-attendance allowance is long overdue in this country. The costs are high, but the benefits potentially greater. Every day that a family continues providing care is beneficial to the state and indirectly to the general public.

The costs of institutional care are very high. Nursing home costs were in excess of $600 per month in 1976, and institutional care for the mentally retarded averaged $800. The costs of institutionalization can also be significant in terms of the handicapped person and his or her family. These costs are more difficult to measure, however, because they are social and psychological rather than economic. A program such as the constant-attendance allowance allows families more meaningful choices.

Once the concept of family support becomes acceptable, the issue becomes one of level of benefit and eligibility. One approach is to peg the benefit to the Supplementary Security Income grant. In 1976 dollars this would mean a monthly allowance of $157.70 or $1,900 per year. This grant, given to the caregiver, would be provided solely on the basis of the severity of the handicapped condition and not on the basis of family income. This program might, of necessity, be limited to families caring for the very severely handicapped.

Such a supportive strategy is, however, somewhat foreign to the social welfare philosophy of the United States. It requires developing policies that provide benefits based solely on need and not on family income. Needs-tested programs are fairly common in many Western countries. Society, through its government, recognizes that certain segments of the population are at risk. Typically, these subpopulations include, but are not limited to, the elderly and the handicapped. The concept of risk is used in a statistical sense in that all elderly or handicapped persons are in need or have problems. Still, these subpopulations are more likely to have problems as compared to other groups within the population. To minimize the economic, physical, and social risks associated with the condition (being old or handicapped), benefits are made available to all members of the designated subpopulation. Once the legitimacy of the claim is determined (membership in the designated group is ascertained), the individual or his or her family is entitled to the benefit. The Social Security program, specifically the old-age pension program, comes closest to these concepts of universal coverage and membership in an at-risk population group. Benefits are not determined by the presence or absence of personal resources. But, even under this program, individuals must not only be of retirement age but must also have contributed to the program while they were working.

In this country it is argued that universal provision of benefits is inherently wasteful, since some of the beneficiaries will in fact not "need" the benefit. It is further argued that if benefits or services were provided on a selective basis, if only those who really need services were eligible, recipients would then be given more services or higher benefit levels. On a theoretical level, this reasoning is quite appealing. For example, why should a family caring for its severely retarded child be given a constant-attendance allowance of $1,900 per year if the family income is $50,000? This argument usually concludes by noting that if those whose income is above a certain level are excluded from the program, it may be possible to give more than the $1,900 to those who need financial support.

On a practical level, this position becomes unsettling. A means-tested program implies that families do not have the right to a benefit. Once benefits or services are no longer rights, their provision usually results in some stigmatization. Even if the means-tested eligibility criteria were to be reasonable (e.g., an income of $10,000 or even $15,000 per year), many families would not subject themselves to the eligibility screening. For many, it means an invasion of privacy; for others, it is a strong dislike for any program that seems to be charity. Furthermore, if benefits are income-related, there is a danger that the income level will be lowered (say, from $10,000 to $8,000) in periods of retrenchment. Such was the experience with Medicaid when large groups of previously eligible individuals and families were dropped from the program. This is not possible in universal programs that are not means-tested. Benefits may be raised or lowered, but recipients are not excluded as long as they are providing care to a handicapped person. The major policy variable then becomes the level of handicap to be used in defining group membership or eligibility. Given the uncertainty of demand, it is reasonable to begin with the most severely handicapped and, at a later date, reassess whether other groups should be included, as the United Kingdom did.

These recommendations, the allocation of resources for respite care services and the inception of a constant-attendance allowance, are only two of many that might have been made. I believe their need and value have been established. Although it might be argued that income support alone should be sufficient and that families receiving the allowance could use it to purchase respite care if they wanted to, the market to date has not been responsive.

At this time, these recommendations cannot be justified in cost-effectiveness or cost/benefit terms. If families were abandoning their caregiving function in growing numbers, this argument would make sense because family care would be less costly than institutional care. Fortunately for society this is not happening. If choices have to be made between at-risk groups based on the best cost/benefit ratio possible, these families will again be penalized. Other groups of at-risk populations will, more than likely, show greater returns for investments as long as the criterion continues to be economic returns.

Unless changes in priorities take place, these families will continue to be ignored and underserved. Families who transfer the caring function to the State are "rewarded" in that resources are made available. Families who maintain the caring function are penalized in that their contribution to society is ignored. To rectify this inequitable situation, to move beyond the current welfare State to the more positive idea of a welfare society, the criterion inherent in the human investment model must be balanced with criteria evolving from the philosophical belief in justice as fairness. These families care, they are providing more care than the organized social welfare system, and they are functioning as social services. To continue benefiting from this situation without attempting to be supportive, without sharing the caring responsibility, is hardly in keeping with the notion of a caring society.

## REFERENCES

Aldrich, F. et al. The mental retardation service delivery system: A survey of mental retardation service usage and needs among families with retarded children in selected areas of Washington state. In *Research report*, vol. 3. Olympia: State of Washington Office of Research, 1971.

Bayley, M. *Mental handicap and community care*. London: Routledge and Kegan Paul, 1973.

Beggs, H. and Blekner, M. *Home aids services and the aged: A controlled study*. Part II. The Service Program. Cleveland: The Benjamin Rose Institute, 1970.

Conroy, J., and Derr, K. *Services and analysis of the habitation and rehabilitation status of the mentally retarded with associated handicapping conditions*. Washington, D.C.: U.S. Department of Health, Education and Welfare, 1971.

Dunlap, W. Services for families of the developmentally disabled. *Social Work* 1976, *21*, 220–223.

Gottleib, J. Public, peer and professional attitudes toward mentally retarded persons. In M. Begab and S. Richardson (Eds.), In *The mentally retarded and society: A social science perspective*. Baltimore: University Park Press, 1975.

Harris, A. *Handicapped and impaired in Great Britain*. London: Office of Population and Census, Social Survey Division, Her Majesty's Stationery Office, 1971.

Hewett, S. *The family and the handicapped child*. London: Allen and Unwin, 1972.

Holt, K. The home care of the severely retarded child. *Pediatrics*, 22, 1958, 746–755.

Justice, R., et al. Foster family care for the retarded: Management concerns of the caretaker. *Mental Retardation*, 1971, *9*, 12–15.

Kershaw, J. The handicapped child and his family. *Public Health* 1965, *80*, 18–26.

Kushlich, A. The presence of recognized mental subnormality of IQ under 50 among children in the south of England with reference to the demand for places for residential care. Proceedings of the International Copenhagen Congress on the Scientific Study of Mental Retardation. *Foundation of Child Psychiatry*. Oxford: Pergamon Press, 1964.

Lowther, C. and Williamson, I. Old people and their relatives. *The Lancet*, December 3, 1966.

Morris, R., et al. *Community based maintenance care for the long-term patient*. Waltham, Mass.: Levinson Policy Institute, Brandeis University, 1976.

Sainsbury, P., and Grad de Alarcon, J. The psychiatrist and the geriatric patient: The effects of community care on the family of the geriatric patient. *Journal of Geriatric Psychiatry*, 1971, *4*, 23-41.

Schonell, F., and Watts, B. A first survey of the effects of a subnormal child on the family unit. *American Journal of Mental Deficiency*, 1956, *61*, 210-219.

Sultz, H., et al. *Long-term childhood illness*. Pittsburgh, Pa.: University of Pittsburgh Press, 1972.

Tizard, J. Implications for services of recent social research in mental retardation *The mentally subnormal*. London: Heinemann Medical Books, 1972, p. 272.

Tizard, J. Epidemiology of mental retardation: Implications for research on malnutrition. *Early malnutrition and mental development*. Uppsala, Sweden: Almquist and Wiksell, 1974.

Tizard, J., and Grad, J. *The mentally handicapped and their families: A social survey*. Oxford, England: Oxford University Press, 1961.

Younghusband, E., et al. *Living with handicap*. London: National Children's Bureau. 1971.

Wilensky, H. *The Welfare State and Equality*. Berkely: The University of California Press, 1975.

# 7 TREATMENT AND CARE OF THE CHRONICALLY MENTALLY ILL

*Mary Hilary Sandall*

A demonstration program in Missouri, the original "Show me" state, has been used by that state's department of mental health to formulate a set of principles and to develop a system of care for the chronically mentally ill. The program consists of cooperative apartments shared by two or three former mental hospital patients and rented on the open market by a private agency that provides support to the tenants, helping them adjust. The agency also runs a psychosocial club where the members learn necessary living skills, practice work skills, and enjoy themselves. The general features of the program are not particularly novel—many apartment programs and psychosocial clubs were developed in the 1970s; what is unusual is the contractual arrangement with the state department of mental health. The contracts specify the services expected from the private agency, thus providing a mechanism for accountability, and outline the responsibility of the department of mental health to provide regular monitoring and psychiatric services, thus providing a mechanism for continuity of care.

Contracts originated in 1959 in the second great wave of deinstitutionalization to roll over Missouri's mental health system and they were probably the result of lessons learned in the first wave, which took place in the closing years of the nineteenth century. The history of the treatment of the mentally ill in Missouri followed what

239

seems to have been the typical course. The state legislature first recognized the existence of a "Suffering, dependent multitude . . . gathered in your alms houses and your jails . . . " in 1848 and appropriated money to construct an Asylum for the Insane (Dix, 1848). This rapidly became overcrowded and further sums were appropriated for new asylums, until the state finally had five, all overcrowded. The legislature began to discuss reorganization in 1872 and, not for the last time, hoped that this would save tax dollars: "Your committee firmly believes that it can be achieved without an additional dollar of expense" (Finney, et al., 1875). The so-called incurables were removed from the St. Louis Insane Asylum to the county farm in the next twenty years; in other words, they were mainstreamed into the social support provided for the indigent and helpless citizens of the locality. This move was strongly contested by the superintendent, Dr. E.C. Runge, who pointed out that the chronically mentally ill continue to require specialized care provided by staff trained in the provision of mental health services. He outlined his objections in an article published in 1903, stating "There never was a greater legislative blunder committed than the one which has taken the complete control of the great bulk of chronic cases out of the hands of the superintendent" (Runge, 1903).

It is possible that his words were remembered when the state legislature was asked to approve a similar transfer of patients in 1959: They agreed only on condition that the superintendent continue to retain full responsibility for the psychiatric treatment and followup required by patients moved from state hospitals to local nursing homes and boarding houses. The patients remained on the census of the hospital and so were able to obtain psychiatric drugs and other forms of treatment from hospital staff. Placement contracts specified the residential and nursing services to be provided by the local operators and included a budget page for each patient, detailing the allowable costs and the source of payment—federal or other insurance programs, individual or family income, and, if necessary, a state supplement from the special mental health placement budget appropriated by the legislature. In 1959 as in 1872 the legislature was told that the transfer would save state dollars, and in 1965 that must have seemed an accurate prediction, because passage of the Medicare and Medicaid amendments to the Social Security Act meant that the federal government paid most of the cost of care in extended-care facilities but *not* in state hospitals.

Currently, the placement programs attached to each of the state hospitals provide followup services to 4,500 patients in local residential facilities and the annual placement budget has expanded to $27 million in state money, not including the cost of the hospital-based placement staff. The placement program is now more complex and oriented toward active treatment. It no longer consists simply of the regular monitoring of the care provided by nursing homes and boarding houses, which was the case between 1959 and 1971.

The demonstration program shows this active approach to placement. In St. Louis, in its first nine years, just over 500 patients have been accepted into the cooperative apartment program. Of that number, 20 percent have been able to move on to further independence, defined as no more placement subsidy and no more services; 20 percent have been transferred to more support, defined as nursing home, boarding house, or group home care; while 60 percent continue to live semi-independently in the apartments, receiving various levels of support from program staff. Easy transfer to the most appropriate level of care available is a keynote of the program, facilitated by the case management by the staff of the state's department of mental health and financially supported, when necessary, by the state placement fund.

Although the statistics show us that the apartment program is successful at keeping many chronically mentally ill citizens out of the hospital, figures alone do not convey essential features of the program—acceptability, the people it does serve, and the people it is not designed for—in short, its overall quality. A film or videotape is probably the most effective method of conveying these aspects, but none has yet been made, so a few case histories will be used to illustrate some basic principles.

Cooperative apartments can provide a home for very disabled people. A significant number of tenants have been in hospitals or nursing homes for many years, but chronicity is no bar to successful adjustment. Matt was in the state hospital for forty-one years, all his adult life, and was the typical helpful patient always ready to run to the canteen for a packet of cigarettes or a soda, keeping himself in pocket money and making friends in the style of institutional life. The same method worked equally well in a city neighborhood. He cleaned tables in the local cafe in return for a discount on the price of his meals, he ran errands for neighbors and so collected spending money and friends. He even found an old woman who never left her apartment and told program staff he thought she needed our kind of services. His new acquaintances knew he was from the hospital and accepted him nevertheless. In fact, their knowledge was important to his safety. The day he failed to show at the cafe, the proprietor called the hospital to voice her concern. We found him in bed with pneumonia and feeling too sick to use the telephone. His roommate was away visiting his family, so Matt's local network was a necessary part of his support.

Neighbors like this are supposed to be found only in small towns and in Norman Rockwell paintings of a bygone age, but we have found several city neighborhoods that accept our clients readily and many ordinary people who take an active interest in their adjustment.

This is partly because apartments require no special zoning changes, partly because low to moderate rental apartments already provide homes for people at similar income levels and life-styles to our clients, and, most important, because we screen out state hospital patients with a history of repeated violence, alcohol or drug abuse, and rape or other kinds of assaultive sexual behavior.

A person who sets fires when feeling upset or aggravated really belongs in a solid building with a sprinkler system and round-the-clock staff. A person who steals money from pockets or pocketbooks is an unacceptable roommate until this behavior changes. The majority of long-term patients do not have this kind of unacceptable behavior. They may have odd habits, high levels of anxiety, or even active delusional systems, but these differences do not necessarily mean that they cannot take care of themselves and make friends. We are finding that many people with a level of disability usually leading to institutional care are adjusting to a place of their own and that the responsibilities of daily life fill the hours previously occupied by symptoms.

Having something to do of real importance, like learning how to housekeep on a limited budget, not only fills the time but also removes that problem of lack of motivation so often attributed to the residents of institutions. The passive people, who sit quietly in the long-term wards, whether they are in a hospital, a nursing home, or a boardinghouse are people who are receiving total care, people for whom almost every decision is being made by someone else. These same people become more alert, lively, and active when they are given responsibility for their own life-style and comfort.

The story of Irene and Louise illustrates this change quite dramatically. They were friends because they sat next to each other for years in the hospital and their beds were in the same dormitory. They were anxious, passive, and depressed and had no links with family or friends outside the hospital. Discharge planning produced a lot of resistance. After the move Irene told me she had been praying every night that I would be unable to locate a landlord willing to rent to "crazies" because she herself thought it was a ridiculous idea. The first few days in the apartment were stormy because everyone involved was anxious. Within a year Irene and Louise had saved up enough to be able to replace the furniture donated by the hospital, to give it away to a young neighbor who was getting married, and to fix their apartment up exactly the way they wanted it. Within two years Irene's family had started visiting her again, for they could see she had "recovered" and within three years she was traveling by bus to California every summer to visit her grandchildren. This was after twelve years of hospitalization and a strong inner feeling that she was a "hopeless case." If she had been placed in a boarding house the same changes would not have occurred as she would have continued to be the passive recipient of care. If she had been placed in a halfway house with a set of goals to reach, the same changes might have occurred, but the transition from halfway house to independence would probably have provoked the same high level of anxiety that she showed when leaving the safety of the hospital.

We have found that people learn living skills rapidly in the apartments, and the reward of success is staying in a home that they have made for themselves. The transitions are made by the visiting staff, who cut down on the number of visits and alter the style of the support they are providing. As transition is famous for provoking anxiety it seems reasonable to minimize it for the patients and to transfer the responsibility to the staff.

The staff accept responsibility for transition and at the same time transfer some of caretaking responsibilities to their clients. Staff teach cooking and cleaning. Except in rare circumstances they do not fix meals and organize the housekeeping routine. Staff rely on clients to care for each other and report only the problems that they believe require more specialized help. Long-term patients have picked up some useful knowledge about drugs and their side effects, events that precipitate adverse reactions, and the idiosyncracies of the people they have lived with for years. Like exalcoholics many of them believe that a person with a history of mental illness can understand the problems of the illness with a special sensitivity not always shown by the paid staff.

In many apartments one person has emerged as a caretaker. He or she takes pleasure in being in charge, organizing the routine, reminding roommates to take medication, and so on. This feeling of responsibility is, after all, an essential feature of self-esteem and it helps to keep the program working, as long as the roommates feel comfortable. Some of the more domineering clients have moved through several roommates before a stable relationship develops. A few of them are living alone. The process of developing good relationships seems to be a natural one; it can perhaps be facilitated by staff, but it cannot be established by following a book of rules and trying to match people up according to some formula.

Although the program is aimed at facilitating independence, its staff are naturally concerned about the safety and well-being of their clients. Leaving people to make their own decisions can carry the special danger of neglecting them; making decisions for them can carry the special danger of inducing dependency.

Institutionalization does not occur only in state hospitals; it is a possibility in any setting where one group of people direct another group, whether in boardinghouses, foster homes, or natural families. Staff must retain a sensitivity to this issue. We have found that the tension between promoting independence and providing adequate support is naturally expressed in dialogues between client and staff, client and family, staff and family, agency staff and department of mental health staff. Keeping the dialogue open and allowing sufficient weight to each point of view is a basic component of treatment philosophy and a large element in client and staff training or retraining.

We have learned that while 80 percent of patients referred to the program benefit from it as shown by development of living skills and social life, not every chronically mentally ill person is best treated in this way. At her first screening for the program Vanessa seemed an ideal client; she was middle aged, depressed, had no ties with her family, and was too anxious to take a job, even in the sheltered workshop. We discovered during the following weeks (in which numerous midnight telephone calls about apparent trivia woke up the staff on call) that her anxiety was too great for her to be able to learn a new life-style. After all the obvious remedies had been tried and had failed, we arranged for her to move to a boarding house. In this environment she relaxed, settled down, began to go to job training and eventually took a job. After a few months of work she herself approached her case manager and asked to be screened for transfer to an apartment. She is now successfully discharged from the apartment program, attending the outpatient clinic regularly, and giving every appearance of stability. About 15 percent of program residents have shown the same pattern: trying independent living, failing at first, returning to more supervision, and then trying again. This can be related to the nature of many severe mental illnesses, with their pattern of recovery and relapse. Although the revolving door sometimes indicates totally inadequate followup programs, it can also be a sign of a cyclical illness and as such should be facilitated by good case management and a treatment philosophy that adjusts the level of care to the level of disability. Vanessa's story also illustrates the benefits of introducing people to the most independent setting first. Although Vanessa failed to adjust initially, the experience left sufficient positive memories for her to ask to try it again. Without her experience of apartment living and consequent solid knowledge of what it involved she might have made an excellent adjustment to the boardinghouse and then given every appearance of someone in the right place. The ability of the mentally ill to adjust to their environment should never be underestimated. This characteristic has positive effects when they are in a challenging environment and negative effects when they are in a total institution. The way people behave is not necessarily a good predictor of the way they will behave in a new setting. Instead of searching for elusive behavioral clues to future adjustment it is more useful to try  the test of screening almost everyone for placement in the most independent level of care possible. If adequate staff support is provided for the first few days or weeks of transition this method is quite safe, quite rapid, and eminently successful.

The essence of a demonstration program is not to provide a panacea for every possible client, but to demonstrate an approach, to serve as a testing ground for ideas, to serve as a training ground and to be an integral part of a larger system. The larger system contains other special programs designed to meet other types of client needs. Case management—or the development of a relationship between staff members of the larger system and its clients—is the mechanism connecting clients with the most appropriate programs. In Missouri we are developing effective case management by making sure that patients released from state hospitals into a whole array of residential programs are followed up by a placement team of workers consisting of nurse, social worker, mental health technician, and consultant psychiatrist. This followup consists of monitoring the care given by nursing homes, boardinghouses, and apartment programs; providing psychiatric treatment when necessary; and facilitating transfers to the most appropriate site of treatment.

The monitoring includes regular review of the financial arrangements, making sure that nursing homes are not continuing to charge for clients after death or removal to another home, making sure that operators are passing on spending money to their residents and not using it to buy toothpaste for them, making sure that the care paid for is actually being provided. There are many honest and scrupulous operators in the business of extended care, but it is a business and sometimes the temptation to make more money can impede the development of high-quality services. The chronically mentally ill residents of such facilities are in particular need of case managers to act as their advocates and to make sure that they are in the right place and receiving what they require.

In the apartment programs case management by staff of the state's department of mental health includes a quarterly review of progress using both subjective and objective criteria. The subjective criteria are hard to define, being based on the case manager's prior knowledge of the client and consisting largely of opinions as to whether the client is doing well. The objective criteria have been developed as a method of keeping good records and of keeping track of various indicators of progress. Clients are reviewed in five dimensions: money management and housekeeping; personal care (hygiene and clothing); work or training; social life; problems with neighbors or the law. If they demonstrate competence in budget-planning, housekeeping, and self-care, if their social life seems to be reasonably supportive and enjoyable, if they are not involved in serious problems, then the case manager considers transfer to outpatient status. This move is more than symbolic, it means that the private agency is no longer paid a fee for providing support services and that the apartment resident is now self-sufficient. The agency is motivated to recruit new clients and this form of aftercare, unlike a halfway house, can never become "full." The only need for a waiting list is when the private agency staff is overextended and can no longer accept more work. The staff can increase along with the client load, as each new referral is a new source of income.

The only limit to growth of the agency is imposed by the style of administration: relationships among staff and clients resemble those of an extended family whose members know one another personally and are mutually supportive. The beginnings of the state hospital movement were somewhat similar. The first superintendents seemed to perceive the asylum as a very large home under their care and direction, with the development of good relationships being the mark of successful treatment. In the early days of the St. Louis Asylum, patients considered ready for discharge were invited to eat with the superintendent and his family and the first annual reports contain several stories indicating a personal interest in the lives of the patients. Accounts of the principles of "moral treatment" have a very familiar ring to them and we should always try to remember that in the practice of psychiatry, most methods have a long history and that if we read more than the latest journals we might save ourselves the repetition of mistakes already made in previous centuries and other societies.

The dangers of an authoritarian and paternalistic approach have been adequately documented over the years and certainly an over-crowded and regimented institution cannot be defended on any grounds. However, in our haste to get rid of state hospitals we should remember that they afford excellent opportunities for the slow development of relationships between the inpatients themselves and between the staff and the patients (especially the aides, or front-line staff). These relationships must be replicated somehow in any program designed to replace the long-term care offered by the state hospitals. The administrative design that allows this development is a team approach to case management, a style of treatment that does not involve moving the clients from place to place as a sign of progress, and a limit to the size of the group involved in the treatment process. We are not yet clear on the optimum size of such a group. The early state hospital superintendents were in favor of limiting the inpatients to about 200 as they felt that their own personal approach was impossible with a larger institution. (Of course they were all disappointed in this idealistic endeavor and they all blamed overcrowding as the cause of their treatment failures.)

In Missouri, we are still looking at this question. Our original demonstration program in St. Louis grew quite rapidly in the first five years and then seemed to stabilize at around 80 apartments, 150 tenants and a psychosocial club with around 90 people attending every day. The inflow of new clients is just slightly larger than the outflow of old clients, and it is possible that this agency is near its optimum size for the personal approach necessary for the development of supportive relationships.

Replication instead of expansion is our method of bringing this style of treatment to more patients of the department. The demonstration program in St. Louis has already been replicated in Kansas City, Springfield, and Columbia, the other metropolitan areas of Missouri, and this year we hope to open a similar program in the most remote rural area of the state. Each replication is somewhat different in detail, but the contractual mechanism is the same, the basic tenets of the treatment philosophy are the same (here the original demonstration serves as an excellent training opportunity), and the case management provided by the department of mental health is identical. In essence we are franchising a successful program.

Moreover, a proliferation of small agencies provides a range of options for our clients. The original demonstration program of apartments and psychosocial club is particularly successful with middle-aged or elderly people who adjust to household routine and seem well satisfied with a fairly quiet life. Younger clients move through the program more rapidly, and while some succeed in using it as a stepping stone toward independence, others present more of a challenge as they move rapidly in and out of the hospital, in and out of employment, and in some cases, in and out of the criminal justice system. The young schizophrenic with no work history and an addiction to alcohol or drugs is a very difficult client for almost any kind of treatment program.

An agency in St. Louis that serves exoffenders is considering accepting some of our clients in their structured programs; methods that sometimes change the behavior of disorderly young people may also assist a very similar group, one that fell into the mental health system instead of the other behavior modifying agency. It is clear that a more effective partnership between the mental health system, the school system, and the criminal justice system is required, and we certainly have not achieved that in Missouri, nor have we yet designed a sorting method that assigns people to the system best designed to meet their needs.

The chronically mentally ill form a group very difficult to define and very difficult to fit into one particular style of treatment. The range of programs they require include custodial care for the dangerous, nursing care for the physically sick or totally confused, and rehabilitation and training for the disabled. Custodial care should not be provided for the nondangerous; nursing care should not be given to the physically fit and to those who can be taught self-care; and environmental rehabilitation (placing people in situations that maximize their independence) should be tried as often as possible for any one who looks even remotely likely to succeed.

Independence is a concept almost as difficult to define as chronic mental illness. We all try to balance the drive toward self-assertion with our social responsibilities, and each of us constructs our own individual and changing mixture of solitary activity and social life. Traditionally the chronically mentally ill have been restricted excessively in these fundamental choices, being given too much in the way of an externally imposed structure.

Without exploring further the nature of the disabilities produced by mental illness it is possible to say confidently, on the basis of experience, that excessive dependency is produced by excessive care and that the appropriate remedy is to match the care exactly to the level of disability. Mental health professionals should assist patients to develop skills and provide them with opportunities to exercise their skills. They need a range of options.

In summary adequate care for the chronically mentally ill can be defined as a system of care with different levels of support and a mechanism to assist clients in the move to the most appropriate level of support. The system includes case management for continuity and monitoring, different programs for different needs, and a constant tension between the patients' need to exercise autonomy and their need for adequate support.

## REFERENCES

Dix, Dorothea, quoted in *Proceedings of the Fifteenth General Assembly of the Senate of Missouri.* Jefferson City, Mo.: 1848.

Finney, J.; Allen, R.; and Heller, M. *Report of the Committee on Penal and Reformatory Institutions.* St. Louis, Mo.: The County Court of St. Louis, 1875.

Runge, E.C. Review of eight years work at the St. Louis Insane Asylum. *Interstate Medical Journal, 10,* October 1903.

# 8 TREATMENT AND CARE OF RETARDED CITIZENS

*Robert L. Carl, Jr.*

At first blush one presumes great progress in the provision of treatment and care of mentally retarded and other developmentally disabled people during the recent past. Considering the almshouses and asylums of two centuries ago and especially in light of such things as special education and legislative–judicial activities affirming certain individual rights for retarded citizens, we are compelled to recognize such progress. I wonder if today's retarded citizens would agree?

A brief review of the history of the treatment and care of retarded persons is in order. In 1846 Dr. Samuel Gridley Howe of Boston initiated the first systematic survey of the mentally defective population. His conclusions that about 2 percent of the general population were defective but that most of these persons could be helped led the legislature to fund the first public residential institution in the United States. Similar state schools were soon established in New York, Pennsylvania, Ohio, and Connecticut. They were designed as small special schools, with preparation for a productive life in the community as the prime goal.

It is ironic that the father of institutional care for retarded persons soon began decrying the institutional mode, for precisely the reasons that motivate many modern reformers. Howe lashed out at the segregation, regimentation, impersonalization, and lack of life-style options characteristic of institutional care. "His was the last voice to speak in this vein for more than half a century" (President's Committee on Mental Retardation (PCMR), 1977).

The last 100 years have seen Howe's notion of temporary special schools bastardized into large, impersonal, custodial care facilities, focused primarily on protecting society from retarded persons. Feebleminded and idiotic children should be institutionalized, thought many, lest they grow up to become depraved and dangerous adults.

The eugenics movement, grounded in Social Darwinism, became popular, giving further impetus to segregating mental defectives from the greater society. In 1901 *Possible improvement of the human breed* was published, in which Galton proposed "that by eliminating the unfit, man could actively assist nature in promoting the survival of the highest quality human being" (PCMR, 1977).

The advent of psychometry in the early 1900s provided but one more opportunity to better control mental defectives, this time by supplying a supposedly scientific base to the detection and subsequent treatment of these persons. After all, if intelligence was a fixed characteristic of an individual, determined by heredity, the treatment implications soon become obvious: segregation, custodial care, sterilization. It must be deja vu, because somehow these issues seem more recent to me! Don't we still struggle with them every day?

For obvious reasons, the 1930s and 1940s were not decades of great progress for retarded persons. Two significant events had great impact, however. First the Social Security Act of 1935, laid the groundwork for much of the present funding for services for retarded citizens; second, World War II allowed many retarded persons to escape the institutions and obtain jobs or serve their country in uniform. I have not seen any literature on the latter topic but personally know more than two dozen persons who found this way out.

Next came the parents' movement of the 1950s and 1960s, and although no immediate changes in care and treatment were uniformly apparent, some basic assumptions were challenged vigorously. The parents and professionals who started the Association for Retarded Children (ARC) embarked on a journey of change that is still unfolding. For the most part they rejected institutional care, demanding better—whatever that meant. In the face of commonly held values and often against the judgment of professionals, these pioneering parents insisted on keeping their children home, started their own special schools, and began to "bang the system." The banging still goes on—but then so does the system!

From a public policy perspective, these advocacy groups forced several issues to emerge:

1. Parent–family roles in decisionmaking about handicapped children became legitimate.
2. Professionals in certain fields, especially medicine, psychology, and social work were now asked to be more accountable.
3. Educational and developmental modes of treatment became more acceptable, with a concurrent rejection of the medical and curative model (since it quite obviously provided neither hope nor help).
4. Parents began to demand a series of services for their children, not as beggars but under the protective cloak of the U.S. Constitution!

Begging the forgiveness of professors of freshman philosophy, we could conceptualize the time up to 1950 as the Age of Darkness in regard to treatment and care of retarded persons and other developmentally disabled. Then comes the Age of Enlightenment of the 1950s and 1960s. The 1970s were the Age of Litigation. The Pennsylvania Association of Retarded Citizens suit focusing on public special education led the way. Other suits followed, including right-to-treatment suits in Alabama, New York, Massachusetts, and many other states, including the landmark Pennhurst decision, once again in Pennsylvania. However, despite court findings and court orders, the problems persist today. It is to be hoped that the 1980s can be the Age of Fulfillment!

Let me identify a few of the many persons who have been instrumental in forcing the retardation issue past the Age of Darkness into enlightenment or at least illumination. Of course, Rhode Island's own congressman, the late John E. Fogarty, toiled tirelessly and imaginatively for more and better services. President John F. Kennedy and the entire Kennedy family helped bring retardation into the open on a very personal basis. Three others have given us significant opportunity, again in very public and meaningful ways, to better understand the complexities facing retarded persons. Burton Blatt is one of these. His publications, especially *Christmas in purgatory, Souls in extremis: An anthology on victims and victimizers*, and his latest (with Fred Kaplan as coauthor) *The family papers: A return to purgatory* (1979), are obligatory reading for any new professional in the field and continue to inspire many of us who are not so new. Gunnar Dybwad, professor emeritus at Brandeis University, along with his wife Rosemary, has sent students to all corners of the globe preaching the dual messages of promise and accountability. Finally Wolf Wolfensberger provided an ideology, which albeit often misunderstood and just as often maligned, has served as a soundingboard against which the whole notion of treatment and care of retarded citizens is tested. To these people, I express my gratitude.

Presuming we are in or near the Age of Fulfillment regarding treatment and care of retarded citizens, several questions remain to be addressed: What principles or assumptions underlie the care and treatment needs of retarded persons? How do these principles play out into a model service system? How do we implement the needed services?

## PRINCIPLES OF TREATMENT AND CARE

We should focus primarily on the caring, because if we care, then we will assure the necessary treatment. Remembering that retardation is not curable, although its effects are subject to amelioration, is it not strange that we commonly seek new staff trained in the curative arts (physical therapy, occupational therapy, speech therapy), but seldom invest money in so-called caregiving staff nor much in teaching custodial-care staff to be actual caregivers? Is it not odd that most state and federal programs still require parents, our best potential caregivers overall, to separate themselves from their children in order that these children may obtain what we call care?

In focusing on care, I mean nonconditional care, I mean that someone deserves care because he or she is a human being, not because he or she will "get better" or is cute, or "will benefit from community living."

Care must be rendered in small, personalized, community-based places. I agree wholeheartedly with Blatt and Kaplan (1979, p. 143): "We must evacuate the institutions for the mentally retarded. There is no time for new task forces and new evaluation teams. The time is long past for such nonsense."

Institutions for retarded persons, indeed for any persons in my view, are an abomination. Segregating from normal growth opportunities persons who are intellectually limited and then decrying their odd and inappropriate behavior, often using such behavior as an excuse for continuing to incarcerate them, is immoral at best. It is also stupid. We violate all of the theories of learning in these institutions and then ask in amazement why our slow learners manifest strange and maladaptive behaviors. Yet I submit that these behaviors we label as maladaptive are quite appropriate for the setting: the environment is maladaptive not the persons. To effect change we should focus on the setting, not the person.

I am not naive enough to believe that merely changing environments will automatically change persons. Much more must be done at an individual, personal level. On the other hand, I can almost guarantee that failing to change the setting—that is, failing to get rid of institutional settings—will ensure the continued promotion of bizarre and nonproductive lives for all persons so incarcerated.

Nothing that passes for care or treatment in an institution cannot be replicated or even improved upon in a smaller, more personalized, normalized setting. Personalizing life experiences are the most critical issues for retarded persons.

## MODEL SERVICE SYSTEM

Retarded citizens ought to live with, where, and like other citizens live. Of course, certain specialized services must be available as well, but these are readily obtainable if we wish.

Retarded persons, like the rest of us, need good places to live, work, and play; or to put it another way, retarded persons need a home (remember, where the heart is) not just a bed or a house. They need something valuable to do during the day; schooling for children and working or some reasonable facsimile for adults should generate in them a positive sense of self as a contributing member of society. They need leisuretime options, not a once-a-year trip to the circus in the company of dozens of similarly involved persons, which are similar to the ways you and I spend our free time. And, finally, they need formal social supports (case management, guardianship, advocacy, and the like) if their families and friends cannot provide the informal support system we are all striving to develop.

Please consider a model service system outline presently utilized by the State of Rhode Island (R.I. Department of Mental Health,

Retardation, and Hospitals (MHRH), 1979). Many such outlines are available. This outline is not proposed as either the most comprehensive or the most usable. Instead, it is merely one example of a conceptual, planning, and operational tool presently being employed in one state. It is an attempt to describe in some detail the various kinds of services that, if available, would best serve retarded citizens in Rhode Island.

The model service continuum implies that a community-based mental retardation system is grounded in the following assumptions:

1. There exist adequate legislation, shared philosophy, sufficient appropriation, and functional organizational structure by which the system is administered and maintained.

2. The consumer will experience continuity of appropriate service.

3. The service options developed and maintained will accommodate the existing or proposed resources, based on the least restrictive, most integrated community settings that meet the present and projected needs of individuals.

4. The system includes services that are flexible enough to account for individual differences and include an array of service alternatives.

The proposed service model comprises four major components:

1. Primary day services that are appropriate chronologically and developmentally and promote the dignity of the clients served;

2. Residential services that promote independence but allow for guidance and specialized supervision as needed;

3. Ancillary services, including all preventive and supportive activities such as case management, family supports, health care, and the like, and

4. Administrative and planning services that enable the state to plan, direct, coordinate, and monitor the service system in ways that are both professionally and fiscally accountable.

Our destination is becoming clearer, I hope. Recognizing that all roads will get you there if you don't care where you are going, how do we steer a proper course?

## IMPLEMENTING THE SERVICES

Usually the reason given for inadequate or inappropriate services is lack of money or too few staff. The pretension is that adding more dollars or hiring new staff would necessarily solve our problems. Nonsense! More money could be useful; generally it just buys more of the same services (should I say disservices) that already exist. Examples of this abound, whether they take the form of new institutional facilities or better staffing ratios in old state school cottages.

In our society change is fundamentally political in nature. Yet too many leaders in the retardation field pretend that improvements are professional and technological in nature. No amount of reform is going to make an intolerable institution tolerable. Maybe we can make it tolerable for administrators or visiting dignitaries but never for the poor souls subject to daily dehumanization there. The reasons preventing rapid community development and the concurrent phasing down of institutions are solely political. We possess the technology; the residential, educational, and vocational service models exist. What we lack is the collective will and the imagination.

We blame unions, local chambers of commerce, legislators, taxpayers, and governors, when in fact most "leaders" in the field are busier protecting their own interests than those of retarded citizens. Admittedly politics is a tough, sometimes brutal, often unfulfilling activity. Yet too many of the common citizenry are still afraid of retarded people, and too many legislators are too busy finding jobs in institutions for their constituents to worry about retarded citizens, and too many businessmen would rather not be bothered; yet without the support of these groups, retarded people are going nowhere fast. It is up to professionals and administrators in the field to educate the public, politicize the electorate, and demonstrate through efficiency and accountability a high-quality service system.

Consider the various "zoning exemption" items of legislation that began surfacing around the country in the 1970s. Two states I have worked in have laws exempting group homes that meet certain criteria from local zoning ordinances designed to prevent group home development. The laws work perfectly; however, no more group homes are opened because of them. The problem is not a zoning problem; it was never a legislative problem. Instead it is a problem of public xenophobia, of public education. People are afraid of the unknown; laws designed to protect the rights of undesirables are bad or communistic or stupid or whatever, we are told time after time. So the citizens call their town councilmen or their legislative representatives and use political influence to keep the group home out of their neighborhood. Meanwhile, all too often, this political action overcomes the law and professional opinion—and the group home is not started.

Take a close look at the way retarded people and those of us who labor in the field are represented in the media. Special Olympics often receive a large dose of public pity from the local television stations. How often have we seen the sportscaster shaking his head, commenting about the "courage these kids possess," and then going back to his real business for another year. Retarded people get lots of headlines: "Retarded Home to Open Here," "Neighbors Vow to Fight Group Home," "Institution Employee Arrested," "Investigation Finds Abuse at State School," and the like. People whose primary responsibility is to inform the public somehow always act surprised and outraged when they uncover inadequate services for retarded persons. Yet the same publications that decry problems chide administrators who ask for new money or new legislative mandates.

We must focus attention on the media; turn the tables on them and force their public accountability to adequately represent the real lives and real needs of retarded citizens. There need be no pity nor humor in retardation; these are the primary messages of the collective media of today. We must show them dignity and promise in the everyday lives of retarded citizens.

Another constituency who are often misrepresented are public employees. How often do we hear "How patient you must be to work with them?" Or how often are our employees denigrated by the occasional but all too consistent stories of client abuse by a fellow state worker? I submit that state employees, like other workers, will perform about as well as their training and supervision allows. We have a ready pool of workers who are already committed or obligated to a career in retardation. The big problem is that their work sites and often their everyday skills are not appropriate to the real needs of retarded people. So we must generate alliances of mutual self-interest with public employees, guaranteeing job security, opportunities for new careers, and the training to fulfill new community-based roles. Such alliances should overcome what is probably the single largest political and economic roadblock to community development: the fear of loss of jobs or of closing down an institution that is a large employer. In fact to serve retarded people adequately we will need more jobs, not fewer, and spread out throughout a state, not segregated into a few isolated locations.

If we are going to retrain public employees for new community roles, then we must rethink the contract-for-services thrust that has so impacted community services in the recent past. I suggest that the contract-for-services model often employed by states is inappropriate for many reasons. First, it sets up an unnecessary and unproductive confrontation with public employee organizations. Second, all too often consumer advocacy organizations serve as the provider organizations that set up questionable conflict-of-interest situations. How many advocacy groups serve as referral points for service, providers of services, and litigants against the state for better services? When advocate/providers threaten to close down unless they obtain higher rates, as opposed to supporting new service development, then they are providers only, not advocates. Let us promote true advocacy, separate and apart from the actual delivery of services, a personal advocacy focusing on retarded persons as individuals, not based on the need to raise rates or stabilize organizations.

Public officials, whether elected or appointed, represent a particularly critical group in general. In my judgment, too many appointed officials stress maintaining their appointments. Not much to be done about them, unless we develop some collective political clout with elected officials. Of course, here comes the rub. Too few elected officials are willing to play a leadership role on behalf of retarded citizens. Too many elected officials see retardation services as opportunities for patronage or to influence state contracts. Too few demonstrate a genuine interest in retarded people. Most simply ignore retardation, vainly hoping it will go away and hoping no group homes show up in their district—at least not during election time. The exceptions stand out. Rhode Island's governor uses reelection ads focusing on improvements in the state's retardation services; but this is highly unusual. Most governors just hope they will not have to hear about retardation problems.

Public accountability is the only answer. Public discussion of the real problems facing retarded people, in the media, during the elections, all the time. Consumers, advocates, and professionals must take a stand, forcing public officials to do likewise.

Earlier, I derided funding problems. This is not to suggest that funding is immaterial. Instead, I suggest that we explore some significantly different funding arrangements, if we are truly interested in retarded people. First, basing most funding streams on state-federal entitlements, must be examined. The whole notion of retarded people being generated independent of the real community (at least that is what many foes of group homes seem to intimate) intrigues me. Above all, retardation is a personal, family, neighborhood community issue. If you doubt this, think back to the last pregnancy you worried about! Yet our funding mechanisms remove almost all responsibility from local folks.

Second, basing retardation funding to a great extent on Medicaid (Title XIX of the Social Security Act), as we do here in Rhode Island and elsewhere, is inconsistent. Retarded people for the most part are not sick, will not be cured, and frankly, most of the medical community avoids them. Yet, we work hard to qualify them for Medicaid so we can chase the federal buck. Now, there is nothing wrong with federal dollars being spent for services for retarded persons. Conservative administrations notwithstanding, I suggest we increase the federal pie for people of all types. Qualifying people with developmental problems as medically needy is not the answer, however. Establishing a fiscal package to support long-term care for certain persons is. Here is another example where political action is in order.

Now we come to governance. It must be clear that state programs, at best, run bad institutions poorly. The evidence is clear that state agencies laden with uncaring, mindless clerks and no-sayers have little interest, nor potential for, operating high-quality small, personalized care systems for retarded people. On the inside, we joke about who the clients are: from the outside the joke is all too cruel.

Now, I am not saying that state workers are bad. Instead, I am saying that state work should be accepted for what it is. But Burton Blatt described some of the problems in *Exodus from pandemonium.* Between the politicians and the state budget types, pandemonium is too kind a word for those who are trying to perform professional services.

I suggest a different system of governance; one that takes into account the forces of public employee unions, the need for degrees of administrative flexibility, and the promise of small personalized services that are linked to real communities. Don't worry, commissioners, there will still be a role for the state agency—as standard setters, monitors, planners, and funders. But this is all the state should do.

Actual operation of services should be taken away from state agencies and nonprofit organizations alike. Instead, we should generate local public corporations, with state and local representative leadership to operate the services directly or, as needed, to contract for services. Such models of governance now exist. Examples include the various bridge and turnpike authorities so commonly found in America. Clearly the state departments of transportation could not operate these services, given the structures of state bureaucracy; just as important, the states could not monitor themselves. And the highways were going to hell. Voila, the turnpike authorities. Surely, people are just as important as ribbons of concrete!

Many doubt that we can afford the necessary system improvements in the 1980s. In fact, we cannot *not* afford to make the necessary improvements. Our collective humaneness demands it. It is time for us to generate a national policy and fund it rather than seeking more money to do more of the same.

In summary, I am calling for a major revamping of retardation services. Such activity would require differential deployment of personnel away from institutions and into community services. Likewise, new governance models will be required and more appropriate funding streams, both focused on local control and local responsibility. Citizen advocacy leading to the political clout to effect the establishment of individualized, personalized, and cost-effective services could result.

## REFERENCES

Blatt, Burton, and Kaplan, Fred. *The Family Papers: A return to purgatory.* New York: Longman, 1979.

President's Committee on Mental Retardation. *Mental retardation: Past and present.* Washington, D.C.: January 1977, p. 6.

Rhode Island Department of Mental Health, Retardation and Hospitals. *Rhode Island long term plan for the mental retardation system.* Cranston: R.I. Department of Mental Health Retardation and Hospitals, July 16, 1979, pp. 71-90.

# NAME INDEX

# SUBJECT INDEX

267

# ABOUT THE EDITOR

Joseph J. Bevilacqua, is the commissioner of the Virginia Department of Mental Health and Mental Retardation, a post he assumed September 1, 1981 after serving for six years as director of the Rhode Island Department of Mental Health, Retardation and Hospitals. The immediate past president of the National Association of State Mental Health Program Directors, he is involved in a number of other national mental health and social service organizations concerned with government policies and services for the mentally disabled. Because of the many conflicting forces that have and will continue to have an impact on social and health services throughout the nation, he organized the First Annual Fogarty Memorial Conference in an attempt to formulate a consensus of how policies can be changed to improve programs for the mentally disabled. Dr. Bevilacqua's past affiliations include work with the President's Commission on Mental Health's Task Panel on Organization and Structure of Mental Health Services. He holds a Ph.D. degree from Brandeis University's Florence Heller School for Advanced Studies in Social Welfare.

# ABOUT THE CONTRIBUTORS

**Elizabeth M. Boggs**, is a mental retardation consultant focusing on national policy and federal legislation. A member of the National Council on the Handicapped, she is an honorary fellow of the American Psychiatric Association and an honorary associate fellow of the American Academy of Pediatrics. For many years Dr. Boggs has been involved with the formulation of national policy for services for the handicapped and disabled, and was one of forty founders of the Association for Retarded Citizens in 1950. She has served on such national policy councils as the President's Panel on Mental Retardation, the National Advisory Council on Services and Facilities for the Developmentally Disabled, and the Joint Commission on the Mental Health of Children. She holds a Ph.D. degree from Cambridge University in England and in 1972 was awarded an LL.D. degree by Ohio State University.

**Valerie Bradley** is President of the Human Services Research Institute in Boston. She participated in the White House Conference on Handicapped Individuals and has worked in a variety of other consulting and government programs. Ms. Bradley is a member of the American Association on Mental Deficiency and the Mental Health Association of Washington, D.C. She holds an M.A. degree in political science from Rutgers University.

**Robert L. Carl, Jr.** is the associate director for Mental Retardation Services in the Rhode Island Department of Mental Health, Retardation, and Hospitals and was formerly deputy commissioner of the Division of Retardation in the Ohio Department of Mental Health and Retardation. A lecturer at numerous colleges and universities and active in American Association on Mental Deficiency, he has acted as consultant and expert witness in right-to-treatment class action litigation. Dr. Carl holds a Ph.D. degree from the University of Michigan's School of Education.

**William C. Copeland** is currently an adjunct professor at the University of Minnesota's Hubert H. Humphrey Institute of Public Affairs and president of the Seneca Corporation, a human service program and finance consulting firm. He was formerly associated with such organizations as the Urban Institute, Interstudy, and the American Hospital Association. Mr. Copeland holds a B.A. from Muskingum College with graduate studies at the University of Pittsburgh, University of Chicago, and the University of Minnesota.

**Iver A. Iversen** is a project coordinator with the Hubert H. Humphrey Institute and a vice president of the Seneca Corporation. Formerly with Sister Kenny Institute and Interstudy, he has developed a number of important applied mathematical applications in human service administration. He holds an M.S. degree in biostatistics from the University of Minnesota.

**Robert M. Moroney** is currently professor of social work at Arizona State University's School of Social Work. He was a professor of social planning at the University of North Carolina's Department of City and Regional Planning when his chapter was prepared. Dr. Moroney has worked with a variety of organizations concerned with the development of social service policy for children and their families, including the Bush Institute on Families and Children, the National Center for the Study of Adolescence, and the President's Commission on Mental Health and the Family. He earned his Ph.D. at Brandeis University's Florence Heller School for Advanced Studies in Social Welfare.

**John H. Noble, Jr.** is presently senior program analyst and special assistant to the deputy assistant secretary for planning and budget in the U.S. Department of Education and was previously director of the Division of Rehabilitation and Disability Policy, Office of the Assistant Secretary for Planning and Evaluation, in the U.S. Department of Health, Education, and Welfare. He has also been a consultant to the secretariat of the World Health Organization and consultant to the National Research Council of the National Academy of Science. Dr. Noble has also served as a member of the editorial boards of *Evaluation Quarterly*, the *Journal of Social Service Research*, and the *Policy Studies Annual.* He holds a Ph.D. degree from the Brandeis University's Florence Heller School for Advanced Studies in Social Welfare.

**E. Clarke Ross** has been director of the United Cerebral Palsy Associations' Governmental Activities Office since 1976. He has also held a variety of positions with other voluntary agencies and educational institutions. A member of the American Academy of Political Science and the American Society of Public Administration, Dr. Ross holds a D.P.A. degree from George Washington University.

Currently a psychiatrist at the Range Mental Health Center in Virginia, Minnesota, **Hilary Sandall** was until recently director of Community Support Services at St. Louis State Hospital. She was previously the hospital's assistant superintendent for medical affairs and earlier served as a medical officer for the Government of Jamaica. Dr. Sandall earned her medical degree at Oxford University in England.

**James J. Skeffington** is an attorney practicing in Providence, Rhode Island, who has long been concerned with the rights and the well-being of mentally retarded citizens. He served as President of the John E. Fogarty Foundation for the Mentally Retarded from 1973 through 1979.

# CONFERENCE PARTICIPANTS

John J. Affleck
Director, Rhode Island Department of
    Social and Rehabilitative Services
Cranston, Rhode Island

Mary Ann Allard
Research Associate
Human Services Research Institute
Washington, D.C.

William S. Allerton, M.D.
Medical Director
Eagleville Hospital
Philadelphia, Pennsylvania

Joan Amundson
Consultant to Assembly
    Mental Health Committee
California Legislature
Sacramento, California

Dennis E. Angelini, Ph.D.
Assistant Director
Manpower Development
Rhode Island Department of Mental
    Health, Retardation, and Hospitals
Cranston, Rhode Island

William A. Anthony, Ph.D.
Director
Center for Rehabilitation,
    Research, and Training
Boston University
Boston, Massachusetts

Leona Bachrach, Ph.D.
Maryland Psychiatric Research Center
Baltimore, Maryland

James P. Benedict
Administrator
Dr. U.E. Zambarano Memorial Hospital
Rhode Island Department of Mental
    Health, Retardation, and Hospitals
Cranston, Rhode Island

Joseph J. Bevilacqua, Ph.D.
Director
Rhode Island Department of Mental
    Health, Retardation, and Hospitals
Cranston, Rhode Island

Elizabeth Boggs, Ph.D.
Consultant
Mental Retardation Services
Hampton, New Jersey

Valerie Bradley
President
Human Services Research Institute
Washington, D.C.

Marsha Buck
Executive Director
Mental Health Advisory Budget Project
Sacramento, California

James J. Callahan, Ph.D.
Director
Levinson Policy Institute
Heller Graduate School
Brandeis University
Waltham, Massachusetts

Robert L. Carl, Jr., Ph.D.
Associate Director for Mental
    Retardation
Rhode Island Department of Mental
    Health, Retardation, and Hospitals
Cranston, Rhode Island

Urbano Censoni
Acting Director
Division of D.D. Services
Michigan Department of Mental Health
Lansing, Michigan

Deborah P. Clarke
Legal Officer
Rhode Island Department of Mental
    Health, Retardation, and Hospitals
Cranston, Rhode Island

Gary Clarke
Director
Intergovernmental Health
    Policy Project
Washington, D.C.

William Copeland
Hubert H. Humphrey Policy Institute
University of Minnesota
Minneapolis, Minnesota

Leona H. Egeland
Chairwoman
California Ways and Means
    Subcommittee on Health
    and Welfare
Sacramento, California

Nathan B. Epstein, M.D.
Medical Director
Butler Hospital
Providence, Rhode Island

Susan Epstein
Mental Health and Mental
    Retardation Consultant
Newtonville, Massachusetts

Richard H. Freeman
Assistant Director
Substance Abuse
Rhode Island Department of Mental
    Health, Retardation, and Hospitals
Cranston, Rhode Island

Donald P. Galamaga
Executive Director for Management
    and Support Services
Rhode Island Department of Mental
    Health, Retardation, and Hospitals
Cranston, Rhode Island

Derril Gay
Director
Division of Mental Health, Mental
    Retardation, and Substance
    Abuse Services
Georgia Department of Human
    Resources
Atlanta, Georgia

Robert Gettings
Executive Director
National Association of Coordinators
    of State Programs for Mental
    Retardation
Arlington, Virginia

Thomas Gilhool
Public Interest Law Center
Philadelphia, Pennsylvania

David S. Greer, M.D.
Associate Dean of Medicine
Division of Biology and Medicine
Brown University
Providence, Rhode Island

George W. Gunther, Jr.
Chief Administrative Officer
Dr. Joseph H. Ladd Center
Rhode Island Department of Mental
    Health, Retardation, and Hospitals
Cranston, Rhode Island

Timothy M. Hennessey, Ph.D.
Department of Political Science
University of Rhode Island
Kingston, Rhode Island

William H. Hollinshead, III, Ph.D.
Medical Director
Division of Family Health
Department of Health
Providence, Rhode Island

Michael Ingall, M.D.
Medical Director
Providence Mental Health Center, Inc.
Providence, Rhode Island

Ruth Knee
Consultant
Long Term Mental Health Care
Fairfax, Virginia

Rudy Mangione, Ph.D.
Director
Ohio Division of Mental Retardation
    and Developmental Disabilities
Columbus, Ohio

Jesse J. McCorry, Jr., Ph.D.
Office of Policy Development/Office
    of Human Development Services
U.S. Department of Health
    and Human Services
Washington, D.C.

Ann Drissel McCuan
Staff Assistant
Office of the Director, Division of
    Mental Health Services Programs
National Institute of Mental Health
Rockville, Maryland

Peter Megrdichian
Administrator
Center General Hospital
Rhode Island Department of Mental
    Health, Retardation, and Hospitals
Cranston, Rhode Island

Neil Meisler
Associate Director
Division of Mental Health
Rhode Island Department of Mental
    Health, Retardation, and Hospitals
Cranston, Rhode Island

Robert M. Moroney, Ph.D.
Department of City and
    Regional Planning
University of North Carolina
Chapel Hill, North Carolina

Arthur Nagle
Program Manager
Division of Substance Abuse
Rhode Island Department of Mental
    Health, Retardation, and Hospitals
Cranston, Rhode Island

John H. Noble, Ph.D.
Office of Assistant Secretary
    for Planning and Budget
U.S. Department of Education
Washington, D.C.

Gail O'Connor
President
American Association of
    Mental Deficiency
Tacoma, Washington

Paul Pisano
Legal Counsel
Rhode Island Department of Mental
    Health, Retardation, and Hospitals
Cranston, Rhode Island

Anderson Pollard
Community Liaison Officer
Neuropsychiatric Institute
University of California
Los Angeles, California

James A. Prevost, M.D.
Commissioner
Office of Mental Health
Albany, New York

Thomas D. Romeo
Associate Director
Rehabilitative Services
Rhode Island Department of Mental
    Health, Retardation, and Hospitals
Cranston, Rhode Island

E. Clarke Ross, D.P.A.
Executive Director
United Cerebral Palsy Associations, Inc.
UCPA Governmental Activities Office
Washington, D.C.

Marlene Ross
Director
Division of Mental Health Services
Department of Mental Health
Lansing, Michigan

Louis Rowitz, Ph.D.
School of Public Health
University of Illinois
    at the Medical Center
Chicago, Illinois

Susan Rubinstein
Cornhill Associates
Newton, Massachusetts

Sister Janice Ryan, Ph.D.
President
Trinity College
Burlington, Vermont

Hilary Sandall, M.D.
Director
Community Support Services
St. Louis State Hospital
St. Louis, Missouri

Leslie Scallet
Mental Health Law Project
Washington, D.C.

Harry C. Schnibbe
Executive Director
National Association of State Mental
    Health Program Directors
Washington, D.C.

Donald Spence, Ph.D.
Director
Program on Gerontology
University of Rhode Island
Kingston, Rhode Island

Richard Surles, Ph.D.
Commissioner
Vermont Department of Mental Health
Waterbury, Vermont

John Talbot, M.D.
Associate Medical Director
Payne–Whitney Psychiatric Clinic
New York, New York

## CONFERENCE COORDINATORS

Robert W. Holmes
Coordinator of Training
  and Education
Division of Substance Abuse
Rhode Island Department of Mental
  Health, Retardation, and Hospitals
Cranston, Rhode Island

Sister Mary Patrick, O.P.
Administrative Assistant to the Director
Rhode Island Department of Mental
  Health, Retardation, and Hospitals
Cranston, Rhode Island

## CONFERENCE CO-FACILITATORS, RHODE ISLAND DEPARTMENT OF MENTAL HEALTH, RETARDATION, AND HOSPITALS

Jeanne Adams
Consultant Public Health Nurse
  for Mental Health

Susan L. Babin
Administrator
Planning and Policy Formulation
  for Retardation

Dante Boffi
Assistant Director
Financial Management

Marklyn Champagne, R.N.
Public Health Nurse Consultant
  for Retardation

Donna Cone, Ph.D.
Assistant Director
Division of Program Standards,
  Planning, and Evaluation

Frank DiMaio
Administrator for Mental
  Retardation Program
  Maintenance

Nicholas Elbaum
Program Analyst for Mental Health

Lauranne Howard
Drug Training Officer
Division of Substance Abuse

Daniel McCarthy
Administrator for Community
  Mental Health Services

Albert J. Quattromani
Administrator for Retardation Program
  Development and Implementation

Dawn Sullivan
Chief of Program Development
Division of Program Standards,
  Planning, and Evaluation

Fred Young
Chief of Social Service for
  the General Hospital

Patricia Zanella
Administrator
Community Services for Retardation